CW00938096

VOICES

ADVANCED

DANIEL BARBER, CHIA SUAN CHONG,
MAREK KICZKOWIAK AND LEWIS LANSFORD

NATIONAL
GEOGRAPHIC
LEARNING

Australia · Brazil · Canada · Mexico · Singapore · United Kingdom · United States

NATIONAL GEOGRAPHIC
LEARNING

National Geographic Learning,
a Cengage Company

Voices Advanced Student's Book, **1st Edition**
Daniel Barber, Chia Suan Chong,
Marek Kiczkowiak and Lewis Lansford

Publisher: Rachael Gibbon

Commissioning Editor: Kayleigh Buller

Development Editor: Stephanie Parker

Director of Global Marketing: Ian Martin

Product Marketing Manager: Caitlin Thomas

Heads of Regional Marketing:

   Charlotte Ellis (Europe, Middle East and Africa)

   Irina Pereyra (Latin America)

   Justin Kaley (Asia)

   Joy MacFarland (US and Canada)

Production Manager: Daisy Sosa

Media Researcher: Leila Hishmeh

Art Director: Brenda Carmichael

Operations Support: Hayley Chwazik-Gee

Manufacturing Manager: Eyvett Davis

Composition: Composure

Audio Producer: New York Audio

Contributing writer: Katherine Stannett
(Endmatter)

Advisors: Catherine McLellan, Bruna Caltabiano,
Dale Coulter and Mike Sayer

© 2022 Cengage Learning, Inc.

ALL RIGHTS RESERVED. No part of this work covered by the copyright
herein may be reproduced or distributed in any form or by any means,
except as permitted by U.S. copyright law, without the prior written
permission of the copyright owner.

"National Geographic", "National Geographic Society" and the Yellow Border
Design are registered trademarks of the National Geographic Society
® Marcas Registradas

For permission to use material from this text or product,
submit all requests online at **cengage.com/permissions**
Further permissions questions can be emailed to
permissionrequest@cengage.com

Student's Book with Online Practice and Student's eBook:
ISBN: 978-0-357-45873-0

Student's Book:
ISBN: 978-0-357-44345-3

National Geographic Learning
Cheriton House, North Way,
Andover, Hampshire, SP10 5BE
United Kingdom

Locate your local office at **international.cengage.com/region**

Visit National Geographic Learning online at **ELTNGL.com**
Visit our corporate website at **www.cengage.com**

Printed in Greece by Bakis SA
Print Number: 01 Print Year: 2021

MIX
Paper from
responsible sources
FSC® C169932

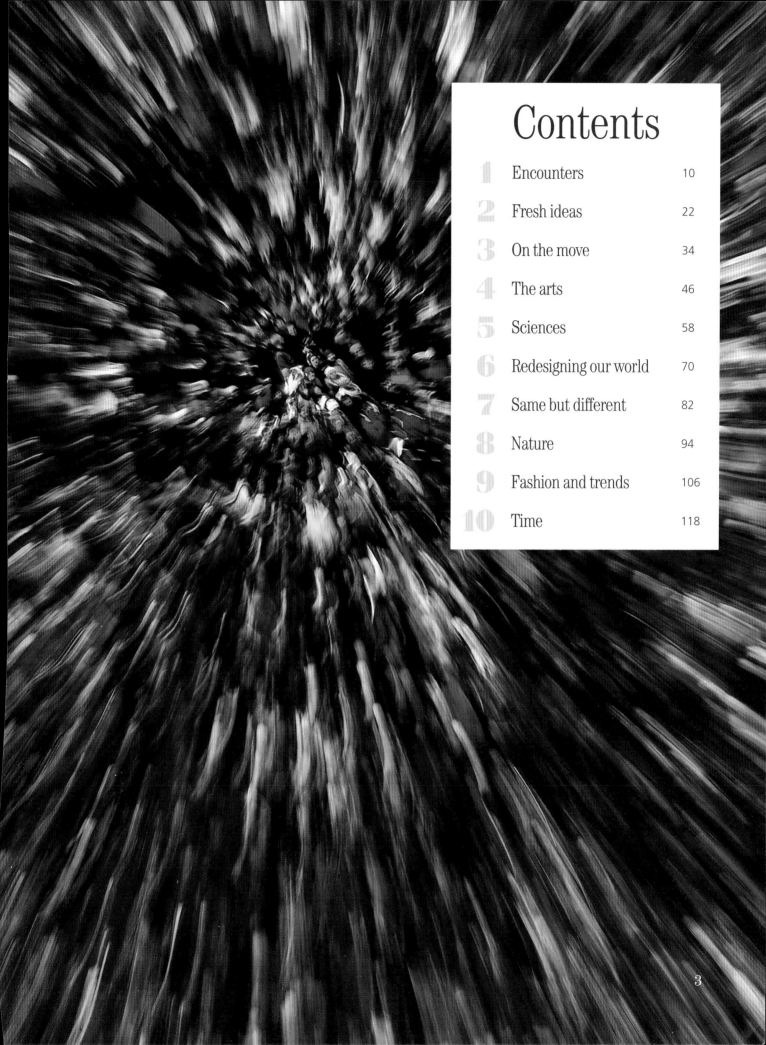

Contents

Scope and sequence

	GRAMMAR	VOCABULARY	PRONUNCIATION
1 Encounters *Pages 10–21*	perfect structures; distinguishing between words with similar meanings	encounters with people; precious finds and possessions	using chunking and intonation in complex sentences; saying words that are difficult to pronounce
2 Fresh ideas *Pages 22–33*	multi-word verbs; irreversible word pairs	features and benefits of new ideas; noun suffixes related to creating ideas	saying consonant clusters across word boundaries; understanding consonant clusters across word boundaries
3 On the move *Pages 34–45*	modals and related verbs; hedging in spoken English	ways of moving; making life choices	using emphatic stress when hedging; understanding consonant sound changes within and between words
4 The arts *Pages 46–57*	discourse markers; using the present tense to tell stories	music; oral narratives	adapting your pronunciation; stressing words to engage listeners
5 Sciences *Pages 58–69*	adding emphasis with cleft sentences; negative and limiting adverbials	describing health benefits; suffixes related to research	saying vowels and diphthongs: length; saying longer vowels before voiced consonants

READING	LISTENING	WRITING	COMMUNICATION SKILL	CRITICAL THINKING	USEFUL LANGUAGE
an extract from a novel; using a dictionary	an explorer talks about a precious find; using mindmaps to help predict what you might hear	a follow-up email; structuring a message	adapting to different personality types	analysing characters	adapting to different personality types; making plans and suggestions
a biography about a scientist; creating a timeline	explorers talk about where their ideas come from; understanding accents: consonant sounds	a proposal; explaining causes and results	encouraging creative problem solving	applying ideas in different contexts	describing a product's features and benefits; encouraging creative problem solving
an extract from a non-fiction book; identifying different ways to indicate cause and effect	explorers talk about their relationship to place; inferring opinions	an email to confirm arrangements; making formal arrangements	supporting others through change	evaluating solutions to problems from different perspectives	supporting others through change
forum posts and poems; identifying and analysing arguments	an explorer talks about oral story-telling traditions in the Caribbean; understanding fast speech (1): final consonants	an online film review; hooking the reader in a review	using humour in international communication	identifying logical fallacies in arguments	using humour in conversations; writing film reviews
an article about two surgeons who are also artists; summarizing the ideas in a text using a Venn diagram	explorers talk about the role of narrative in science; using abbreviations when taking notes	a video brief; supporting a text with images	convincing someone who questions the evidence	assessing supporting evidence	trying to convince someone

Scope and sequence

	GRAMMAR	VOCABULARY	PRONUNCIATION
6 Redesigning our world *Pages 70–81* 	alternative conditional forms; compound adjectives	representation; design	using the correct stress on words with suffixes; stressing key words and using pauses
7 Same but different *Pages 82–93* 	the continuous aspect; homophones and homographs	similarities and differences; using the voice	understanding /ʌ/, /əʊ/ and /aɪ/ across accents; feeling comfortable with your accent
8 Nature *Pages 94–105* 	dependent prepositions; the definite article used with natural features	natural talent; natural world	saying /dʒ/, /tʃ/ and /ʃ/; adapting your pronunciation to say /w/, /v/, and /b/
9 Fashion and trends *Pages 106–117* 	ellipsis and substitution; expressing change and trends	fashion; green business trends	saying elided expressions with the correct stress; saying consonants clearly
10 Time *Pages 118–129* 	the future in the past; expressions with *take*	expressions with *time*; expressions related to the passing of time	saying /r/ vs /l/ at the end of words; saying voiceless consonants in stressed syllables

READING	LISTENING	WRITING	COMMUNICATION SKILL	CRITICAL THINKING	USEFUL LANGUAGE
an article about maps; summarizing with a visual concept map	explorers talk about design fails and successes; learn new words and phrases while listening	a report about website design; writing from visual data	accommodating your conversation partner	identifying the writer's opinions	accommodating your conversation partner; referring to different aspects of a subject
an extract from a memoir; dealing with unknown words in literary texts	three conversations relating to different aspects of the voice; dealing with non-linguistic challenges	an opinion essay; structuring an argument	finding your voice in English	understanding analogies in literature	managing the impression you make; expressing opinions in an impersonal way
an opinion article about modified and lab-grown foods; creating an outline of a text	explorers talk about significant experiences in nature; understanding fast speech (2): merging and disappearing sounds	an essay suggesting solutions to problems; using cautious language	confronting difficult issues	understanding and avoiding biases	confronting difficult issues; discussing effects and solutions
a blog post about toys and games; using topic sentences	a news report about green business trends; understanding hedging	an anecdote; starting a story	increasing your trustworthiness	recognizing commercial interests	increasing trustworthiness; describing problems with clothes, shoes and accessories
an article about rhythm; finding meaning: using definitions	five conversations about time; synthesizing information from multiple sources	a letter; making a personal timeline	managing turn-taking in group conversations	evaluating the degree of certainty	managing turn-taking

Meet the explorers

ALEC JACOBSON

Lives: Canada
Job: I'm a journalist, photographer and adventurer. My goal is to shine a light on important issues and give a voice to the people who experience them first hand. I do that by taking photos and telling human stories.
What would you be doing if you weren't doing this job? My parents keep asking me that question!
Find Alec: Unit 6

ALISON WRIGHT

Lives: US
Job: I'm a photographer, author and speaker. I've travelled to more than 150 countries and have written ten books, including one about how I recovered after a terrible bus crash in Laos. I enjoy sharing my photographs and stories with travellers.
What advice would you give someone who wants to explore the world? Have a sense of purpose. I really love my work because it gets me so much deeper into the culture than just an average traveller.
Find Alison: Unit 10

ALYEA PIERCE

Lives: US
Job: I'm a performance poet and educator. I work with young people to help them find their voice through creative writing and theatre. As a black woman writer, I am also interested in telling the stories that are not being told.
Where is 'home'? Home for me is anywhere close to nature and art.
Find Alyea: Unit 4

ANDREJ GAJIĆ

Lives: Albania
Job: I'm a shark research scientist. I work in the conservation of sharks and study the diseases caused by sea pollution in the Mediterranean and other marine environments. I'm also a biology professor, author, underwater photographer and pilot of remotely operated underwater vehicles.
Describe yourself in three words: Committed, enthusiastic, focused.
Find Andrej: Unit 2

ANUSHA SHANKAR

Lives: US
Job: I'm a wildlife biologist – and interested in how animals live in extreme conditions. I'm a PhD student at Stony Brook University in New York and my research is on hummingbirds and how they save energy.
How many languages do you speak?: I can speak about five languages. English is my best, Spanish second best, and then Tamil, Hindi and Malayalam in order of fluency.
Find Anusha: Unit 3

CAROLINA CHONG MONTENEGRO

Lives: Australia
Job: I am a fisheries ecologist and am also doing research for my PhD at the University of Queensland. I'm studying a kind of grouper fish from the Tropical Eastern Pacific, which has become rare because of too much fishing.
What advice would you give to someone who wants to explore the world? Don't be afraid to go by yourself. It can be challenging, but it's worth it.
Find Carolina: Unit 7

FRANCISCO ESTRADA-BELLI

Lives: US
Job: I'm an archaeologist and I run an archaeological project in the Maya Biosphere Reserve in Guatemala. I have written about the Maya civilization and I'm also an assistant professor at Tulane University in New Orleans.
If you didn't do this job, what do you think you'd be doing?: I never wanted to do anything but archaeology. I'd be lost if I didn't do this.
Find Francisco: Unit 2

GABBY SALAZAR

Lives: US
Job: I'm a conservation and wildlife photographer. Now, I'm also a doctoral student. I'm studying how environmental images and education change how people feel about the environment and the actions they take to protect it.
What did you want to do when you were younger? I wanted to be a Broadway singer (I had a lot of confidence, but not so much singing talent!). I also wanted to be a pastry chef because I love sweets.
Find Gabby: Unit 7

IMOGEN NAPPER

Lives: UK
Job: I'm a marine scientist, specializing in plastic pollution. My work recently helped stop the use of microbeads in cosmetics all over the world. With National Geographic, I'm working to identify technology that can catch the tiny microplastic fibres that enter the water when clothes are washed.
What do you do to relax? Play my guitar (badly)!
Find Imogen: Unit 4

JEFF KERBY

Lives: Denmark
Job: I'm an ecologist and photographer, interested in how climate and the seasons affect how species interact with each other in extreme environments. I'm also a photojournalist. I want my stories to show people that we need to protect the Earth.
What's your signature dish to cook? Salsa – using very fresh and simple ingredients.
Find Jeff: Unit 8

MARIA FADIMAN

Lives: US
Job: I'm a conservationist, studying the relationship between people and plants. I work mostly in rural areas with a special interest in the rainforests of Latin America. I am also an associate professor at Florida Atlantic University.
What do you miss when you are away from home? My family and my cats. And pizza.
Find Maria: Unit 8

MIKE GIL

Lives: US
Job: I'm a marine biologist. I am interested in understanding how animal social networks can shape ecosystems that provide valuable services to people. I'm also very involved in teaching people about science.
What do you always take with you when you travel? No matter what: a toothbrush and a positive attitude – both simply make life better anywhere.
Find Mike: Unit 1

NORA SHAWKI

Lives: Egypt
Job: I'm an archaeologist and spend my time digging and doing research. Now, I'm working in the Delta in Egypt to try to protect areas that are being taken over by the modern world.
Describe yourself in three words: Goofy, curious and fun.
Find Nora: Unit 9

PABLO 'POPI' BORBOROGLU

Lives: Argentina
Job: I'm a marine biologist and I specialize in penguins and marine conservation. I am president of the Global Penguin Society, an international conservation group that protects the world's penguins. I'm also currently leading a worldwide effort to help penguins by creating protected areas on both land and sea.
What's your fondest memory? Listening to my grandmother's stories about penguins when she visited them 100 years ago in Patagonia.
Find Pablo: Unit 5

REBECCA WOLFF

Lives: Canada
Job: I'm a researcher in the Andes of Peru and Ecuador. I look at the relationship between people and their environment and study how our environments can make us feel healthy or unhealthy.
How many languages do you speak? I speak English and Spanish fluently. I also speak a little bit of French, Hindi and Quechua.
Find Rebecca: Unit 3; Unit 6

TERESA CAREY

Lives: US
Job: I'm a science journalist and sailor. In 2008, I sailed the ocean on a small boat with only my cat for company. After many years as a professional sailor, I wanted to tell more science stories. I hope to inspire people to come together and create solutions.
What did you want to do when you were younger? What didn't I want to do?! I wanted to do everything!
Find Teresa: Unit 5

Grace meets her great-granddaughter, named after her, for the first time, in St Francis hospital, Columbus, Georgia, US.

Encounters

GOALS

- Use a dictionary to understand a literary extract
- Use the perfect aspect to talk about events as seen from a later point
- Talk about encounters; describe finds and possessions
- Use mindmaps to help predict what you might hear
- Learn to adapt to different personality types
- Write a follow-up email

1 Work in pairs. Discuss the questions.

1 Look at the photo. What do you think Grace wants to say to her great-grandchild?
2 How might her relationship with her great-grandchild make a difference to her life?

WATCH

2 ▶ 1.1 Watch the video. Answer the questions.

NATIONAL GEOGRAPHIC EXPLORER

MIKE GIL

1 What was Mike's first impression of his PhD advisor? How was it inaccurate?
2 What was Mike's first impression of his college professor? What influence did the professor come to have on him?

3 Make connections. Discuss the questions.

1 Have you ever formed a first impression that turned out to be accurate? What happened?
2 Have you ever formed a first impression that turned out to be wrong? What happened?

11

1A
First impressions

LESSON GOALS
- Use a dictionary to understand an extract from a novel
- Analyse characters in a novel
- Talk about a first encounter

READING

1 Work in pairs. Discuss the questions.

1 How often do you meet new people?

2 The book *Anne of Green Gables* is a children's classic written in 1908. Have you heard of it or seen a film of it?

3 Read the introduction to the book on page 13. What do you think is going to happen next?

2 Skim the novel extract. Answer the questions.

1 How does Matthew feel about meeting Anne?

2 How does Anne feel about meeting Matthew?

3 Who does most of the talking?

3 Look at the Reading skill box. Then choose the best dictionary definition (a–f) for each word (1–6) from the extract. For a–c you will also need to choose the correct meaning.

READING SKILL
Using a dictionary

When looking words up in a dictionary, ask yourself:

- Does the word have more than one meaning? Use the context to help identify the most relevant meaning, as well as the correct part of speech.

- Is the word part of a longer word, an expression or a phrase? You may be able to look up the whole phrase or expression.

- Is the word useful to learn? Many dictionaries show whether the word is frequently used or is more formal, literary or old-fashioned.

1 spare (line 1)

2 shabby (line 2)

3 dwell (line 9)

4 marble (line 9)

5 scrawny (line 11)

6 worldly (line 19)

a i *n* a small ball made of coloured glass

  ii *n* a type of hard stone

b i *n* an extra thing you keep in case you need it

  ii *adj* not being used at the present time

  iii *v* save somebody from pain or unpleasantness

c i *adj* having experience and knowledge of life

  ii *adj* of possessions, all that someone owns

d *adj* very thin

e *v* (literary) live in a certain place

f *adj* old and in bad condition

4 Look at the Critical thinking skill box. Then look at adjectives 1–8. Do they describe Anne (A) or Matthew (M)? Tick (✓) the correct answer. Where possible, underline any parts of the extract that tell you.

CRITICAL THINKING SKILL
Analysing characters

When you 'meet' a person in fiction, you form an impression of their character and personality. Understanding how an author has helped form your impression will make you understand the writer's technique and the story better. When you analyse your first impression, ask yourself:

- What words, if any, **describe** the character? Look for adjectives and adverbs e.g. *happy* or *shyly*

- What actions **show** the character's personality? Look for things the person does or doesn't do that reveal the sort of person they are.

		A	M			A	M
1	confident	☐	☐	5	optimistic	☐	☐
2	adventurous	☐	☐	6	talkative	☐	☐
3	nervous	☐	☐	7	quiet	☐	☐
4	responsible	☐	☐	8	happy	☐	☐

5 Work in pairs. Discuss the questions.

1 What else do we learn about Anne and Matthew from the extract?

2 What kind of person do you imagine Marilla to be? Why? How do you think she will react to Anne?

SPEAKING

6 Work in pairs. Can you think of an interesting first encounter you have had? Talk about it and ask and answer follow-up questions. Could you use any of the characteristics mentioned in Exercise 4 to describe the person you met?

Anne in the contemporary TV series based on *Anne of Green Gables*.

INTRODUCTION

Matthew Cuthbert, a sixty-year-old farmer, lives and works with his sister Marilla on their farm called Green Gables. The pair have decided to adopt an orphan boy – a boy with no living parents – to help them run the farm. However, when Matthew goes to the railway station of the local town, Bright River, expecting to meet the boy for the first time, he discovers that a girl has arrived instead. Matthew, a shy person, is shocked and surprised. As he worries about how to introduce himself, the girl – eleven-year-old Anne Shirley – takes control of the situation.

Chapter 2

1 ... Matthew, however, was spared the ordeal of speaking first, for as soon as she concluded that he was coming to her, she stood up, grasping with one thin, brown hand the handle of a shabby, old-fashioned carpet-bag; the other she held out to him.

'I suppose you are Mr Matthew Cuthbert of Green Gables?' she said in a peculiarly clear, sweet voice. 'I'm
5 very glad to see you. I was beginning to be afraid you weren't coming for me and I was imagining all the things that might have happened to prevent you. I had made up my mind that if you didn't come for me tonight, I'd go down the track to that big, wild cherry tree at the bend, and climb up into it to stay all night. I wouldn't be a bit afraid, and it would be lovely to sleep in a wild cherry tree all white with bloom in the moonshine, don't you think? You could imagine you were dwelling in marble halls, couldn't you? And I was
10 quite sure you would come for me in the morning, if you didn't tonight.'

Matthew had taken the scrawny little hand awkwardly in his; then and there he decided what to do. He could not tell this child with the glowing eyes that there had been a mistake; he would take her home and let Marilla do that. She couldn't be left at Bright River anyhow, no matter what mistake had been made, so all questions and explanations might as well be
15 deferred until he was safely back at Green Gables.

'I'm sorry I was late', he said shyly. 'Come along. The horse is over in the yard. Give me your bag.'

'Oh, I can carry it', the child responded cheerfully. 'It isn't heavy. I've got all my worldly goods in it, but it
20 isn't heavy. And if it isn't carried in just a certain way the handle pulls out – so I'd better keep it because I know the exact knack of it. It's an extremely old carpet-bag. Oh, I'm very glad you've come, even if it would have been nice to sleep in a wild cherry tree.
25 We've got to drive a long piece, haven't we? Mrs Spencer said it was eight miles. I'm glad because I love driving. Oh, it seems so wonderful that I'm going to live with you and belong to you. I've never belonged to anybody – not really.'

From *Anne of Green Gables* by L.M. Montgomery

EXPLORE MORE!

Search online for 'how to make a good first impression' for tips and ideas about making first encounters positive.

1B
The start of something special?

LESSON GOAL
- Talk about encounters with people
- Talk about events as seen from a later point
- Learn to say complex sentences clearly

SPEAKING

1 Work in pairs. Look at the photo and discuss the questions.

1 How do you think these two people might have got talking? Improvise a short conversation.

2 Can you remember a time you started talking to someone like this? What happened?

VOCABULARY

2 Read the sentences. Decide whether the expressions in bold suggest: a) a good; b) a poor; c) an unexpected start to a relationship.

1 I **bumped into** him outside my flat. **It turns out** we're neighbours! We **struck up a conversation** and realized we have a lot in common!

2 I **didn't think much of** him to begin with. My first impression was that he was a bit **distant**.

3 I thought the **conversation flowed** really naturally. I may have talked too much, though! I hope I didn't **come across as** over-confident.

4 They were both so **approachable**, even though they're a lot older than me. And they really **took me under their wing**.

5 We met at one of those conferences where you **get thrown together**. We **just happened to** be in the same place at the same time.

3 Work in pairs. Using words and expressions from Exercise 2, make five questions to ask other classmates about their experiences of meeting new people. Then change partners and ask them your questions.

Go to page 135 for the Vocabulary reference.

READING FOR GRAMMAR

4 Read the three accounts of chance encounters on page 15. Which account (Citra's, Károly's or Travis's) describes …

a a coincidence?

b the start of a long-term relationship?

c an encounter with someone famous?

5 Work in pairs. Underline all the examples of perfect structures (*have* + past participle) in the chance encounter texts. Then answer questions 1–3. Read the Grammar box to check.

> **GRAMMAR** Perfect structures
>
> Use perfect structures to look back at past, present and future events from a later point in time.
> *I asked her what she'**d been doing** there.*
> Perfect forms can also be used …
> - as an infinitive: *someone who just happened to* ***have met*** *my daughter?*
> - after a modal: *The woman* ***must have noticed*** *…*
> - with *-ing* forms: ***having grabbed*** *that empty double seat on a crowded bus, …*

Go to page 145 for the Grammar reference.

1 What is the perspective of the person talking in each case, relative to the event they describe?

2 What form of the structure is used after:
a) a modal verb? b) the preposition *to?*
c) other prepositions?

3 Look at the examples with no subjects. What is the subject of a) *having grabbed?* b) *to have met* and c) *having said?*

6 🎧 1.1 Complete the sentences using the verbs in brackets in a perfect form. Then listen to check.

1 I still don't understand why we _____ (never / say) hello until that day.

2 I'm really pleased _____ (meet) you, but this is my stop.

3 Evgeny and Lily are getting married after _____ (insist) they would wait five years.

4 How do you know about my new job? Who _____ (you / talk) to?

5 I decided I might as well go to the supermarket, _____ (wake up) at four.

6 Tomorrow's too soon. The invitation _____ (not / arrive) by then.

CHANCE ENCOUNTERS

Most journeys aren't very memorable, but every now and then, having grabbed that empty double seat on a crowded bus, train or plane, you end up sitting next to someone fascinating, unforgettable … special. Chance encounters like these can be life changers.

Citra

I was so nervous going to Jakarta, the capital, for the first time by myself. The woman next to me on the bus must have noticed I'd been crying and was very kind. She took me under her wing after that and, incredibly, we're still friends to this day. She and I get together regularly for lunch in Jakarta. In fact, we'll have been seeing each other like that for eight years next month.

Károly

In 2018 I was in Berlin. It was my first time there, and I didn't know anyone. Anyway, in this café I struck up a conversation with a woman who told me she'd worked in Hungary, where I'm from. I asked her what she'd been doing there and if she ever visited Dunaújváros, the town I grew up in. Not only had she been there, but it turns out she'd been to my favourite diner and knew my daughter! What are the odds of getting into conversation with someone in another country who just happened to have met my daughter hundreds of kilometres away?

Travis

I'd been in Ohio and was struggling to get home, it having snowed so much the previous few days. After three cancelled flights I was finally on my way home. This lady with an accent I didn't recognize was sitting next to me. She was very approachable and we got chatting. It turned out she was a musician from Mali. After having said our goodbyes at the airport, I got into a taxi. My driver was Nigerian, so I told him the story. He freaked out when he heard who I'd been talking to. So I gave him an autograph she'd given me. Her name didn't mean much to me, but apparently she's a really big name if you know anything about the West African music scene.

PRONUNCIATION AND SPEAKING

7 🎧 **1.2** Look at the Clear voice box. Then listen to sentences 1–3. Mark pauses with a line |. Notice any intonation changes.

CLEAR VOICE
Using chunking and intonation in complex sentences

To make the structure of sentences with more than one clause easier to follow, speakers can use slight pauses to divide them into 'chunks'. Speakers might signal the beginning and end of chunks using changing intonation. For example, a rising intonation could suggest that the sentence is incomplete.

1 I decided | I might as well go to the supermarket having woken up at four.
2 I'd been in Ohio and was struggling to get home, it having snowed so much the previous few days.
3 They are getting married after having insisted they would wait five years.

8 Practise saying the sentences from Exercise 7.

9 Work in small groups. Think of a person you dream of meeting. Imagine you have met them and make up a story about the encounter. Tell your group about it as if it happened a few years ago.

EXPLORE MORE!

Find true accounts online of other chance encounters. Search for 'chance + encounters + strangers'.

1C

A precious find

LESSON GOALS
• Use mindmaps to help predict what you might hear
• Discuss important finds and possessions
• Say words with difficult pronunciation
• Distinguish between words with similar meanings

SPEAKING

1 Work in pairs. Discuss the questions.
1 What interesting objects have you found …
  a while travelling?
  b on a walk in your city?
  c in your own house?
2 Which of these objects might you keep if you stumbled upon them? Why? / Why not?

a colourful stone or seashell
a piece of old china, e.g. a cup or plate
an old photo of you   a letter   an expensive watch

LISTENING

NATIONAL GEOGRAPHIC EXPLORER

2 You're going to listen to Mike Gil talk about the object in the photo. Work in pairs. Look at the Listening skill box. Then, using the headings in the mindmap, try to predict words and phrases Mike might use.

An abalone shell.

3 ∩ 1.3 Listen and try to complete the mindmap with what Mike says. Compare with a partner.

4 ∩ 1.3 Listen again. Try to add to your notes from Exercise 3. Discuss the questions.
1 What does Mike believe about our relationship with objects?
2 Why is the shell important to him?

LISTENING SKILL
Using mindmaps to help predict what you might hear

Before listening, it might help to use a mindmap to note down ideas for words or phrases you're likely to hear. For example, when listening to descriptions, you might hear words describing shape, size, where an object was found and how someone feels about it. If you don't understand part of the description, listen for synonyms and definitions – the speaker is likely to use more than one way to describe the same thing.

VOCABULARY

5 Use these phrases to summarize what Mike said. Use a dictionary to check the meaning of any new vocabulary. Then check in the audioscript on page 168.

feel emotionally/deeply attached to
has sentimental value for me
aesthetically pleasing
(collect things) of all shapes and sizes
a vivid/vague memory/recollection   it takes me back to
it evokes emotions/memories of
stumble across/upon   be/serve as a manifestation of

Go to page 135 for the Vocabulary reference.

6 Rewrite the sentences using the words in bold, so that the sentences have the same meaning. Use three or four words in each gap.

1 I remember very well the day I found this seashell. **vivid**

I _____ of the day I found this seashell.

2 This old photo is very valuable to me, emotionally speaking. **sentimental**

This old photo has great _____ me.

3 My house is really crammed with all sorts of furniture. **shapes**

My house is really crammed with furniture of _____.

4 I found this old bus ticket in a drawer the other day. Just touching it takes me back to that trip. **evoke**

I only need to touch this ticket to _____ that trip.

5 I have a deep connection to this old toy. **attached**

I feel _____ this old toy.

7 Change the objects in Exercise 6 so that the sentences are true for you. Discuss in pairs.

PRONUNCIATION

8 🎧 **1.4** Look at the Clear voice box. Then listen to the sentences from Exercise 6. Practise saying the words that are difficult for you to pronounce.

CLEAR VOICE
Saying words that are difficult to pronounce

The spelling of words in English often has little connection to how words are pronounced. Many words also have letters that are silent; other words might look similar to words in your first language, but be pronounced quite differently. Finally, some English sounds might not exist in your first language. Make a note of the pronunciation of new vocabulary and practise as much as you can. Record your voice if it helps.

9 Read the Focus on box. Then look at these words. Can you think of one similar word for each? How is their meaning and use different? Discuss in pairs. You can use a dictionary to help.

attached to   come across   emotional   evoke   vague

FOCUS ON Distinguishing between words with similar meanings

Some words (e.g. *vivid* and *vibrant*) can have very similar meanings. However, often they do not collocate with the same words. For example, although you can talk about both *vivid/vibrant colours*, you can only talk about *a vivid/~~vibrant~~ memory*.

Similar words are also often used to convey slightly different ideas. For example, *vibrant* suggests something is exciting and full of life, while *vivid* suggests something (e.g. *a memory* or *description*) is strong and detailed.

When you look up words with similar meanings, it is important you check both what their specific meaning is and what words they collocate with.

Go to page 146 for the Focus on reference.

10 Look at these pairs of words with similar meanings. Complete sentences a and b below with the correct form of one of the words.

awake / evoke   emotional / sentimental
vague / ambiguous

1 a She had a _____ suspicion that he wasn't telling the truth.

b A number of the points included in the report were highly _____.

2 a The chance meeting _____ the old feelings.

b The sound of rain always _____ memories of my childhood in Cambodia.

3 a Why are you so _____ about these ugly old shoes?

b The last few weeks have been tough. I think he might need our _____ support.

SPEAKING

11 Think about an object you have come across at some point that is important to you. In pairs discuss ...

• what it looks like and the story behind it is (how, when and where you found it).

• what memories or emotions it evokes for you.

• how it reflects who you are.

• whether you'd ever consider throwing it away.

1D
Adapting to different personality types

LESSON GOALS
- Learn about the different personality types
- Consider the different goals and preferences of each personality type
- Practise adapting the way you manage your different encounters

SPEAKING

1 Think of a good friend. Write down three qualities that describe them. In pairs, discuss the questions.

1 How similar is your friend's personality to yours?
2 What drew you to each other? What keeps you together?

2 Do the personality quiz. Then compare your answers with a partner.

Personality quiz

Look at the statements and tick (✓) the option (a or b) that you feel best describes you.

1
a ☐ I prefer to be efficient and do things quickly.
b ☐ I prefer to take things slowly and carefully.

2
a ☐ I like collaborating with people.
b ☐ I like working independently.

3
a ☐ I'm outspoken and tend to speak my mind.
b ☐ I often keep my opinions to myself.

4
a ☐ Being liked is more important than being right.
b ☐ Being right is more important than being liked.

5
a ☐ People say I'm full of life.
b ☐ People say I'm a calming influence.

6
a ☐ When making decisions, it's more important to me to consider other people's feelings
b ☐ When making decisions, it's more important to me to consider the facts and the end result.

7
a ☐ I tend to get on with things without thinking too much about them.
b ☐ I spend time thinking about things before I do them.

8
a ☐ People see me as being positive and agreeable.
b ☐ People see me as being logical and analytical.

3 Work in pairs. Check your results on page 165 Do you agree with the quiz results? Why? / Why not?

4 Look at the infographic on page 19. Which quadrant do the quiz results say describes your personality best? In pairs, answer the questions.

1 What do quadrants 'D' and 'i' have in common? What about 'C' and 'S'?
2 What do quadrants 'i' and 'S' have in common? What about 'D' and 'C'?
3 Which characteristics are usually seen as positive and which might be seen as negative in each quadrant?

MY VOICE

5 ▶ **1.2** Watch the video about different personality types. In pairs, answer the questions.

1 What examples does the video give to illustrate how one person might display personality traits from different quadrants?
2 How does the video suggest we adapt and adjust to our conversation partners? How easy or hard do you think this might be to do?

6 Look at the Communication skill box. Using these tips and the infographic, decide what each type tends to value. What might they fear the most?

COMMUNICATION SKILL
Adapting to different personality types

When adapting to the 'dominance' type …
- be confident, direct and concise; focus on the task at hand; provide solutions; remain objective.

When adapting to the 'influence' type …
- be friendly; use humour; focus on building rapport and commonalities; relate personal anecdotes; show appreciation for their ideas.

When adapting to the 'steadiness' type …
- be warm, sincere and empathetic; show interest and concern for them; be patient even when they are slow to embrace change.

When adapting to the 'conscientiousness' type …
- be logical and systematic; pay attention to details; use facts and evidence; be diplomatic.

The DiSC model

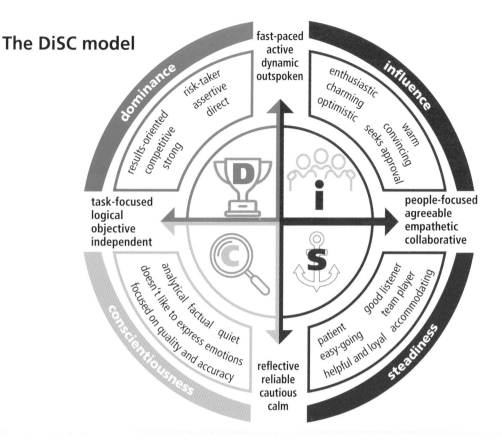

7 OWN IT! 🎧 1.5 Listen to three scenarios and take some notes. What personality types do you see in Min-woo, Cara, Soha and Lev?

8 Work in pairs. Compare your notes. Discuss what the four people in Exercise 7 should do in each situation.

9 Look at the Useful language box. Would you use similar phrases in your own language?

> **Useful language** Adapting to different personality types
>
> **Being direct and concise**
> The point I'm trying to make is that …
> I hope you don't mind me being direct.
>
> **Building rapport**
> I find your (work/ideas) on (the topic) fascinating!
> It's interesting that we both (know/like) …
>
> **Showing interest and concern**
> I'm really interested to hear your thoughts on this.
> You seem a little (preoccupied/upset). Is something bothering you?
>
> **Backing up what you say with evidence**
> Scientific research has proven that …
> I'm not making this up. I read somewhere that …

10 🎧 1.6 Listen to how Min-woo deals with the first scenario when he goes to speak to Cara, his manager. What does Min-woo do to adapt to Cara's personality type?

11 Look at your notes on the other two scenarios in Exercise 7 or read the audioscript on page 169. With a partner, roleplay each scenario using the Communication skill tips and Useful language to help you adapt to each other.

SPEAKING

12 Think of someone you know whose personality is very different from yours. Answer the questions. Then work in pairs and tell each other about the person you've chosen.
  1 What do you think are the differences between you? Are there any similarities?
  2 What personality type do you think they are?
  3 What's your relationship like with them? Is there anything you could do to build a stronger relationship with them?

EXPLORE MORE!

Find out about more complex DiSC personality assessments. Search online 'DiSC model assessment' to find other questionnaires you can do.

It was great meeting you!

LESSON GOALS
* Learn to structure a follow-up message
* Make plans and suggestions
* Write an email to follow up a meeting

SPEAKING

1 Work in pairs. Discuss the questions.

1 When you meet someone new and want to arrange to meet them again, which of the following do you usually do?
   * Nothing
   * Find them afterwards on social media and try to connect with them
   * Ask for their phone number or email address
   * Suggest a specific meeting, for example going for a coffee
   * Something else

2 Do you find it easy or difficult to arrange a follow-up meeting with someone you've recently met?

READING FOR WRITING

2 Read the three messages (two emails and a text) on page 21, which each suggest a follow-up meeting. Tick (✓) the statements that are true for all three messages.

1 The writer and the recipient of the message recently met for the first time.

2 They were introduced to one another by a mutual friend or acquaintance.

3 They both do the same sport or hobby.

4 The writer would like to meet their new acquaintance again.

5 The writer suggests a phone call or online meeting.

3 Look at the Writing skill box. Then read the messages again and identify the three stages of each message.

WRITING SKILL
Structuring a message

When you arrange a follow-up meeting, whether it's formal or informal, you will usually structure it in the same way:

1 Mention the first meeting and what you talked about.

2 Explain why the writer would like another meeting.

3 Suggest next steps or a future meeting and ask for a response.

4 Work in pairs. Answer the questions.

1 Which messages are the most and least formal? What specific features of the text show this?

2 Are the three texts equally polite? Why? / Why not?

A

Hi Elena

It was lovely meeting you at Hana's party last weekend. I was fascinated to hear that you're as interested as I am in local history. I'd love to hear more about some of the discoveries you mentioned. How about meeting for a coffee? Saturday afternoons are good for me. Let me know if you'd like to get together.

All the best,
Ania

B

Dear Mr Ong

I really enjoyed meeting you at the conference last week. I wonder if you managed to get out for a morning run by the river as you'd hoped? I found your approach to social media marketing extremely interesting.

Since our meeting, I've been thinking that there might be some ways in which our two groups could beneficially collaborate. Certainly your technology could be usefully applied in the products my team is currently promoting. I'd be keen to take this discussion further, if you agree.

Would you be interested in having a video call to discuss some ideas? If so, would you be able to make time in the next week or two? I think a half hour to begin with would be enough for me to outline what I have in mind. Then if you're interested, we could take it from there. Thursday or Friday morning next week would work well for me. If either of those days suits you then suggest a time. If not, let me know what would work for you.

I look forward to talking to you again.

Best regards,
Helene Lacroix

C

Great talking to you at the climbing gym last Monday. You said you'd like to have a go at outdoor climbing some time. Two friends and I are planning a day out next weekend and we could use a fourth. Want to come along? Let me know!

5 Look at the expressions in the Useful language box. Which phrase is the most formal and which is the least formal?

> **Useful language**   Making plans and suggestions
>
> Would you be interested in (-ing)?
> Let me know if you'd like to (get together).
> How about (-ing?)
> I'd be really grateful if you could …
> Would (one day next week) be convenient?
> I'd be keen to (collaborate).
> Let me know what works for you.
> Would (Friday) suit you?
> If you're interested, we can take it from there.
> I look forward to (meeting you again).

WRITING TASK

6 **WRITE** Choose one of the following situations. Write a more formal email. Use B as a model.

- At a trade show you met someone who works for a company you may want to work for. Suggest a call or video chat to find out more about the company.
- An acquaintance introduced you to a teacher on a university course you might want to apply to. Suggest a call or video chat to find out more about the course.
- On a work-related training course you met someone who does a similar job to yours in a different company that isn't a competitor. Suggest meeting to discuss what you could learn from each other.

7 **CHECK** Use the checklist. I have …

☐ used an appropriate subject line.
☐ mentioned our first meeting and what we talked about.
☐ explained why I'd like another meeting.
☐ made a specific suggestion for a future meeting.
☐ asked for a response.
☐ used the appropriate level of formality.
☐ used the Useful language to make plans and suggestions.

8 **REVIEW** Work in pairs. Read your partner's email. Does it include all of the items on the checklist? Is the tone appropriate? Why? / Why not?

Go to page 130 for the Reflect and review.

GROW, is a 20,000m² artwork on a leek farm, developed by Daan Roosegaarde to celebrate the beauty of agriculture and showcase the innovative technologies that aim to help plants grow more sustainably, Lelystad, the Netherlands.

2

Fresh ideas

GOALS

- Create a timeline to understand a biography
- Use multi-word verbs to talk about innovation
- Explain features and benefits; use noun suffixes
- Understand consonant sounds in English
- Encourage creative problem-solving
- Write a formal proposal

1 **Work in pairs. Discuss the questions.**

1 Look at the photo. What connection does this image have with the topic of fresh ideas?
2 Have you seen other examples of light being used to create an interesting effect?

WATCH

2 ▶ 2.1 Watch the video. Answer the questions.

NATIONAL GEOGRAPHIC EXPLORERS

FRANCISCO
ESTRADA-BELLI

ANDREJ GAJIĆ

1 What way of doing things did Francisco see in Guatemala? Why did he admire it?
2 What did Andrej notice about fishermen in the Adriatic Sea?
3 What new habit did each explorer pick up?

3 **Make connections. Discuss the questions.**

1 Do you have any ways of doing things that reduce waste or use resources more efficiently?
2 Have you discovered a new style of food or a new way of serving a meal? What was it?

2A
Finding inspiration in the past

LESSON GOALS
- Create a timeline
- Apply ideas in different contexts
- Talk about combining old and new ideas

READING

1 Work in pairs. Discuss the questions.

1 A home remedy is a traditional treatment for an illness, such as drinking mint tea for a stomach ache. What home remedies have you heard of?

2 Do you use any home remedies, for example when you have a cold?

2 Read the biography on page 25. Which statements best apply to Tu Youyou's work?

1 Modern, science-based medicine has replaced traditional medicine because it works better.

2 Traditional ways of doing things may have become tradition because they are effective.

3 Progress isn't about replacing old ideas with new ones, it's about finding out what works.

4 When someone is trained in old-fashioned ideas and techniques, they sometimes need to return to education for more updated information.

5 A thorough understanding of different systems can lead to powerful new developments.

3 Look at the Reading skill box. Read the biography again and complete the labels (1–7) on the timeline with the events (a–g).

READING SKILL
Creating a timeline

When a text describes a series of events, these may not be described in the order they happened in. A timeline can provide a clear picture of what occurred on specific dates, as well as showing events that go on for longer. When you make a timeline …

- decide the start and finish dates.
- determine the scale of the timeline.
- add the important events.

a Tu's further studies in plant-based medicine
b Artemisinin approved
c Tu attends university
d Tu has a serious illness
e Stronger artemisinin approved
f Artemisinin successfully extracted
g Artemisinin saves millions of lives

SPEAKING

4 Look at the Critical thinking skill box. Then answer questions 1 and 2.

CRITICAL THINKING SKILL
Applying ideas in different contexts

Writers often discuss and explore ideas in connection with a specific context. However, the concepts may also apply to other areas of life.

A central idea in a biography of an inventor might be the important role that luck played alongside hard work. The relationship between those two concepts could also be applied to athletes, artists or anyone else who works hard at something.

1 Tu Youyou's story is one of valuing both tradition and new ideas. Can you think of other examples of traditional methods being used along with modern ones in these fields?
- education
- farming and food growing
- making music
- your own ideas

2 Can you think of some things that are still done in a traditional way where you live, even though there are newer, more modern ways of doing them?

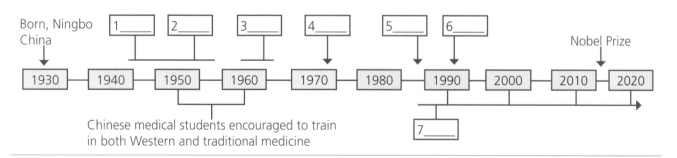

Born, Ningbo China — 1930 — 1940 — 1950 — 1960 — 1970 — 1980 — 1990 — 2000 — 2010 — 2020 — Nobel Prize

1____ 2____ 3____ 4____ 5____ 6____ 7____

Chinese medical students encouraged to train in both Western and traditional medicine

INSPIRING LIVES

Tu Youyou, a pharmaceutical chemist whose innovations in drug development have saved millions of lives

Nobel Medicine Prize co-winner Tu Youyou leaves the stage after receiving her medal during the award ceremony at the Stockholm Concert Hall on December 10, 2015.

Bringing together the past and the future

Scientist Tu Youyou knew from her studies in ancient Chinese medicine that a plant called sweet wormwood or *Artemisia annua* could
5 be used to treat malaria, a serious disease which, spread by mosquitoes, affects millions of people every year. However, Tu Youyou and her colleagues struggled to extract it through boiling. After repeated failures, Tu
10 remembered one of the recipes from traditional Chinese medicine that she'd copied into her notebook. According to this ancient formula, the plant should be soaked, not boiled. Once they changed to this method, artemisinin – the
15 chemical compound that fights malaria – was extracted. The year was 1972.

Early education and inspiration

Born on December 30, 1930 in Ningbo, China, Tu Youyou was the only girl of five children
20 in her family. Her parents valued learning and made sure that Youyou and her four brothers all had a good education. At the age of 16, Youyou had to take a two-year break from high school because of a serious illness.
25 'This experience led me to make a decision to choose medical research for my advanced education and career,' she says. 'If I could learn and have medical skills, I could not only keep myself healthy but also cure many other
30 patients.' She was soon studying Pharmacy at the Medical School of Peking University.

The best of both worlds

In the 1950s, students of medical science in China were encouraged to study traditional Chinese medicine in addition to their training in
35 Western medicine. At the same time, traditional Chinese medicine practitioners were given the opportunity to formally study modern medical techniques. This meant that at university, along with learning the latest research in developing medicines, Tu also did research in traditional medicines and the use of plants for healing.

40 After completing her studies with a PhD in 1955, she joined the Academy of Traditional Chinese Medicine, overseen by the China Ministry of Health, which is now called the China Academy of Chinese Medical Sciences. The group tested the effectiveness of traditional remedies in treating serious illnesses. Tu participated in two research
45 projects, then from 1959 to 1962, joined a full-time course for more in-depth study of traditional plant-based medicines. When she returned to research, she was assigned to a group trying to identify plants that could be used to treat malaria.

Success at last

50 After Tu's 1972 breakthrough discovery and further careful research and testing, artemisinin was approved to treat malaria in 1986. In 1992, a much stronger version of the drug was given a new certification. As of now, it has been used to treat more than two hundred million patients with malaria. Tu has continued to work to find new ways to
55 make the drug more effective and adapt to new variants of the disease.

'From our research experience in discovering artemisinin, we learned the strengths of both Chinese and Western medicine. There is great potential for future advances if these strengths can be fully integrated.'

In 2015, Tu's contribution to medicine was honoured with a Nobel
60 Prize. 'Every scientist dreams of doing something that can help the world,' she says. 'Exploring the treasury of traditional Chinese medicine has provided us with a unique path leading to success.'

EXPLORE MORE!

Search for 'new drugs from traditional medicines' to find other examples.

Features and benefits

LESSON GOALS
* Explain a product's features and benefits
* Learn how to use multi-word verbs
* Pronounce groups of consonants across words

SPEAKING

1 Work in pairs. Discuss the questions.

1 What are some of the most useful products you use every day?

2 Think of a new product that has been introduced in your lifetime. What does it do differently from or better than products that came before it?

VOCABULARY

2 Look at the infographic and complete the short article with these words.

adaptation   affordable   corporations   cutting-edge
emerging   infrastructure   luxuries   market   reverse

Traditional innovation

Created for a
developed market

Adapted for
developing markets

Reverse innovation

Adapted for
developed markets

Created for a
developing market

A NEW WAY TO INNOVATE

A developed ¹_____ economy is one that is mature and has an advanced technological ²_____. A developing market economy is one that is ³_____, i.e. it is at an earlier stage of development. Typically, businesses in a developed economy design products to sell at home and then try to find ways to adapt them to be more ⁴_____ in economies with less money to spend. However, the Freedom Chair was created first for Tanzania – a developing market – and then adapted for sale in the United States, going against the usual flow of innovation and ⁵_____. This unusual product-development model is called ⁶_____ innovation. The main benefit is seen as the development of products that meet the needs of people who can afford few ⁷_____. They typically don't involve the absolute latest, ⁸_____ technology, but instead, use simpler existing technologies to provide what is really needed. However, despite the apparent advantages, some critics claim that what large ⁹_____ are really doing by this method of innovation is trying to save money on developing new products for the rich.

Go to page 136 for the Vocabulary reference.

LISTENING AND GRAMMAR

3 🎧 **2.1** Listen to a business student give a short case-study presentation about the Freedom Chair. Take notes on the features and benefits of the chair.

4 Read the sentences from the presentation. Underline the multi-word verbs.

1 Wheelchair users come up against serious practical challenges every day.

2 They can have real problems getting out and being active in the community.

3 Getting around in the countryside involves coping with rough roads.

4 If heavy use wears out some of the parts, replacement parts will be available locally.

5 Answer questions 1 and 2 about the sentences in Exercise 4. Then read the Grammar box to check.

1 Which of the multi-word verbs can be separated?

2 Which have an object?

GRAMMAR Multi-word verbs

Multi-word verbs are made up of a verb and one or two particles or prepositions such as *up, over, on, out* or *down*.

Phrasal verbs

Intransitive phrasal verbs have no object.
If the chair breaks down, replacement parts are available.

Separable phrasal verbs are transitive, which means they need a direct object. The object can go between the verb and the particle or after the particle. *I'd like to point out a second feature. / I'd like to point a second feature out.*

Prepositional verbs

The object must go after the particle. *I'll go over the main features.*

Go to page 147 for the Grammar reference.

---

6 Delete the incorrect phrases. In some items, both options are correct.

Sabina relies ¹*on her chair / her chair on* to get around. She really couldn't do ²*without it / it without*. When we were in town, she pointed ³*out some places / some places out* where she used to have problems – for example the bank, which had steep stairs. However, a few years ago they put ⁴*a lift in / in a lift*, which has really helped. She can cope ⁵*with most shops / most shops with* because they tend to be wheelchair-accessible in her city. When she needs medication, her doctor orders it and then Sabina ⁶*picks it up / picks up it* at the pharmacy.

7 Rewrite sentences 1–5 adding these words in the correct position.

---

against   away   on   to   with

---

1 The engineers want to do with expensive features.

2 I'm looking forward trying it.

3 People with disabilities come up regular challenges when cities do not take their needs into account.

4 They have to put up a lot of inconvenience.

5 This material cuts down extra weight.

EXPLORE MORE!

Search for 'examples of reverse innovation' to find other stories.

PRONUNCIATION AND SPEAKING

8 🔊 **2.2** Look at the Clear voice box. Then listen and repeat phrases 1–9.

CLEAR VOICE
Saying consonant clusters across word boundaries

When words are combined to make phrasal verbs, compound nouns or common expressions, they are often pronounced as if the words are joined together. When a word that ends in a consonant is followed by a word that begins with another consonant, a consonant cluster across words is formed.

breaks_down

When you speak, if you find the consonant cluster difficult to say, pause briefly between the two words.

---

1 developed_market

2 product_ development

3 breaks_down

4 cutting-edge_ technology

5 existing_technology

6 the main_feature

7 the main_benefits

8 personal_transport

9 let's_look

9 Think about a product you know and use. Make notes about its …

• **features:** technical aspects of the product, for example, size, shape, material, construction.

• **benefits:** the ways in which features make the product good or useful for users.

10 Prepare a case study presentation to tell a small group about your product. Use your notes from Exercise 9 and the Useful language to help you.

Useful language Describing a product's features and benefits

I'd like to tell you a bit about …
It is/isn't cutting-edge technology.
The engineers/designers who came up with … set out to provide …
I'll go over …
I'd like to point out …
Let's look at …
The main feature is …
The main benefits of this feature are …

11 Work in a small group. Take turns to introduce the product, explaining its features and benefits.

2C
Where ideas come from

LESSON GOALS
• Use suffixes to form nouns
• Understand consonant sounds
• Use irreversible word pairs
• Talk about ways to come up with ideas

'There is no such thing as a new idea. It is impossible. We simply take a lot of old ideas and put them into a sort of mental kaleidoscope. We give them a turn and they make new and curious combinations. We keep on turning and making new combinations indefinitely; but they are the same old pieces of coloured glass that have been in use through all the ages.'

Mark Twain, American writer

A kaleidoscopic image of Times Square, New York City.

SPEAKING

1 Read the Mark Twain quotation above. Work in pairs. Do you agree or disagree? Why?

VOCABULARY

2 Use the words in brackets and these endings to make noun forms to complete 1–9.

-dom   -hood   -ion   -ity   -ment   -ness   -ship

The following habits can increase the
¹_____ (probable) that you will come up with good ideas:

- **Seek opportunities for** ²_____:
  (collaborate). Working in ³_____ (partner) with people you trust means your ideas can be tested, questioned and improved.

- **Actively pursue** ⁴_____: (involve) with new people, ideas or activities. (Never made music? Take guitar lessons!) This will stimulate your mind and increase the ⁵_____ (likely) of new ways of thinking.

- **Develop your** ⁶_____: (aware) of when ideas come. Do you get inspired when you go for a walk? Turn walking into a way to generate ideas.

- **Schedule your work. Making a**
  ⁷_____: (commit) to a deadline – even if it's set by you – can help focus your mind to be creative.

- **Use the power of** ⁸_____: (boring). Instead of always grabbing your phone to check social media, sometimes just let your mind be empty. This can give it the ⁹_____ (free) to come up with new ideas.

3 Work in pairs. Discuss which ideas in Exercise 2 you agree with or have successfully tried. Try to use the noun forms.

Go to page 136 for the Vocabulary reference.

LISTENING

NATIONAL GEOGRAPHIC EXPLORERS

4 🎧 **2.3** Listen to Francisco Estrada-Belli and Andrej Gajić talking about where their ideas come from. Which ideas from Exercise 2 do they mention?

5 🎧 **2.4** Look at the Listening skill box. Listen and write the phrases you hear.

LISTENING SKILL
Understanding accents: consonant sounds

A speaker's accent in a second language is often influenced by their first language. Speakers of some languages might pronounce the *v* sound more like *b*, so you may hear *debelop* rather than *develop*. Speakers of other languages may tend to say *dewelop*, using a *w* sound for *v*. Knowing about these different ways of pronunciation may help you understand other people better.

6 🎧 **2.3** Listen again to Francisco and Andrej in Exercise 4. Are the sentences true (T) or false (F)?

1 Francisco usually meditates only when he has a problem to solve.
2 Ideas can come to Francisco at many different times throughout the day.
3 Francisco often becomes bored while trying to come up with a good idea.
4 Andrej is usually most successful at solving problems when he concentrates on them.
5 Andrej says that developing new ideas requires understanding other people's ideas.
6 For Andrej, working closely with colleagues is important for developing fresh ideas.

7 Look at the Focus on box. Work in pairs. How would you use the word pairs in the box? How would you say them in your language?

FOCUS ON   Irreversible word pairs

Some common expressions used by fluent speakers of English are pairs of words that are generally said only in one order. For example, people often say *more or less* but very rarely say *less or more*. Other examples include:
back to front, in and out, plain and simple, clean and tidy, life or death.

Go to page 148 for the Focus on reference.

8 Complete sentences 1–6 with these irreversible word pairs.

back and forth	day in, day out	first and foremost
peace and quiet	rain or shine	tried and tested

1 Meditation is a _____ method for clearing your mind.
2 After a busy day, I need some _____ so I can relax.
3 I go to the office and have the same routine _____ .
4 I texted _____ with Kati until we were finally able to agree a time to meet up.
5 I go for a morning walk come _____ – even in winter!
6 He's a teacher _____ , but also does some research.

PRONUNCIATION AND SPEAKING

9 🎧 **2.5** Look at the Clear voice box. Circle the examples of consonant clusters across words in 1–6. The listen to the sentences and notice where sounds are deleted.

CLEAR VOICE
Understanding consonant clusters across word boundaries

When a word that ends with a consonant sound is followed by a word that begins with a consonant sound, one of the consonant sounds is often softened or deleted. For example, *next to* would naturally be pronounced /nɛks tuː/ (*nex-to*) rather than /nɛkst tuː/ (*next to*).

1 I had a hard time focusing.
2 That's another tried and tested activity.
3 We had some good back and forth discussions.
4 These are some tasks that might need my help.
5 I've learned not to force myself.
6 It wouldn't have been possible without collaboration.

10 Read the questions. Note down your answers.

1 Do you tend to get good ideas at a certain time or place?
2 Can you think of a time when you were trying to get ideas for an important decision? How did you go about it?
3 Have you ever collaborated with others to come up with ideas? How? What was the result?

11 Work in small groups. Discuss your answers to Exercise 10. Decide which story of ideas and decision-making you like best.

EXPLORE MORE!

Search for 'How to come up with new ideas' to find more examples.

Encouraging creative problem solving

LESSON GOALS
- Learn how to encourage creative problem-solving
- Identify ways to mediate problems
- Practise using questions to encourage creative problem-solving

SPEAKING

1 Look at the matchsticks below. With a partner, can you work out the biggest possible number you can make just by moving two matchsticks?

2 Read the clue on page 167 and try again.

3 Look at page 165 for a possible answer. Then discuss the questions below with a partner.
1 Why might this be a tricky puzzle for most people?
2 What does it tell us about problem solving?
3 How does the clue help us think outside the box?

4 Read about Yury and Marcia. Then discuss the questions (1 and 2).

Yury has problems sleeping and struggles to wake up on time for work in the mornings. As a result, he's often late for work and is getting into trouble. His friend Marcia tries to help.

M: It can help to have a hot bath before you sleep.

Y: I don't have a bath in my flat, only a shower. And showers wake me up.

M: How about reading a boring book in bed?

Y: I've tried that. I just get bored.

M: You're probably not getting enough vitamins.

Y: I do. I eat really healthily.

M: Why don't you try counting sheep? That works for me …

Y: Counting what? Why would I count sheep?

1 Do you think Marcia was successful in helping Yury solve his problem? Why? / Why not?
2 What are the advantages and disadvantages of giving someone advice when they approach you with a problem?

MY VOICE

5 ▶ 2.2 Watch the video about creative problem-solving. In pairs, answer the questions.
1 Why do many people consistently apply similar solutions to their ongoing problems?
2 When someone comes to us with a problem, why is responding with advice not always a good idea?
3 How is the role of a mediator different from the role of an adviser?
4 Yury is focusing on his inability to sleep as the cause for his lateness. How might reframing the problem help him?
5 How can *What If?* questions help Yury?

6 Look at the Communication skill box. In pairs, look at the scenarios (1–4) on page 31 and take turns to be Student A and Student B.

COMMUNICATION SKILL
Encouraging creative problem solving

In order to encourage creative problem solving, it's important to move away from offering advice and instead support the other person in coming up with their own creative solutions. You can do this by …
1 getting them to reframe their problem e.g. to describe their issue in five words or rephrase their problem as a question.
2 using questions to help them explore their problem, examine their reality and see things from different perspectives.
3 encouraging them to come up with their own solutions.

Student A: Describe the problem in five words.
Student B: Rephrase the problem as a question.

1 Beyza works from home, but finds it hard to stay focused. She is easily distracted by social media and spends too much time watching videos on her phone. She feels she needs a few breaks, but she's been falling behind on her deadlines recently.

2 Dino moved out of his parents' house a year ago and has been getting takeaways every evening since then. He says he doesn't know how to cook, but takeaways are expensive and aren't always healthy.

3 Yen's husband Tuan likes Yen coming along when he goes out with his friends. But Yen doesn't enjoy these gatherings because she feels like an outsider and can't really follow their conversations. Yen tried to suggest that she didn't join these evenings, but this is causing a lot of upset between them.

4 Paulo loves shopping and often justifies it by saying 'Life is too short. We need to enjoy it!' However, he has difficulty managing his money and tends to run out of money before the end of the month. This is becoming a problem for him.

7 Look at the Useful language box. How might these questions encourage creative problem solving?

> **Useful language** Encouraging creative problem solving
>
> **Reframing the problem**
> Can you describe your problem using five words?
> Are you basically asking ('What can I do to avoid being late for work?')
>
> **Examining reality**
> Is there anything you could do differently?
> Is that a fact or might it just be an assumption?
>
> **Seeing things from a different perspective**
> What would you do if you were (your best friend)?
> How might (your family) want you to deal with this?
>
> **Coming up with solutions**
> What do you need to do to make that happen?
> What if there were no obstacles? What would you do?

Competitors prepare for the Rubik's Cube European Championship in Prague, Czech Republic.

8 **OWN IT!** Beyza, Dino, Yen and Paulo from Exercise 6 decide to talk to a friend about their problem. Work in groups of three to roleplay the situations. Take turns to be Student A, B and C. Use the Communication skill tips and the Useful language to help you.

Student A: You are the person with the problem – choose Beyza, Dino, Paulo or Yen.

Student B: You are the friend supporting A to solve their problem.

Student C: You are the observer. Interrupt if you hear Student B giving advice instead of asking questions. Offer Student B feedback at the end of their roleplay.

SPEAKING

9 Work in small groups. Discuss the questions.

1 Have you ever told someone about a problem and felt frustrated by their response? What happened?

2 What do you tend to do when someone tells you about their problem? Might you change how you approach such a situation after this lesson?

EXPLORE MORE!

How can you help yourself or others think outside the box? How can you develop those lateral thinking skills? Find out more by searching online for 'develop + lateral thinking'.

2E

As a next step ...

LESSON GOALS
• Explain causes and results
• Introduce the sections of a proposal
• Write a proposal

SPEAKING

1 Work in pairs. Look at the photo. Discuss the questions.

1 Is there any area near you where this kind of situation happens?

2 What problems does this sort of situation create?

3 What are some possible solutions?

READING FOR WRITING

2 Read the proposal. Match the topics (a–f) with the sections (1–5) in the proposal. There is one extra topic.

a Current situation

b Expected outcomes and benefits

c Introduction

d Potential obstacles

e Recommended next steps

f Proposed solutions

3 Look at the Writing skill box. Underline the sentences in the proposal that use these expressions.

WRITING SKILL
Explaining causes and results

Both for explaining problems and proposing solutions, it's useful to state clearly the consequences of an existing situation and to describe the results of proposed changes. This will help the reader clearly understand why change may be necessary. The following expressions are useful for calling attention to results:

As a result, ...
... has led to ...
Consequently, ...
... therefore ...
... thus ...
... resulting in ...

1 This proposal suggests ways of improving traffic flow and visitor experience in the town centre.

2 In recent years, road traffic has greatly increased in the town centre. As a result, there are frequent traffic jams. Many of the journeys are made by local residents coming into town to shop. The congestion has led to increased noise and air pollution in the area and also to slow bus journeys. Consequently, the area has become unpleasant for drivers, pedestrians, cyclists and public transport users alike.

3 The situation would be greatly improved through the following three measures.

• **The creation of a network of cycle lanes and paths leading into the town centre taking bicycles away from the routes with the most traffic.** This would make cycling safer and more enjoyable and would therefore encourage people to cycle rather than drive into town.

• **A reduction in the amount of provision for parking in the town centre.** This would provide an incentive for people not to drive into the town centre and instead to walk, cycle or take the bus, thus reducing the number cars coming into and out of the area.

• **The closure of Centre Street to motor vehicles between Gale Lane and Green Lane.** This would create a pleasant outdoor space for people to enjoy on foot, away from the noise and air pollution of the busy city streets.

4 Taken together, the above three measures would significantly cut car traffic in the area, encourage people to cycle into town rather than drive, and make bus journeys faster and more convenient. The reduction in car traffic would in turn lower the amount of noise and air pollution, resulting in a better experience for all users of the town centre.

5 Before proceeding further, an investigation of the practicalities and costs of implementing the above proposed changes should be carried out. In addition, local residents and businesses should be consulted to determine the level of support for the proposed changes.

A traffic jam in Pune, India.

4 Match the causes (1–5) with the results (a–e) according to the text.

1	An increase in road traffic	a	Noise and air pollution
2	Traffic congestion	b	Reduction in driving
3	Noise and air pollution	c	Frequent traffic jams
4	Safer cycling routes	d	Less pollution and a better experience
5	A reduction in traffic	e	Area unpleasant

5 Think of a situation or area of your city or town that could be improved. Make notes on …:

- the situation.
- possible ways to improve the situation.
- benefits and outcomes of the suggested plan.
- recommended next steps.

6 Look at the Useful Language box and note the phrases for introducing each section of a proposal (1–5). Then underline the phrases used to introduce each section in the proposal on page 32.

> **Useful language** Introducing the sections of a proposal
> 1 The aims of this proposal are to …
> 2 There is a strong feeling among (residents) that …
> 3 It is recommended that …
> 4 Implementation of the above ideas would result in …
> 5 As a next step, …

7 Work in pairs to discuss your notes from Exercise 5. Then write a one-sentence introduction to use for your proposal.

This proposal suggests ways of dealing with rubbish and improving the visitor experience in the town square.

WRITING TASK

8 **WRITE** Using the text on page 32 as a model, write a formal proposal in five sections. Include some explanations of causes and results. Use the Writing skill box, your notes from Exercises 5 and 7 and the Useful language to help you.

9 **CHECK** Use the checklist. I have …

- [ ] included an introduction.
- [ ] explained the situation, including specific problems and their causes.
- [ ] proposed a solution including hoped-for results.
- [ ] explained benefits and outcomes.
- [ ] suggested next steps.

10 **REVIEW** Work in pairs. Read your partner's proposal. Do you think the proposal would be approved? Why? / Why not?

Go to page 130 for the Reflect and review.

US skier Nicholas Fairall, competes in a ski jumping event in Innsbruck, Austria.

3

On the move

GOALS

- Identify connections between cause and effect
- Practise ways to interpret and speculate about events
- Describe ways of moving; talk about life moves
- Infer a speaker's opinions
- Support others through change
- Write an email to confirm arrangements

1 Work in pairs. Discuss the questions.

1 Look at the photo. What physical skills are involved in an activity like this one? What mental skills are required?

2 Do you have any unusual physical skills?
Well, I can wiggle my ears!

WATCH

2 ▶ **3.1** Watch the video. Answer the questions.

NATIONAL GEOGRAPHIC EXPLORERS

ANUSHA SHANKAR   REBECCA WOLFF

1 What physical skills are Anusha and Rebecca happy they have? When and why did they learn them?

2 What physical skills do they wish they had?

3 Make connections. Discuss the questions.

1 What can you do with your body that you didn't use to be able to?

2 Which of these skills would you like to have?

be really flexible   dance well   juggle   ride a horse

Moving around freely?

LESSON GOALS
* Understand an extract from a book about data bias
* Identify different ways to indicate cause and effect
* Evaluate solutions to problems from different perspectives

SPEAKING

1 Work in pairs. Discuss the questions.
1 What forms of transport do you usually use?
2 How many places do you travel between on a typical day?

2 Read an online review of *Invisible Women* on page 37. What is the problem that *Invisible women* addresses? How does snow clearing relate to the book's themes?

3 Match the words and expressions (1–6) in the review with the definitions (a–f).
a information to be used to help decision-making
b a lack of similarity and equality between things
c regular journeys between home and work
d not giving an advantage to either men or women
e elected members of a local government
f consider something carefully again

READING

4 Read the extract from *Invisible Women* and label the two travel patterns (a and b) in the diagram with 'men' or 'women'.

5 Look at the Reading skill box. Find three cause and effect expressions in the review. Which introduce a cause and which an effect?

READING SKILL
**Identifying different ways
to indicate cause and effect**

The link between an action or situation and its effects can be clearly signposted with words and expressions such as *As a consequence/ result,* and *Therefore.* However, there are many other ways to express cause and effect, such as with …
* nouns, e.g. *The outcome is that … / … the added benefit of …*
* verbs, e.g. *can affect / contributed to / may disadvantage …*
* expressions, e.g. *thanks to / owing to / What this means is that …*

Look for these less obvious signposts to better understand the arguments.

6 Read the extract again. Find the effect of the following causes. In pairs, discuss what word or expression tells you the connection in each.
1 In Karlskoga, snow was cleared from the major roads before walkways and bicycle paths.
2 Women do 75% of the world's unpaid care work.
3 There are differences in the way men and women travel and the reasons for travel.
4 The town councillors switched the order of snow-clearing to prioritize pedestrians and public-transport users.

SPEAKING

7 Look at the Critical thinking skill box. Which of the perspectives listed are not explored in the extract?

CRITICAL THINKING SKILL
**Evaluating solutions to problems
from different perspectives**

To more comprehensively evaluate a proposed solution, try looking at it from different points of view. This might involve you imagining yourself in other people's shoes or, if you are able, asking them directly for their opinion. Consider the impact of a proposed solution …
* on different groups (based on wealth, gender, ethnic background, age, ability, etc).
* on the climate and the living planet.
* from a financial point of view.

8 Work in groups. Look at page 167. Read about a problem. Then follow these steps (1–5) to decide on the best solution.

Step 1 Decide whose perspectives might be particularly important to consider.
Step 2 Evaluate each solution from those perspectives.
Step 3 Brainstorm other solutions that might be worth considering.
Step 4 Identify any 'data gaps' in your understanding that would help reach a good decision.
Step 5 Make a decision as to the best solution (with the information you have).

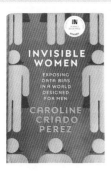

In her book *Invisible women* Caroline Criado Perez looks at a number of areas of life where an absence of [1]**data** on women has led to decisions in government policy, technology, the workplace and medical research which have had a negative impact on women. This has not usually been deliberate, but stems from a tendency to think that what's good for men is good for everyone. In Chapter One, Criado Pérez tells the story of Karlskoga, a town in Sweden, where they are trying to [2]**re-evaluate** all their policies to ensure gender equality. When it came to decisions about clearing snow from roads and walkways, town [3]**councillors** initially assumed that these, at least, would be a [4]**gender-neutral** issue. However, when they dug a bit deeper, they discovered a [5]**disparity** between how snow clearing affected men and women, owing (in part) to the differences in their daily [6]**commutes** ...

Chapter one From *Invisible Women* by Caroline Criado Perez

1   ... At the time, snow-clearing in Karlskoga began with the major traffic arteries, and ended with pedestrian walkways and bicycle paths. But this was affecting men and women differently because men and women travel differently. The data we have makes it clear that women are more likely than men to walk and take public transport. In France, two-thirds of public transport passengers are women; in Philadelphia, in the US, the figure is 64%. Meanwhile, men around the world are more likely to drive and if a household owns a car, it is the
5   men who dominate access to it.

And the differences don't stop at the mode of transport: it's also about why men and women are travelling. Men are most likely to have a simple travel pattern: a twice-daily commute in and out of town. But women's travel patterns tend to be more complicated. Women do 75% of the world's unpaid care work and this affects their travel needs. A typical female travel pattern involves, for example, dropping children off at school before going to work; taking an elderly relative to the doctor and doing the grocery shopping on the way home. This
10 is called 'trip-chaining', a travel pattern of several small, interconnected trips that has been observed in women around the world.

What these differences meant back in Karlskoga was that the snow-clearing schedule was in fact not gender neutral at all, so the town councillors switched the order of snow-clearing to prioritize pedestrians and public-transport users. After all, they reasoned, it wouldn't cost any more money, and driving a car through snow is easier than pushing a buggy (or a wheelchair, or a bike) through snow.

What they didn't realize was that it would actually end up saving them money. Since 1985, northern Sweden has been collecting
15 data on hospital admissions for injuries. Their databases are dominated by pedestrians, who are injured three times more often than motorists in icy conditions and account for half the hospital time of all traffic-related injuries. And the majority of these pedestrians are women.

A five-year study in Skåne County found that the injuries cost money in
20 healthcare and lost productivity. The estimated cost of all these pedestrian falls during just a single winter season was 36 million Kronor (around £3.2 million). This is likely to be a conservative estimate; many injured pedestrians will visit hospitals that are not contributing to the national traffic accident register: some will visit doctors; and some will simply stay at home. As a result,
25 both the healthcare and productivity costs are likely to be higher.

But even with this conservative estimate, the cost of pedestrian accidents in icy conditions was about twice the cost of winter road maintenance. In Solna, near Stockholm, it was three times the cost, and some studies reveal it's even higher. Whatever the exact disparity, it is clear that preventing injuries by
30 prioritizing pedestrians in the snow-clearing schedule makes economic sense.

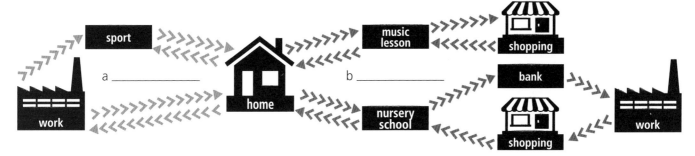

3B
The world at walking pace

LESSON GOALS
- Describe ways of moving
- Practise ways to interpret and speculate about events
- Use emphatic stress when hedging

Finish

Humans migrated out of Africa around 60,000 years ago, making it to the tip of South America about 10,000 years ago.

Start

Total distance:	30 million footsteps (33,800 km)	Journey started:	Jan, 2013
Means of travel:	on foot / by boat	Planned duration:	7 years
Starting point:	Rift Valley, Ethiopia	Latest estimated duration:	11 years
End point:	Patagonia, southern Argentina	National borders crossed	36

VOCABULARY AND SPEAKING

1 Work in pairs. Look at the photo, map and fact file about Paul Salopek's journey and discuss the questions.

1 What kind of journey is Paul on?
2 Where is he going?
3 Why might he be travelling this way?

2 Using a dictionary to help you, decide which of these expressions might describe the way Paul is travelling. Work in pairs to compare answers.

be in no rush   creep past   dash around
go for a leisurely stroll   make a flying visit
a race against the clock   take your time
trek through the mountains
walk at an unhurried pace   wander around

Go to page 137 for the Vocabulary reference.

3 Complete each sentence with the correct form of a word or words from Exercise 2.

1 We took it easy today. After _____ the museum for an hour, we just went for a gentle _____ around the city.
2 I like the _____ pace of life in the countryside.
3 It was very late, so I tried to _____ upstairs, but my father still woke up.
4 I won't be home until 7, so you can _____ making dinner!
5 On the first day they _____ for eight hours, covering more than 30 kilometres.
6 She was in a _____ to get home to see her son before he went to bed.
7 Sorry, this is just a _____. I can't stay.
8 The whole team was working _____ to finish the project on time.
9 I've been _____ all morning getting ready to go away. There's so much to do before we leave.

LISTENING AND GRAMMAR

4 🎧 **3.1** Listen to a podcast about Paul Salopek's journey around the world. Make notes about …

a the route. b the reasons for doing it.

c what Paul has learned.

5 🎧 **3.2** Listen to six extracts from the podcast. Change the words and expressions in bold to the ones you hear. How does the meaning change?

1 Paul is trekking the pathways the first humans who migrated out of Africa **took** → _____.

2 They **didn't make** → _____ a journey right across the world like this, **did** → _____ they?

3 He's **listened** → _____ carefully to all these stories of human life …

4 … how complete strangers, who **had** → _____ nothing in common with him, …

5 As you're listening to this, who knows where he **is** → _____?

6 He **is going to** → _____ arrive at his finishing point sometime in the next …

6 Look at the sentences in the Grammar box. Which of the structures in bold express ideas 1–4? Which express more than one idea.

> **GRAMMAR** Modals and related verbs
>
> Modal verbs express an attitude or interpretation of what is being spoken about.
> *They **couldn't have made** a journey like this.*
> But modals aren't the only verbs that have these functions. Semi-modal verbs share the same functions, but not the same structure as modal verbs.
> *You**'d better** find somewhere to sleep.*
> Sometimes semi-modal verbs are necessary because modals don't have tense forms.
> *He**'s been able to** listen carefully. (not He's can…)*
> Other structures, such as *be supposed to, needn't, allow* fulfil the same function as modal verbs.
> *You**'re not supposed** to walk …*
>
> **Go to page 148 for the Grammar reference.**
>
> 1 permission, obligation or necessity
> 2 possibility or ability
> 3 speculation about the past, present or future
> 4 suggestions or advice

7 Work in pairs. Make notes about the following things. Show each other your notes and ask anything you'd like to know more about.

- a journey you'll have to make this week
- something you'd better do before next week
- a thing that ought to arrive soon
- behaviour that isn't permitted at school or work
- something you do but aren't supposed to
- something you needn't have worried about
- something you might be able to do in the future

PRONUNCIATION

8 🎧 **3.3** Look at the Clear voice box. Then listen to the examples. Practise saying the sentences.

> **CLEAR VOICE**
> **Using emphatic stress when hedging**
>
>
>
> Modals and related verbs are useful when you want to state an opinion or give advice in a less confident, less certain or less direct way, i.e. to 'hedge'.
> To hedge clearly it's often helpful to give emphasis to the hedging words (i.e. the words in bold):
> *Paul ~~wouldn't~~ **might not** have made (or **It's possible** that Paul wouldn't have made) the same connections if he hadn't arrived on foot into their communities.*
> *You ~~should buy~~ **might** want to buy warmer clothes before spending the night in the desert.*

9 Use modals and related verbs to make this text less direct. Then practise reading it aloud. Which words will you emphasize?

Walking is better for you than any other exercise. It helps you reduce the risk of heart disease. Walking reduces stress too. You must walk for at least thirty minutes each day to avoid a heart attack. If you do this, you will feel better and will even live longer.

SPEAKING

10 Work in groups. Prepare a walk for visitors to your town or country: choose either a three-hour stroll around your town or city, or a three-day trek somewhere in the countryside. Discuss …

- where the best places may be to go.
- what time of day or year they should do it.
- any other important advice.

EXPLORE MORE!

Find out where Paul is now and whether he has finished his journey. Read the last reports he made. Search online for 'Paul Salopek + walk'.

Moving on

LESSON GOALS

Talk about progress and change using metaphors of movement
Inferring opinions
Practise more ways of hedging

► have identity tied to places and local group

► form strong group attachments

► value familiarity and security

► find it easy to answer 'Where are you from?'

THE 'SOMEWHERES'

THE 'ANYWHERES'

► have identity tied to global groups or to individual achievement

► have fewer, weaker attachments to groups

► value change and being open with people different from themselves

► find it hard to answer 'Where are you from?'

SPEAKING AND VOCABULARY

1 Work in pairs. Look at the infographic and answer the questions.

1 Would you describe yourself as a 'somewhere' or 'anywhere' person, or do you think the distinction is not a useful one to make? Why? / Why not?

2 To what extent do you think people have a choice as to whether they are a somewhere or an anywhere person?

2 Choose the question you think is the most interesting from each pair. Check you understand the meaning of the phrases in bold. Then ask and answer your questions in pairs.

1 a Do you feel like **settling down** yet, or are you about to **embark on** a new adventure?

b Do you think you'll **stay put** in one place or will you **feel stuck** if you do?

2 a Are you someone who plans ahead or do you tend to **stumble into** things?

b What advice would you give someone who finds themselves **at a crossroads** in their life?

3 a Do you sometimes feel the need to **get away** from your current situation?

b What would be **a backward step** for you now?

4 a What plans do you have? If they **fall through**, do you have a plan B?

b Is life **an uphill struggle** at the moment? What would ease things for you?

5 a Are you someone that needs to **stand out** from the crowd?

b Are you happy to **follow the crowd**, or do you prefer to **do your own thing**?

6 a Do you see **a bright future** ahead for you or are you more pessimistic?

b What's the next step in order to **further** your career?

Go to page 137 for the Vocabulary reference.

3 Find expressions in Exercise 2 that contain the following ideas.

a looking into the future (two phrases)
b making progress (four phrases)
c staying in the same place (two phrases)
d finding it hard to make progress (four phrases)
e being the same as others (one phrase)
f being different from other people (two phrases)

4 Work in pairs. Write three pieces of advice using expressions from Exercise 2.

LISTENING

NATIONAL GEOGRAPHIC EXPLORER

5 🎧 **3.4** Look at the Listening skill box. Then listen to Anusha Shankar and Rebecca Wolff. Do you think each speaker considers themselves to be more a 'somewhere' or an 'anywhere' person?

LISTENING SKILL
Inferring opinions

We often need to listen for evidence of a speaker's opinion even though they don't state it directly. Evidence can come in many forms, such as …

- biographical information, e.g. things they did, family background and other facts about their life.
- aspects of their personality they mention, such as fears, desires, strengths and weaknesses.
- particular words that suggest attitude towards an idea or other people, especially emotive words like *fantastic* or *frightened*.

6 🎧 **3.4** Listen again. Are the statements true (T) or false (F)?

1 When they were children, both women moved for the same reason.
2 One benefit of Anusha's attitude to moving is that she has an exciting social and professional life.
3 Anusha is one of the only people in her family to travel outside India.
4 Rebecca's mother had taken her to Nova Scotia before she eventually moved there.
5 Although she has travelled a lot for work, Canada will always be Rebecca's home.

SPEAKING

7 Work in pairs. Read the Focus on box. Then underline the ways Anusha and Rebecca hedge in sentences a–d.

> **FOCUS ON** Hedging in spoken English
>
> Hedging is using words or expressions to reduce the directness or force of what you are saying.
>
> There are different ways of hedging, not just using modal verbs (see page 39).
>
> You can make information seem less important or certain, e.g. with a *bit, just, almost, probably, maybe*, or add uncertainty to the way you express them, e.g. *I think, kind of, you know.*
> **I think** *my adaptability is a handy skill.*
> **Sometimes** *it is strange to feel rootless.*
> Another way to hedge is to use words like *appears* and *suggests.*
> *My American friends* **seem** *to travel for fun.*
> You can also hedge by adding expressions that limit the information in some way.
> *It doesn't take me long to settle,* **at least socially**, *into new jobs.*

Go to page 150 for the Focus on reference.

a My American friends … rarely live for more than a few months in a new place, except maybe for a study abroad programme during college.
b I don't know if I can say I'm more of a traveller or a settler. I can see the appeal for both, …
c I've never felt super attached to any particular place.
d Not associating the idea of home with a place, but rather with the people is beautiful to me.

8 Work in pairs. Take turns to answer the questions. Before you answer, plan how you will hedge your answers.

1 Would you be happy living a travelling lifestyle without one place to call home?
2 Are people who are comfortable in unfamiliar situations more successful in life?
3 If the future of work is online, will people be able to live wherever they like?
4 Is the idea of staying in one place your whole life unrealistic these days?

EXPLORE MORE!

Search online for 'David Goodhart + Road to Somewhere' to find out more about the idea of *Somewhere* and *Anywhere* people.

3D Supporting others through change

LESSON GOALS
- Learn about how people respond to change
- Identify how we can support people affected by the life changes we make
- Understand how consonant sounds change in context
- Practise ways of managing change

SPEAKING

1 Work in pairs. Discuss the last time you dealt with a big change in your life and how you felt about it. Use these ideas or your own.

> moving   work   changes to your family unit

2 ∩ 3.5 The book *Who Moved My Cheese?* looks at different ways people deal with change. Listen to the summary and answer the questions.

1 How did the different characters (Sniff, Scurry, Hem and Haw) react to the change in their situation? What were some of the different emotions that Hem and Haw experienced?
2 What motivated Haw to find new cheese?

3 Look at the change curve on page 43. Decide which of these words might describe each stage of change. Use a dictionary to look up any words you are unsure of.

> anger   commitment   experiment   fear   shock

MY VOICE ▶

4 ▶ 3.2 Watch the video and check your answers. Fill in the change curve with the correct words from Exercise 3. Then answer the questions.

1 Why might change be difficult?
2 What might happen if we don't handle Stage 2 well?
3 How might recognizing someone's commitment to change in Stage 4 help them in the future?

5 Read some statements about change. Which stage do you think they are in?

1 'I can't imagine why we didn't do this sooner!'
2 'We've always done things that way. They'll bring the old way back, you'll see.'
3 'This is causing me more hassle than it's worth! What have I done to deserve this?'
4 'I can see how this might not be such a bad thing.'

6 Look at the Communication skill box. Then read the scenarios 1–3 and say which stage Samira, Dwayne and Winek are in. What would you do if you were Greta, Leong or Irina?

COMMUNICATION SKILL
Supporting others through change

The changes we make can have an impact on the people around us and how we respond can help them manage these changes.

Stage 1: be open with information, answer questions and help them understand the change.

Stage 2: listen actively, ask questions and show support. Handle their emotions with sensitivity.

Stage 3: allow them time and space to try things out. Highlight the benefits of this change.

Stage 4: recognize their commitment to embracing the change.

1 Greta has been driving her colleague Samira to work for the last three years, but Greta has recently decided to start cycling to work instead. Samira doesn't know how she'll get to work now and got upset with Greta for causing her 'unnecessary stress'.

2 Leong and Dwayne are housemates who enjoy cooking and eating together. Leong has now become vegetarian and suggests that Dwayne could either join him or they could prepare their meals separately. Dwayne doesn't believe this change will last and constantly reminds Leong of how much he used to enjoy eating meat.

3 Winek used to manage a team at the office but his boss Irina recently told him that he had to start working from home. He now has to find new ways of managing his team and is feeling overwhelmed and fed up.

THE CHANGE CURVE

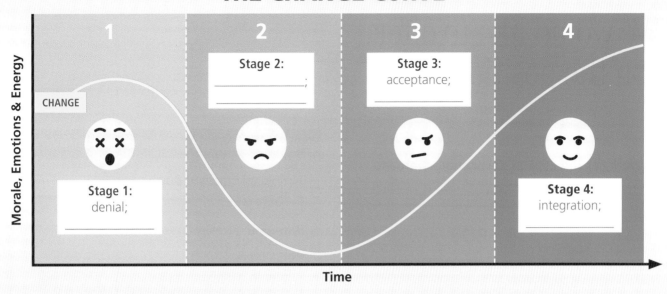

7 Look at the Useful language box. Which of these phrases do you think might be useful for Greta, Leong and Irina to use in the situations in Exercise 6?

Useful language Supporting others through change

Being open with information
Would you like me to talk you through my (plans)?
Could I explain this to you in more detail?

Listening actively and showing support
How do you feel about this? / How does this affect you?
I do understand that this isn't easy.
What can I do to make this easier for you?

Highlighting the benefits
The upside to this is (you don't have to commute to work anymore)
It must be (refreshing) to not have to (commute to work anymore).

Recognizing commitment
I'm so happy you're on board with all this.
I'm really glad to see you embracing the change.

PRONUNCIATION AND SPEAKING

8 🎧 3.6 Look at the Clear voice box. Then listen to the sentences (1–3) said slowly then fast and underline the /tʃ/ and /dʒ/ sounds in the fast version.

EXPLORE MORE!

CLEAR VOICE
Understanding consonant sound changes within and between words

In fast speech, consonant sounds can be affected by adjacent consonants. This can happen in the middle of words, e.g. the first *t* in *states* and *illustrates* sound like /t/ and /tʃ/ respectively. It can also happen between words, e.g. the *d* in *do* may be pronounced /dʒ/ in the question *Do you ...?*
These changes are normal features of fast speech, so it's important to understand them. However, you may decide to speak more slowly and clearly, depending on your listener.

1 Would you like me to talk you through my plans?
2 Could I explain this to you in more detail?
3 How do you feel about this?

9 **OWN IT!** Work in pairs. Choose two scenarios from Exercise 6 to roleplay, taking turns to be the person bringing about the change. Remember to use the Communication skill tips, the Useful language and the phrases in Exercise 7 in your roleplay.

10 Work with another pair. Discuss the questions.
1 Have you ever had someone help you through a big change in your life? What did they do?
2 Have you ever helped someone through a big change? What did you do?

In *Who Moved My Cheese?* the character Hem wrote several life lessons about change on the wall. What did he write and do you agree with him? Search online for 'Who Moved My Cheese?'.

3E

We would like to offer you the position

LESSON GOALS
* Make arrangements in a formal email
* Use appropriate language in an email
* Write an email to confirm arrangement

SPEAKING

1 Work in pairs. Look at the agency advert and discuss the questions.

JOB SPOT

Looking to start your career in hospitality and food catering?

Want to improve your languages 'on the job'?

Good Reception puts together promising candidates (like you!) and top hotel employers worldwide!

Contracts from 3 months to 1 year.

Send your CV to GoodReception.agency

---

1 Would you consider an opportunity such as this one to work abroad or in another city? Why? / Why not?
2 What benefits to living and working abroad are there, other than improving your language skills?

READING FOR WRITING

2 Read the email and answer the questions.
1 What are Deepa's reasons for writing to Lukács? Make a list.
2 Choose the best subject for the email (a, b or c)
  a Travel arrangements
  b Kovalam visit September and accommodation
  c Work placement confirmation

3 Read the email again. What does Lukács have to include in his reply? Make notes on the different points.
Thank Deepa for the job offer & accept – confirm start date – etc…

New Message

To: lukacskemeny92@mail.com

Cc: Gurpreet

Date sent: 28 May

Dear Lukács,

Further to our phone conversation, I am writing to inform you that we would like to offer you a front-desk position at the Coconut Grove Hotel commencing September.

You said that you would be free the week starting 5 September after your final exams in Budapest. I wonder whether you might be able to start work the following Monday. We would be happy to sign an initial contract until 3 March, that is for 6 months.

As discussed, we would be willing to arrange suitable accommodation while you are working with us. Please inform Gurpreet, my assistant, of any special requirements or preferences you may have. He is copied in to this email, so you have his address.

Can I suggest that you arrive a day or two earlier, in order to get settled in to life in Kovalam? You will need to get a train from Mumbai to Trivandrum and we can arrange a car to collect you from there and bring you to Kovalam, which is only half an hour away.

Please find attached the terms and conditions. You will need to return it to us digitally signed, after which we can draw up your contract.

Should you have any other questions regarding the company or any aspect of your relocation here, please do not hesitate to get in touch.

I wish you all the best in your forthcoming exams and I look forward to meeting you in person.

Yours, with kind regards,

Deepa Mirchandani

Human Resources Manager

---

4 Work in pairs. Look at the text message and ticket. How are they relevant to Lukács's reply?

> Lukács, have you heard? Karina & JJ getting married 1st March! So early!?? Just letting you know before you make plans for India.

Mumbai Lokmanya Tilak Terminus	Trivandrum Central
Departs on: 07-09-23	Arrivals on: 08-09-23
S M T W **T** F S 04:30	S M T W T **F** S 07:55

Coach 2	Seat 27	Adult 1	Child 0

5 Look at the Writing skill box. Identify one more example of each of the formal features mentioned in Deepa's email.

WRITING SKILL
Making formal arrangements

When writing emails, using the right level of formality for the person and situation is essential to give a good impression. If you are too informal in formal situations, you will seem unprofessional. Some general differences between formal and informal correspondence include ...

- vocabulary, e.g. *organize* vs. *sort out, conversation* vs. *chat*.
- expressions, e.g. *I will be in contact* vs. *I'll drop you a line*.
- punctuation, e.g. lack of contractions, exclamations and emojis in formal emails.
- grammar, e.g. use of relative clauses in formal emails; omission of sentence subject in informal messages.

6 Find expressions in Deepa's formal email that mean the same as these more informal equivalents.
1 After our chat on the phone ...
2 This is just to let you know you've got the job.
3 Do you think you can start the Monday after?
4 We'd be happy to sort out a place for you to stay.
5 I'm cc'ing him here.
6 How about getting here a couple of days before you start?
7 We can pick you up if you like ...
8 Here's the contract (attached).
9 If you want to know anything else about us ...
10 Feel free to drop us a line.
11 Looking forward to meeting you face-to-face.

WRITING TASK

7 WRITE Write a reply to Deepa. Include the points you identified in Exercises 3 and 4 and use the order of information in Deepa's email as a guide.

8 CHECK Use the checklist. I have ...
- ☐ opened and closed the email in a suitable way.
- ☐ included all the essential points in my email.
- ☐ used vocabulary and expressions appropriate to the reader.
- ☐ used structures and punctuation suitable to the level of formality of the email.

9 REVIEW Work in pairs. Read your partner's email. Would it leave the reader with a positive impression? Can you suggest anything to improve it?

Go to page 131 for the Reflect and review.

Sophie De Oliveira Barata at the Alternative Limb Project applies an artistic approach to her designs, to create unique and personalized prosthetic limbs, London, UK.

46

4

The arts

GOALS

- Analyse arguments in a forum thread
- Use discourse markers
- Talk about music and oral traditions
- Understand final consonants in fast speech
- Use humour in international communication
- Write a film review

1 Work in pairs. Discuss the questions.

1 Look at the photo. Do you think designing prosthetic limbs is a form of art? Why? / Why not? How would you define art?
2 If you could only have one, would you choose: a novel, a music album, a painting, a book of poems, a film? Why?

WATCH

2 ▶ 4.1 Watch the video. Answer the questions.

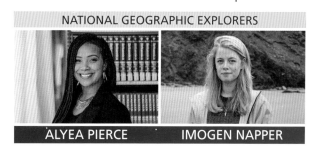

NATIONAL GEOGRAPHIC EXPLORERS

ALYEA PIERCE   IMOGEN NAPPER

1 How do other art forms help Alyea be a better writer?
2 How does Imogen express her creativity?
3 Could Alyea and Imogen live without art? Why? / Why not?

3 Make connections. What is your connection with art? Compare your answers with Alyea's and Imogen's.

Is this literature?

LESSON GOALS
• Identify and analyse arguments in a forum thread
• Identify logical fallacies
• Debate the future of AI in the arts

READING

1 Look at the introduction to the forum thread and the two poems on page 49. Work in pairs to discuss the questions.

 1 Which of the poems do you like better? Why?

 2 Can you guess which poem was written by a) a well-known poet, b) by Artificial intelligence (AI)? How do you know?

2 Skim the forum thread. Which writers think AI is capable of writing literature? Which disagree?

3 Look at the Reading skill box. Work in pairs. Choose two of the comments in the thread and use the questions in the box to identify and evaluate the writer's opinion.

READING SKILL
Identifying and analysing arguments

When supporting their arguments, writers might use different techniques. Some of these will be more and some less objective, so it is important that you are able to identify and analyse them to ultimately evaluate how valid the writer's opinion is. Ask yourself:

• Does the writer use personal examples only?

• Do they make broad generalizations?

• Are their arguments balanced or very one-sided?

• Do all the arguments and examples logically support the opinion?

4 Compare your ideas on Exercise 3 with another pair. Which opinions and arguments in the forum thread are the most valid? Why?

5 Read the forum posts more carefully. Choose the correct options.

 1 According to ana234, the authorship of a text is *important / not important* when you are classifying something as literature.

 2 Metacritic uses comic books as an example of *what is not literature / a new type of literature*.

 3 Almaniac thinks that AI *cannot yet be creative / is capable of original literature*.

6 Look at the Critical thinking skill box. Find an example of each kind of logical fallacy in the online thread.

CRITICAL THINKING SKILL
Identifying logical fallacies in arguments

Logical fallacies are common mistakes in reasoning. Here are some of the most common:

• *Ad hominem* – when someone makes an attack on a person, rather than their arguments.

• Appeal to ignorance – when someone states we lack facts or information about something and uses it to support their argument.

• Slippery slope – when someone suggests that very unlikely outcomes are very probable.

SPEAKING

7 You are going to take part in a debate on the subject 'AI will replace not only writers and poets, but also other artists, such as painters and musicians'. Follow these steps:

• Divide into A and B. Student A: you are in favour, Student B: you are against.

• Work with someone who has the same opinion (i.e. Student A with another A and Student B with another B) to list arguments and examples to support your opinion.

8 Look at the Useful language box. List any other phrases to help you agree, disagree and express your opinion.

Useful language   Debating

While I agree to a certain extent, I'd say …
I'm convinced / I have no doubt whatsoever that …
The chances/likelihood of … are quite high/slim.
Surely we can all agree that …
I wouldn't say that …
I'm afraid I strongly disagree that …
Let's just agree to disagree.

9 Work with another pair who has the opposing point of view and debate the topic.

EXPLORE MORE!

Look for AI-written poems or books. Search online for 'AI + poems' or 'books by AI'. Read a short piece. What is your opinion on it?

litfan1987

Forum subject:
Can AI produce literature?

I recently read that an artist and coder, Andreas Refsgaard, has used AI to write whole books! He even started an online store with AI-written books. AI can also write pretty good poetry. I bet you won't be able to guess which of the examples below was written by AI.

The Old Pond

The old pond,
A frog jumps in:
Plop!

Sun Rays

the sun rays struck my face
warm tingles to my fingertips
the light showed me a path
i should walk down
i spoke and the whispers of the breeze
told me to close my eyes
i lost my way in a paradise

123   15   543   3

---

ana234

According to Sian Cain, books site editor for *The Guardian* newspaper, 'What one person regards as an outstanding example of literature, another will consider drivel'. And I would have to agree with her. Whether these poems are written by humans or AI is irrelevant — and should not be the basis for whether something is deemed literature. After all, there are no objective criteria for evaluating literatureness, if I can coin a new word. So if people read poems, etc. by AI, and find them well written, then they're literature.

23   5   10

---

metacritic

This is utter nonsense! You're not thinking straight if you think AI can produce literature. This whole debate is just another example of a very worrying lowering of standards that you see everywhere. Soon anyone will be able to call anything literature. If AI-generated poems are literature, then what about a song, or a love note, or even a comic book? And while we're about it, why not a post on social media? It's crazy really. AI can't write poetry or literature. Go and read real poetry and you'll see.

10   25   5

Almaniac

I think we have to take a step back here for a sec. First, AI poems aren't exactly the result of AI creativity, but of training with datasets of tens of thousands of actual poems. This means that AI is simply trying to mimic human creativity and originality and is still incapable of creating literature on its own. Having said that, it is interesting to note that one study has shown that it can be difficult to tell AI and human-generated poems apart, even for literary experts. So while AI might not be able to create original pieces of literature, it *can* produce works that are almost indistinguishable from those written by humans.

54   2   23

49

4B
The soundtrack of my life

LESSON GOALS
• Use discourse markers
• Adapt your pronunciation
• Talk about about music

SPEAKING

1 Look at the infographic. Work in pairs to discuss the questions.

1 Which of the music genres mentioned do you enjoy? Which are the most popular in your country? Would you add any to the list?
2 Which songs or music genres make you feel …
• upbeat and cheerful?
• nostalgic or emotional?
• energetic and ready for any challenge?

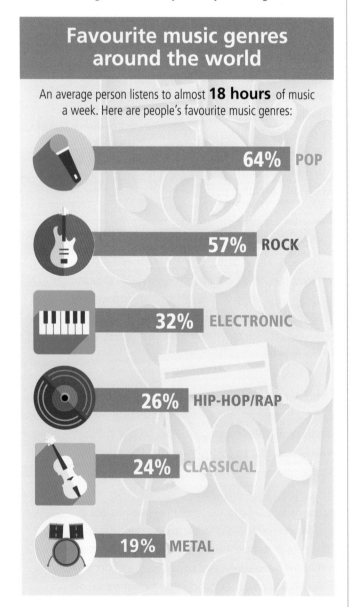

Favourite music genres around the world

An average person listens to almost **18 hours** of music a week. Here are people's favourite music genres:

64% POP

57% ROCK

32% ELECTRONIC

26% HIP-HOP/RAP

24% CLASSICAL

19% METAL

LISTENING AND GRAMMAR

NATIONAL GEOGRAPHIC EXPLORER

2 🎧 **4.1** Listen to Imogen Napper talk about the role music plays in her life. How similar or different is it to the role it plays in your life?

3 🎧 **4.1** Listen again. Complete 1–6 with the word you hear.

1 **As a** _____ **of fact**, I always joke that I was **basically** born in the wrong music era …
2 _____ **to think of it**, it is **actually** my mood that defines what I want to listen to.
3 … I have playlists for different moods and occasions: when I'm walking, exercising, working, cooking, **you** _____ **it**.
4 Music is _____ the fuel to my day.
5 **To be** _____, there is no better feeling when you hear a new song you absolutely love.
6 **For one** _____, listening to a whole record really gives you a more complete story and makes you appreciate the music in a whole new way.

4 Look at the sentences in Exercise 3 again. Discuss what the words and expressions in bold mean. Read the Grammar box to check.

GRAMMAR Discourse markers

There are many words and expressions that you can use when speaking, to …
• organize your ideas (*for starters, for one thing, on top of that*).
• show your attitude (*to be perfectly honest, literally, you name it*).
• clarify a viewpoint (*come to think of it, basically*)
• introduce a different idea (*as a matter of fact, actually, mind you*).
• change the direction of a conversation (*anyway, at any rate*).

The meaning of some expressions is quite clear (e.g. *to be honest*), but in other cases, (e.g. *mind you, you name it*) the meaning is more idiomatic.

Go to page 151 for the Grammar reference.

5 Choose the correct option to complete the sentences.

1 I listen to all sorts of music: jazz, reggaeton, metal, *you name it / for one thing*.
2 I'm not sure what my favourite kind of music is. *Come to think of it, / By any chance*, I don't listen to music that much.
3 I really hate electronic music now. *As a matter of fact / Mind you*, I used be a big techno fan as a teenager.
4 Metal is not really my bag, *so to speak / literally*.

PRONUNCIATION AND SPEAKING

6 🎧 4.2 Listen to how these discourse markers are said fast and then slowly. Write down what you hear when the words are said fast. Discuss in pairs which pronunciation you prefer and which might be easier to understand.

1 Actually
2 As a matter of fact
3 Mind you

7 Look at the Clear voice box. Work in pairs. Say the discourse markers from Exercise 6 first quickly and then more slowly and carefully.

CLEAR VOICE
Adapting your pronunciation

When people speak quickly, sounds change or disappear, and words merge together or are barely pronounced at all. For example, while the careful pronunciation of *actually* is /ˈæktʃuəli/, in fast speech it can sound like /ˈæʃli/. Similar things can happen to many other common discourse markers.

This might make your speech less clear, so consider the listener and, if necessary, adapt your pronunciation saying the words slower and in their full form.

8 Prepare to answer the questions and think about which discourse markers you will use. Then work in pairs to discuss the questions.

1 How important is music in your life?
2 What types of music do you listen to in different contexts, e.g. when you are working, having dinner, trying to relax, feeling down/happy, exercising? Why?

3 Do you have special songs or types of music that evoke certain memories of places, people or events? Say more about this.
4 What music did you used to listen to when you were younger? How have your music tastes evolved over the years?

9 Talk to as many people in the class as possible. Ask each person one question from Exercise 8 and one follow-up question. Then move to the next person. When answering the questions, use appropriate discourse markers.

VOCABULARY

10 Work in pairs. Look at these words and phrases and discuss any you don't know the meaning of. Then complete sentences 1–6 so that they are true for you. Compare your ideas.

---

a catchy tune/song   go to a gig / live performance
an instant hit   lyrics   (my) music tastes have evolved
(the song) is on everywhere   stream (music)
top the charts   a track   be trending

---

1 _____ topped the charts for a long time when I was younger.
2 One song that I think has great lyrics is _____.
3 _____ is currently trending / is on everywhere in my country.
4 _____ can make a song an instant hit.
5 One really catchy tune I can't get out of my head at the moment is _____.
6 Many people go to gigs because _____.

Go to page 138 for the Vocabulary reference.

SPEAKING

11 Work individually. Prepare a 2–3 minute presentation entitled 'The soundtrack of my life'. You can use the questions in Exercise 8 and the vocabulary from Exercise 10 to help you.

12 Work in groups of three. Present the soundtrack of your life to each other. How similar or different are they?

EXPLORE MORE!

Choose one of the bands, songs or music genres your classmates have mentioned and find out more information about it.

The art of storytelling

LESSON GOALS
- Understand final consonants in fast speech
- Use the present tense to tell stories
- Learn how to use stress when telling stories

SPEAKING

1 Work in pairs. Discuss the questions.

1 Do you enjoy telling stories? What kind?

2 How important is storytelling in your culture? Are there any traditional stories you know?

3 Are storytelling traditions a thing of the past or should they be preserved for future generations? Why?

LISTENING

NATIONAL GEOGRAPHIC EXPLORER

2 🎧 **4.3** Listen to the phrases (1–3) said by Alyea Pierce. What happens to the final consonant sounds in bold? Look at the Listening skill box to check.

1 cultures throughou**t** the region

2 becau**se** of their sensitivity

3 ca**n** be seen

LISTENING SKILL
Understanding fast speech (1): final consonants

When people speak English fast, they might not pronounce all the sounds clearly or words might merge together.

- When one word ends with a /t/, /d/ or /v/ and the next starts with a consonant, the final sound might be dropped (e.g. *passed down*). (See the Clear Voice box on page 29).

- When the following word starts with a vowel, the final consonant of the preceding word might get attached to it (e.g. *developed under* → *develop-dunder*).

- The final sound can also change depending on the first sound of the following word (e.g. *can be* → *cambe*) Pay attention to these processes to understand fast speech better.

3 🎧 **4.4** Listen to Alyea discuss oral storytelling traditions. Take notes on why the preservation of oral storytelling is important. Then work in pairs to discuss whether you agree. Why? / Why not?

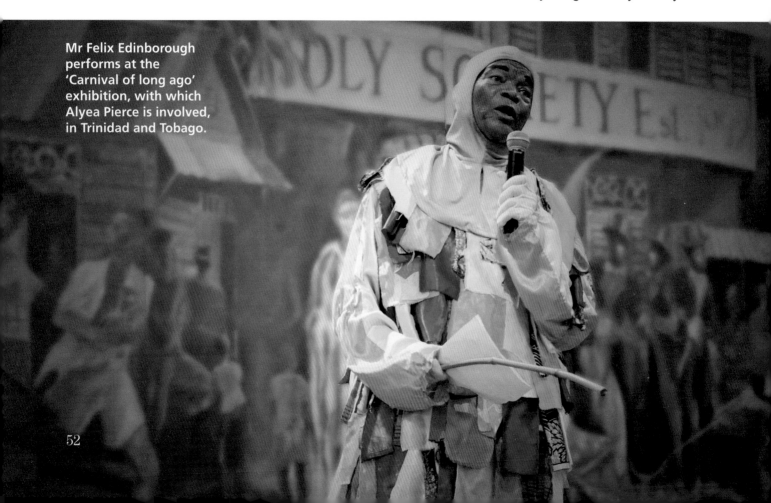

Mr Felix Edinborough performs at the 'Carnival of long ago' exhibition, with which Alyea Pierce is involved, in Trinidad and Tobago.

4 🎧 **4.4** Listen again. Are these statements true (T) or false (F)?

1 Oral traditions have remained largely unchanged throughout ages.
2 In the Caribbean, stories are only told on special occasions during the year.
3 The listener plays a more important role in oral stories than the speaker.
4 Being historically accurate is not crucial to most oral stories.

VOCABULARY AND SPEAKING

5 Look at these phrases. Check the meaning of any new ones in the dictionary. Can you remember which Alyea used and how?

our ancestors   based on facts / true events
historically accurate   indigenous peoples
pass on/down traditions
preserve for future generations
records of the distant past   share stories/legends
storytelling traditions   transcend time

6 Complete the questions with the correct form of one of the words from Exercise 5. Then discuss the questions.

1 How _____ accurate are traditional oral stories? Are some _____ partly on true events?
2 What do you know about your _____? Have stories about them been _____ in your family?
3 How important is it for _____ peoples to construct their own narrative through stories?
4 How are these stories _____ down through generations? Do you think the stories are altered as this happens?
5 Is _____ stories important in your culture? What _____ traditions are there?

Go to page 138 for the Vocabulary reference.

GRAMMAR

7 🎧 **4.5** Listen to a traditional Amerindian story from Oregon. Work in pairs to discuss what you understood of the story. Is the story mainly told in the present or past tense? What effect does this have? Read the Focus on box to compare what it says.

FOCUS ON   Using the present tense to tell stories

When telling stories, jokes and anecdotes, present tenses might often be used instead of past tenses, even though the story is about a past event. This can help make the listener experience the story as if it was happening right now, thus making it more engaging. The listener is likely to feel more immersed in the events as if they were happening to them.
*A cloud **came** and **made** some shade.*
*A cloud **comes** and **makes** some shade.*

Go to page 152 for the Focus on reference.

8 Read a story on page 166. Change the underlined verbs to an appropriate present tense to make the story feel more immediate and engaging.

PRONUNCIATION AND SPEAKING

9 🎧 **4.6** Listen to the phrases (1–3) from the story in Exercise 8. Underline the words that are stressed the most? What effect does this have? Look at the Clear voice box to find out more.

CLEAR VOICE
Stressing words to engage listeners

When telling stories, you want to engage listeners and keep them wondering what might happen next. Stressing certain words or syllables can help you do this. For example, you can …
• stress the new or unexpected information.
  *I would like a **cloud**.*
• show contrast.
  *Coyote is **still** hot.*
• indicate what might happen next.
  *The sky begins to look **ve**ry stormy.*
• show what the listener should pay attention to.
  *a **huge**, **swirl**ing river.*

1 And it rained like it had never rained before.
2 The Rainbow Serpent was hungry and tricked the young men
3 … turning his body into a big arc of beautiful colours.

10 Work in pairs. Prepare a short story to tell. Use stress and present tenses to make it more engaging. Then tell the story to another pair.

EXPLORE MORE!

Search online for 'oral storytelling traditions from [a country you're interested in]' Choose a story you like. What did you enjoy about it?

4D

Using humour in international communication

LESSON GOALS
- Learn about different types of humour
- Consider how we use humour in international communication
- Identify the types of humour to avoid in international communication

SPEAKING

1 Scottish presenter Craig Ferguson once said, 'Being funny is a gift, and when done well, is an art form.' In pairs, discuss these questions.

1 Do you agree with Ferguson's quotation? How important is a sense of humour to you? Why?
2 Is there someone you know who you think is very funny? What do they do to be funny? Do you know people who <u>don't</u> think they're funny?
3 Do you use humour in your conversations? How and why do you use humour?
4 Have you ever said something tongue-in-cheek but it was taken seriously? What happened?

2 Work in pairs. Look at these different kinds of conversational humour. Use a dictionary to look up any words you are unsure of. Then match them with the examples (1–5).

irony   putdown   self-deprecating humour
teasing   witty wordplay / puns

1 A mother, on seeing her children screaming and making a terrible mess, says, with a smile, to her visitor, 'Aren't children delightful?'
2 A: I'm having trouble sleeping.
  B: Come and see one of my presentations. That should fix it.
3 You've lost your phone again? You'd lose your head if it wasn't screwed on!
4 A: I'm going to call the guys in IT to help me with my laptop.
  B: Well, whatever you do, don't ask Miles. He's about as useful as a chocolate teapot.
5 A: How do you find your new boss?
  B: I usually open his office door and there he is!

3 Look at the different types of humour in Exercise 2. In pairs, say which types of humour you tend to use and which ones you are not comfortable using.

54

4 ▶ **4.2** Watch the video. Answer the questions, then compare your answers with a partner.

1 According to the video what are five reasons for using humour?
2 Is behaving in a silly manner always a good way to break the ice? Why? / Why not?
3 How might self-deprecating humour be perceived? What about irony?
4 The video mentions two British expressions used to describe teasing someone. Do you have an expression like that in your language?
5 What's the danger in using cultural references or wordplay in conversational humour?

5 Look at the Communication skill box. Which of these do you naturally do in your conversations? Which do you think are particularly important when communicating internationally?

COMMUNICATION SKILL
Using humour in international communication

Here are some top tips for using humour in international communication:
1 Think about what is appropriate depending on the context and your conversation partner.
2 Avoid putdowns (making fun of people), insults and teasing your conversation partner.
3 Be careful with irony, wordplay and what you assume to be shared knowledge – it might exclude people who don't understand it.
4 Be aware that not every culture sees humour as a good way of coping with nerves and embarrassing situations.
5 When laughing in a group, be aware that some people might not see the humour in what is said and think they're being mocked.
6 Listen and get a feel for your conversation partner's sense of humour and adapt where you can.

6 Look at these situations. Work in pairs. Discuss which of the tips from Exercise 5 you might give Ada, Kit, Matteo and Rosa?

1 Thuy joined Ada and her friends for dinner one evening but couldn't really understand what they were talking about. She felt like they were laughing at her and was miserable all evening.

2 Zhong and Kit were talking about a mutual friend, Iker. Kit started to make fun of Iker's dancing style. Zhong found Kit's behaviour insulting.

3 When Naira pointed out that Matteo had booked the wrong meeting room, Matteo laughed and said 'Oh silly me! It's the second time I've done that this month!' Naira was appalled that Matteo was taking his mistake so lightly.

4 Tyson asked his friend Rosa if she liked his hair as he had just been to the barber's. Rosa replied, 'Yes, it'll be lovely when it's finished!' Tyson felt a bit hurt.

7 In a situation where humour is being used, you may need to clarify what is meant. Look at the Useful language box. Which phrases might be useful for Thuy, Kit, Matteo and Rosa in Exercise 6?

Useful language   Using humour in conversations

Clarifying your intentions
Sorry, I was only joking. I didn't mean to cause offence.
Where I come from, we use humour when (we feel nervous).
I only tease people I'm close to. And I think of you as a close friend.

Clarifying your conversation partner's intentions
Was that meant as a joke?
I'm sorry but you lost me. Why was that funny?
Are you being serious or was that tongue-in-cheek?

8 OWN IT! Work in pairs. Choose two scenarios to roleplay from Exercise 6. Take turns to be the person trying to be humorous. Try to use the Communication skill tips and the Useful language.

SPEAKING

9 Work in small groups. Discuss the questions.
1 What type of comedy do you enjoy watching? What kind of humour are you not so keen on?
2 Have you ever met anyone who had a very different sense of humour from you? How was it different? How did you handle the conversation?

4E
A daring debut

LESSON GOALS
- Learn language for writing film reviews
- Engage the reader when writing a review
- Write a film review

SPEAKING

1 Work in pairs. Discuss the questions.

   1 What's a film that you've seen that …
     a kept you interested from beginning to end?
     b was better than you expected?
     c was not as good as the reviews or others said?
   2 How often do you read film reviews? How accurate are they usually in your opinion?
   3 What's the most important thing for you in a film (e.g. the plot, characters, special effects, actors)?

2 Look at the film and review titles. Have you seen any of the films? If not, which synopses make you want to see the film? Why? / Why not?

Nobody Knows I'm Here

Strange, surreal and suspenseful story of childhood trauma

Nomadland

Gently compassionate portrait of people living nomadic lives in America.

Veins of the World

A heart-warming and heart-breaking family struggle to preserve millennial traditions

---

READING FOR WRITING

3 Read the film review on page 57. If you've seen the film, do you agree with the reviewer? If you haven't, does the review encourage you to watch the film? Why? / Why not?

4 Look at the Useful language box. Underline the phrases from the box the critic uses in their review? Find any others that could be useful.

Useful language   Writing film reviews

It's set in (19th century Japan).
It's based on (a novel by … / a true story).
The tragic/male/protagonist …
The film was shot (on location).
dazzling/spectacular special effects
star-studded/talented cast
an epic/action-packed/Hollywood blockbuster
an acclaimed/understated/underrated independent film
a gripping/compelling plot
(The action) keeps you on the edge of your seat.
It was a box office flop/hit.
It's an (absolute) must-see / a (real) tear-jerker.

5 Think about a film you have seen that you would like to talk about. Work in groups of three. Try to use some of the Useful language to review your film. Do you want to see your classmates' films? Why? / Why not?

6 Look at the Writing skills box. Which ways to hook the reader can you find in the title and content of the review of *Nobody Knows I'm Here*?

WRITING SKILL
Hooking the reader in a film review

Here are several common ways in which film critics try to interest their readers:

- The title: use strong adverbs (*shockingly*) and adjectives (*spectacular*) to generate interest and express your opinion; use noun phrases (*classic family drama with a twist*) to keep it short and snappy
- Opening lines: hook the reader in the opening with an interesting fact about the film (*booed by the public at Cannes*), a compelling opinion (*daring debut*) or an interesting comparison with another movie.
- Rhetorical devices: use groups of 2–3 words starting with the same letter (*bold, brave and baffling*), and repeat the same structures for rhythm (*once a celebrated cop, now a hardened criminal*).

7 Use the tips from the Writing skill box to write the title and the opening sentence of your review from Exercise 5.

Strange, surreal and suspenseful story of childhood trauma

★★★★☆

52   15   125   0

Gaspar Antillo's slow-moving, sweet, yet slightly strange debut tells the story of gentle recluse Memo, who lives with his uncle on a remote sheep farm in the south of Chile. Breathtaking landscapes, beautiful music and superior acting make this film a rare work of art.

The plot moves gracefully between the protagonist's current uneventful life and his childhood as a budding singer. These flashbacks gradually uncover the events that still haunt Memo such that now he stubbornly refuses to use his voice at all, even to speak to his uncle. Locked in his body, mute and indifferent, he spends his time listening to the same heart-rending tune that we see him sing as a child. After a local girl, Marta – played by Millaray Lobos – posts a video of Memo singing, Memo must confront the trauma of his past to regain his voice and present life.

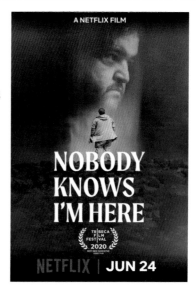

The lead actor's Jorge Garcia's performance as Memo is compelling despite the almost complete lack of dialogue. His portrayal of the gentle giant is deeply emotional and turns a seemingly dull character into a vividly real person. He is also well supported by impressive performances from the other members of the cast.

In the age of action-packed Hollywood blockbusters, the film's slow-moving and almost uneventful plot could be a potential drawback. Yet, Sergio Armstrong's masterful camerawork and Carlos Cabezas Rocuant's superb soundtrack keep you on the edge of your seat. Stunning shots of Chilean landscapes reflect Memo's sombre and secret inner life.

Nobody knows I'm here is a daring debut for Gaspar Antillo: mysterious despite there not being much of a mystery and gripping despite a rather uneventful plot. It's an emotionally charged story that will leave no one indifferent.

---

8 Use these words to replace the words and phrases in bold in the sentences (1–4) to make them more engaging. Then decide if you can use or adapt any of the sentences for your own review.

breathtaking glides musically narratively
surprisingly thoroughly

1 The camera **moves** gracefully creating a gentle atmosphere.
2 The plot is **very** simple, yet **more** entertaining **than I thought it would be**.
3 The fast-moving story and **beautiful** photography make for an unforgettable experience.
4 Visually stunning, **music that is** charming, and **with a story that is** compelling, this film is a modern masterpiece.

9 Decide how you will structure your review. Make some notes under the headings: *Plot, Acting* and *Camerawork*. Add any other headings you think are important for your film.

EXPLORE MORE!

WRITING TASK

10 WRITE Write a film review for an online film magazine. Write approximately 300 words.

11 CHECK Use the checklist. I have …
- [ ] hooked the reader in the title and the opening lines.
- [ ] organized the review into 4–5 paragraphs.
- [ ] reviewed at least two of the following elements: plot, characters, special effects, music, acting.
- [ ] used adjectives, adverbs, words starting with the same letters, or phrases with similar structure to engage the reader.
- [ ] used a range of appropriate film review vocabulary.

12 REVIEW Work in groups of three. Exchange the reviews with a classmate. Which film …
- is the most action-packed?
- has the most gripping plot?
- has the best acting performance?

Go to page 131 for the Reflect and review.

Find out more about the best films and directors from a country of your choice. Which films would you like to see?

A diver measures sea turtle 'Speedy' at a science aquarium in Timmendorfer Strand, Germany.

5

Sciences

GOALS

- Summarize ideas using a Venn diagram
- Learn how to add emphasis with cleft sentences
- Talk about health benefits; learn to build words related to research
- Use abbreviations when taking notes
- Convince someone who questions the evidence
- Write a video brief

1 Work in pairs. Look at the photo and discuss the questions.
1 Have you ever visited a large public aquarium?
2 What are the benefits of experiencing ocean life like this?

WATCH ▶

2 ▶ 5.1 Watch the video. Write Teresa (T), Popi (P) or both (B).

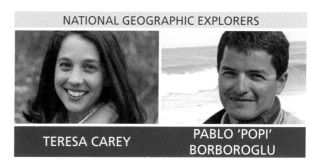

NATIONAL GEOGRAPHIC EXPLORERS

TERESA CAREY   PABLO 'POPI' BORBOROGLU

1 Had a job working on the water.
2 Originally planned to work in government.
3 Now works as a writer.
4 Works to communicate science to the wider world.

3 Make connections. Has the path to where you are now in your life been direct or has it taken unexpected turns?

5A
Science and art

LESSON GOALS
• Assess supporting evidence
• Use a Venn diagram to summarize a text
• Discuss the relationship between science and art

READING

1 Work in pairs. Discuss the questions.

1 If you had to describe yourself as more arty, more scientific, or neither, which would you choose? Why?

2 Do you know people who are good at both the arts and science?

2 Read the article. Which paragraph (1–5) discusses each topic (a–e)?

a Lisa's current work

b Questioning the traditional art-science divide

c A description of how Donald uses drawing

d Lisa's background

e A suggestion for changing school buildings

3 Read the article again. Are the sentences true (T) or false (F)?

1 The author associates creativity more with art than with science.

2 Lisa wanted to be a doctor from early childhood.

3 As a surgeon, Lisa aims to make people look natural rather than perfect.

4 For Donald, his understanding of the situation is as important as his surgical skills.

5 Donald uses drawing to explain procedures to patients.

6 In the final paragraph, the writer says that Lisa and Donald are like architects.

4 Look at the Critical thinking skill box. Answer questions 1–3.

CRITICAL THINKING SKILL
Assessing supporting evidence

A statement or idea can be supported by facts, which are objective, or by anecdotes, stories or experiences, which are subjective. Facts, even if they are generalizations, can be proven to be true or false. Anecdotes, stories and experiences reveal individual examples that may or may not represent universal truths.

Noticing whether supporting evidence is objective or subjective can help you decide whether or not you agree with a writer's ideas.

1 What is the main idea of the article?

2 Is this idea supported objectively or subjectively?

3 Do you think subjective support and objective support can be equally effective? Why? / Why not?

5 Look at the Reading skill box. Copy the Venn diagram below. In pairs, add these words and phrases to the diagram. Can you add any other ideas?

creativity   description   discovery of facts
exaggeration is OK   experimentation
generally objective   often subjective   practice
self-expression   skill

READING SKILL
Summarizing the ideas in a text using a Venn diagram

For certain reading passages, it can be useful to summarize information using a Venn diagram. A Venn diagram provides a way of comparing two or more things and presenting similarities and differences visually.

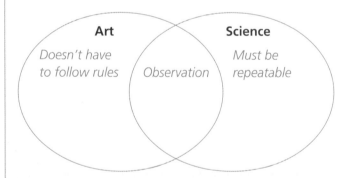

Art — Doesn't have to follow rules — Observation — Science — Must be repeatable

SPEAKING

6 Work in small groups. Discuss the questions.

1 Do you think art lessons in school are as important as science lessons? Why? / Why not?

2 Do you think a child with natural artistic talent should focus only on art, or be encouraged to study science as well? Should kids with a talent for science also pursue art? Why? / Why not?

EXPLORE MORE!

Search online for other 'Scientists who were artists'.

The art of surgery

Looking at the human body through the eyes of both artist and scientist

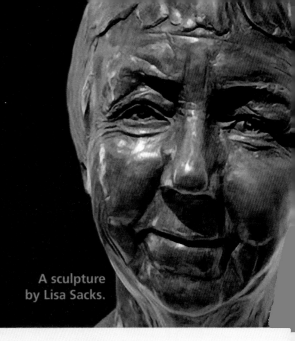

A sculpture by Lisa Sacks.

❶ In most schools, you walk down the hall and turn one way for the art room and another for the science lab – two different worlds seen by some as representing opposite ways of looking at and interpreting the universe. However, in reality, art and science have more in common than most people realize: Both involve looking intensely at, understanding and describing the world – and both require skill and creativity. Look around you and you'll find examples of art and science working together everywhere – in disciplines from architecture and automotive design to map making and music technology. And as Leonardo da Vinci famously showed, even in medicine. He drew detailed images of the human body to understand how it worked and to inform his sculpture and painting. Two doctor-artists working today demonstrate that art and science continue to go hand-in-hand.

❷ Surgeon **Lisa Sacks** made her first sculpture aged 13. 'I was attracted to making sculptures of the human form right from the start,' she says. 'I went to an art, ballet and music secondary school in Johannesburg and majored in sculpture.' At 17, she read a book that featured photographs of sculptures that a plastic surgeon had made of people's bodies. Lisa thought, 'I can do that' and went to medical school.

❸ Her work as a sculptor has helped her understand the human form. When seeing patients before surgery, she can often 'envision how they will look afterwards' and aims to 'make things look naturally harmonious'. She adds, 'People often think that because I'm a plastic surgeon I look at someone with a big nose and want to make it smaller, or that I see wrinkles and want to do a facelift. But that's not the case at all, because as a sculptor I love to see a face full of character.' At the same time, her work as a surgeon has also improved her art. 'My eye is much better informed as I have seen many of the structures from the inside.'

❹ **Donald Sammut** is a surgeon who specializes in hands, especially in reconstructing hands that have been damaged by injury or illness. When he was a teenager, he constantly copied the drawings of Leonardo da Vinci.

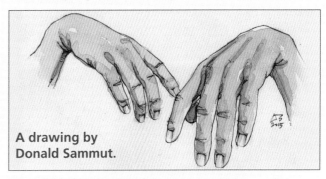

A drawing by Donald Sammut.

Now Sammut uses drawing as an essential part of his clinical work. 'I will draw the hand, while taking a history and notes. This forces the discipline of examining every millimetre,' he says. 'In the operating theatre, before operating, while everything is being prepared, I will sketch the hand.' The drawings form part of Sammut's records of the surgery. 'This again enables me to examine all aspects, and also to "see" the steps of the operation, to concentrate on what is planned.' According to Sammut, 'Just as drawing is about "seeing" more than about execution', so surgery is as much about 'listening' as carrying out a 'technical exercise'.

❺ As Sacks and Sammut demonstrate, two apparently very different disciplines have common ground in terms of creativity, ability to see clearly and necessary levels of focus and skill. Architects take note: next time you design a school, put the science lab next to the art room and make sure there's a doorway connecting the two. The fact that the two disciplines seem to view the world from such different perspectives is the reason why they work so well together – not art *or* science, but art *and* science.

TOP PHOTO:

Portrait bust of Professor Averil Mansfield, vascular surgeon and first woman professor of surgery in the UK.

61

5B
The best medicine

LESSON GOALS
- Describe health benefits
- Practise using the correct vowel length
- Use cleft sentences to add emphasis
- Give a short talk on something beneficial to health

SPEAKING

1 Discuss the questions.

1 When did you last laugh? What made you laugh? What are the benefits of laughing?

2 How would laughter affect the atmosphere at a party? In English class? In a business meeting?

Laughter …

… can be inappropriate – for example when it interrupts a serious business meeting; it can be infectious, as one person's laughter spreads to the whole group; but above all, science says laughter is good for you. Why?

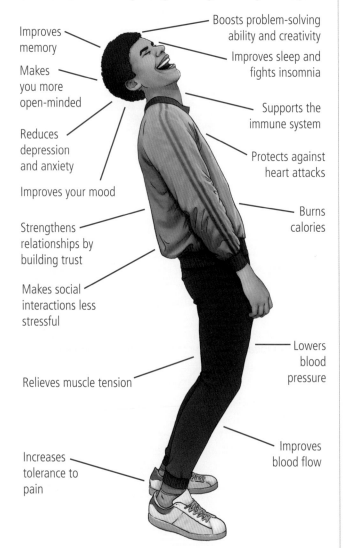

Improves memory

Makes you more open-minded

Reduces depression and anxiety

Improves your mood

Strengthens relationships by building trust

Makes social interactions less stressful

Relieves muscle tension

Increases tolerance to pain

Boosts problem-solving ability and creativity

Improves sleep and fights insomnia

Supports the immune system

Protects against heart attacks

Burns calories

Lowers blood pressure

Improves blood flow

VOCABULARY AND PRONUNCIATION

2 Look at the infographic. Match the words (1–8) with their meanings (a–h).

1 calories
2 immune system
3 insomnia
4 inappropriate
5 infectious
6 open-minded
7 social interactions
8 tolerance

a easily passed to another, like a disease
b willing to consider new ideas
c not suitable for the situation
d serious problems sleeping
e the processes in the body that fight disease
f the ability to experience something without being harmed
g conversation and communication
h the energy in food

3 Look at the Clear voice box. Then complete the table on page 63 with the words in the box above it, according to the vowel sound in bold.

CLEAR VOICE
Saying vowels and diphthongs: length

Speakers of different varieties of English often use a different vowel sound in a word, but if the length of the vowel is similar, it can help with clear communication. It can even help to emphasize the difference in length when distinguishing between words that might be confused.

Short vowels:

/ɪ/ sl**i**p, /i/ happ**y**, /ɛ/ fr**ie**nd, /æ/ **a**ttack, /ʌ/ f**u**n, /ʊ/ g**oo**d, /ɒ/ b**o**dy, /ə/ **a**bout

Long vowels and diphthongs:

/iː/ f**ee**l, /ɑː/ l**au**gh /ɔː/ m**ore**, /ɜː/ b**ur**n, /uː/ gr**ou**p, /eɪ/ s**ay**, /əʊ/ fl**ow**, /aʊ/ s**ou**nd, /ɪə/ cl**ear**, /eə/ sh**are**, /ɔɪ/ v**oi**ce, /aɪ/ f**i**nd, /ʊə/ t**our**

feelings	**h**appy	inapp**ro**priate	inf**e**ctious
ins**o**mnia	m**oo**d	open-m**i**nded	**sy**stem

Short vowels	Long vowels and diphthongs
/ɪ/ **i**mmune 1	/uː/ impr**o**ve 5
/e/ depr**e**ssion 2	/iː/ d**e**tail 6
/ɒ/ t**o**lerance 3	/aɪ/ f**i**ght 7
/æ/ c**a**lories 4	/əʊ/ s**o**cial 8

4 🎧 **5.1** Listen and check your answers.

Go to page 139 for the Vocabulary reference.

5 Write five sentences you believe to be true about health using some of the words from Exercise 2. Work in pairs to compare your ideas. Do you agree with each other's sentences?

LISTENING AND GRAMMAR

6 🎧 **5.2** Listen to people answering the question 'When do you usually laugh and why?' Match each speaker with a reason for laughing.

Speaker 1	a	Being with friends
Speaker 2	b	The way children communicate
Speaker 3	c	The way someone tells stories
Speaker 4	d	Feeling uncertain
Speaker 5	e	Being in a situation where laughter isn't appropriate

7 Notice how sentences 1–3 are constructed. Can you remove/change some words and/or write the words in a different order without changing the meaning?

1 What I love is that they have such a fresh view of the world.
   I love that they have such a fresh view of the world.
2 It's his enjoyment that gets everyone else laughing.
3 The reason we laugh is not usually because someone's made a joke.

8 Look again at the sentences in Exercise 7. Underline the information that each sentence is emphasizing.

9 Read the Grammar box. Then rewrite sentences 1–6 as cleft sentences.

> **GRAMMAR** Adding emphasis with cleft sentences
>
> A cleft sentence is divided into two parts. The introductory part often uses *wh-* words, *It* or *The thing* + *be*.
> *When I'm a bit nervous I tend to laugh.* →
>   ***It's** when I'm a bit nervous **that** I tend to laugh.*
> *Knowing I'm not supposed to starts me laughing.* → ***What** starts me laughing **is** knowing I'm not supposed to!*
> *My grandfather telling a story makes me laugh.* → ***The thing that** makes me laugh **is** my grandfather telling a story,*

Go to page 152 for the Grammar reference.

1 I slipped and fell and then started to laugh.
   Wh- …
2 My friend's social media posts make me laugh.
   It …
3 Laughter makes a party fun.
   The thing …
4 Timing is important in humour.
   Wh- …
5 The eyes show when laughter is real.
   It's …
6 Khaled tells the best jokes.
   The person …

SPEAKING

10 Prepare to tell a small group about something you think is physically and mentally beneficial.

1 Choose something that has a positive effect on your body or mind. Your idea can be serious or funny. Use one of one of the following or your own idea: drinking coffee, swimming, having celebrations with friends, eating chocolate.
2 Think about the following:
   The mental benefits: *Chocolate improves my mood.*
   The physical benefits: *It's good for me because it gives me energy.*
   The time or place you do it: *I have a chocolate bar after lunch with coffee.*
   The thing you like the best about it: *The combination of chocolate and coffee.*

11 Work in a small group. Take turns describing what you prepared in Exercise 10.

5C
Narrative in science

LESSON GOALS
• Use abbreviations when taking notes
• Build words related to research
• Learn about negative and limiting adverbials
• Say vowels before consonants clearly

SPEAKING

1 Work in pairs. Discuss the questions.

1 Which of the following ways have you learned about science, either in school or since leaving formal education?
   • Memorizing facts, formulas, equations or data
   • Doing experiments or other types of research
   • Reading about science or scientific concepts in the context of the wider world – for example in magazines such as *National Geographic*
   • Watching television shows or listening to radio shows or podcasts about science

2 Which of the above are more interesting or more effective ways of learning for you personally?

LISTENING

NATIONAL GEOGRAPHIC EXPLORERS

2 🎧 **5.3** Look at the Listening skill box. Listen to Teresa Carey and Popi Borboroglu talking about the role of narratives in science. Make notes about what you hear.

LISTENING SKILL
Using abbreviations when taking notes

In a situation where you need to take in new information, using abbreviations can make your note-taking faster and more effective.

Use abbreviations for common words and terms that are repeated. Common ones include:

w/ (with)
incl (including)
cf (compare with)
e.g. (for example
i.e. (that is)
re (regarding)

You can also come up with your own abbreviations to suit a particular set of notes.

3 In pairs, compare notes. What information did only one of you note down?

4 🎧 **5.3** Listen again. Discuss the questions.

1 According to Teresa, why are stories so important in science?
2 Why does Popi prefer using a narrative to simply giving scientific facts?

Popi with Magellanic penguins in Punta Tombo, Argentina.

VOCABULARY

5 Add new endings to these words and put them under the correct heading below. In some cases you may need to remove or add some letters.

---
analyse available human individual inform
manipulate person persuade statistic

Verb + *ive* = adjective
imagine ➜ imaginat**ive**

Adjective + *-ity* = noun
necessary ➜ necess**ity**

Noun or verb + *-al* = adjective
arrive ➜ arriv**al**

6 Complete the text about the science of stories with eight of the words you wrote in Exercise 5.

Cave paintings from tens of thousands of years ago show that stories have been important to [1]_____ for a very long time. Some scientists believe that stories helped ancient people make a [2]_____ connection to ideas and possibilities because we naturally relate to characters we hear about. *That could be me*, we think. Today, advertisers often use the [3]_____ power of stories to try to make people buy things instead of [4]_____ evidence. In this way they appeal to our emotions rather than to our [5]_____ thinking. Since the 2000s, the increased [6]_____ of social media has meant that many people are now telling stories all day long. In some cases, the stories are [7]_____ – sharing news, for example, but sometimes they are [8]_____ and cleverly try to make people believe things in a dishonest way.

Go to page 139 for the Vocabulary reference.

7 🎧 **5.4** Read the Focus on box. Then listen to the story about a scientific breakthrough and notice how the four phrases in the box are used.

FOCUS ON Negative and limiting adverbials

Certain adverbial expressions at the beginning of a sentence are often used in both written and spoken storytelling to add emphasis. They are always followed by inversion.
Little did (he) know … / *Only when* … did …
Not only (did)… / *Never before* had …

Go to page 153 for the Focus on reference.

8 Match the beginnings of the sentences (1–4) with the endings (a–d) to describe other scientific breakthroughs.
1 Never before
2 Not only
3 Little
4 Only when we
a did Mária Telkes's parents know that she would become known as 'the Sun Queen' for her work with solar energy.
b did Marie Curie win a Nobel Prize in physics, she also won one in chemistry.
c photographed the deep ocean did we begin to understand it.
d had Mars been seen through a telescope.

PRONUNCIATION

9 🎧 **5.5** Look at the Clear voice box. Then listen and repeat the pairs of words (1–6).

CLEAR VOICE
Saying longer vowels before voiced consonants

The duration of the vowel sound before a voiced consonant as in *had* is slightly longer than the duration of the vowel sound before a voiceless consonant as in *hat*. To help you pronounce the final /d/ as a voiced consonant, try extending the vowel sound a little. This will help make the distinction between the two words clearer even if you aren't perfectly voicing the final consonant sound.

1 heart	hard		4 back	bag
2 close	close		5 wrote	rode
3 hit	hid		6 proof	prove

10 Work in pairs. Take turns to say one of the words in Exercise 9. Your partner points to the word.

SPEAKING

11 You're going to tell a story about a time you learned something new or important or made a breakthrough. Choose one of these topics or use your own idea and make some notes.
- A mistake that taught you to be more careful
- A difficult situation you faced and learned from
- A new skill you developed

12 In pairs, tell your stories. Try to use the expressions from the Focus on box.

Convincing someone who questions the evidence

LESSON GOALS
• Learn about confirmation bias
• Identify ways of convincing someone who doesn't believe in your evidence
• Practise language for trying to convince someone

SPEAKING

1 Think of a time when you were trying to convince someone of your point of view. Work in pairs to discuss the questions.

1 How did you try to convince them? Did you …
   • appeal to their emotions?
   • appeal to their logical reasoning?
   • tell personal anecdotes?
   • quote scientific evidence

2 Did you manage to convince them? What happened?

2 Look at Liying and Eng's story. Then work in pairs to answer questions 1–3.

Childhood friends Liying and Eng are discussing the 'good old days'. Eng feels nostalgic about how parents used to be able to let their kids run around freely, and feels it is dangerous for kids to run around the neighbourhood on their own these days because there is too much crime. Liying disagrees, stating that the rate of crime has actually fallen over the decades. She explains that it's the media that gives us the impression that the streets are a lot less safe, but this only provokes Eng to tell Liying about the 'true crime stories' she's heard from friends. Later, Liying emails Eng some evidence of the falling crime rate but this seems to make Eng feel more strongly about protecting her kids and keeping them at home.

1 How does Liying's point of view differ from Eng?
2 How does Liying try to convince Eng of her point of view? Why do you think Liying wasn't successful?
3 If you were Liying, how would you try and convince Eng?

MY VOICE

3 ▶ 5.2 Watch the video. Answer the questions. Work in pairs to compare your answers.

1 What is confirmation bias?
2 When someone holds very strong beliefs and is presented with evidence that contradicts those beliefs, what might they do?
3 Why does confirmation bias exist?

4 According to the video, which of these should you <u>not</u> do when trying to convince someone with a different point of view to your own?

1 Get angry and emotional.
2 Make them accept the compelling evidence you're presenting.
3 Acknowledge that accepting certain facts does not mean changing their beliefs.
4 Present a clear set of advantages and disadvantages.
5 Encourage them to prioritize accuracy.

5 Look at the Communication skill box. Which of these things do you naturally do when you have conversations with people who don't share your point of view? Which of these things do you feel you need to work on?

COMMUNICATION SKILL
Convincing someone who questions the evidence

In order to make someone more likely to want to listen to – and believe in – your evidence, try to do the following:

1 Listen carefully and with respect.
2 Show that you understand their opinions.
3 Help them feel secure about their identity.
4 Have a collaborative discussion.
5 Encourage a scientific curiosity.
6 Keep the tone of the interaction positive.

6 Work in pairs and look at the scenarios (1–3) below. What are Taiba, Siong and Marcin's beliefs? Why do you think they might be resistant to anyone telling them something different?

7 Look at the Useful language box. The way you say these phrases can make a difference between sounding positive and sounding sarcastic or aggressive. With a partner, practise saying the phrases in different ways. How can you make them sound genuine and positive?

Useful language Trying to convince someone

Showing you understand their opinions
I can see why you might think that.
I get that this is really important to you.

Keeping the discussion collaborative
Like you, I just want to find out more.
Do you get where I'm coming from?

Encouraging a scientific curiosity
Let's see if we can find some scientific evidence to back this up.
I always think it's worthwhile finding out what the research says about it.

8 OWN IT! Work in pairs. Roleplay the scenarios from Exercise 6, using the Communication skill tips and Useful language to help you. Try to convince each other of your point of view. Take turns to be the one who doesn't believe in the evidence.

SPEAKING

9 Work in small groups. Discuss the questions.

1 Can you think of examples of confirmation bias that you've seen? What role do you think social media plays in encouraging confirmation bias?
2 What are some common beliefs that you share with your friends or family? Have you sometimes met people with different beliefs from your own? What happened?
3 What are the benefits of having conversations with people who have different beliefs from your own?

1 Taiba always buys branded clothes and expensive products. When her friend Doro bought an average-priced bag, Taiba said 'That bag isn't going to last! You get what you pay for! You have to pay if you want something that looks good and is of good quality!' Doro tries to convince Taiba that non-branded goods can also look good and then shows her evidence that expensive things don't always mean better quality but Taiba refuses to believe it.

2 Siong is talking to Alex about a new female colleague who was friendly and chatty at their initial meeting. Siong goes on to say that women are known to say more words during an average day. Alex tells him that research has proven that men and women actually say almost the same number of words in a day, but Siong doesn't believe it.

3 Marcin drives everywhere, even when he's going to a shop that is a five-minute walk away. His colleague Katja tries to talk to Marcin about the impact of his actions on climate change but Marcin firmly states that climate change is a hoax and states that the recent cold winters is evidence that there is no global heating happening. Katja shows him evidence of the alarming changes in global temperatures, but Marcin dismisses it as fake news.

EXPLORE MORE!

Scientifically curious people are more likely to want to learn about things that might contradict their world view. Find out more about by searching online for 'scientific curiosity + confirmation bias'.

Life hacks

- Choose images to support a text
- Identify a problem and offer a step-by-step solution
- Write a video brief

Video brief: How to cool a hot car	
Voice	**Visuals**
When you get into your car on a hot day, the first thing you do after starting your car is turn on the air conditioner, right? But if that's what you do, you're doing it wrong!	Driver looking very hot and sweaty getting into a car on a hot day and pressing the air conditioner button.
The problem is it's probably hotter inside the car than outside.	Close-up on driver looking hot and miserable.
This is because of the greenhouse effect. The energy from the sun can pass through the glass into the car and create heat inside, but the heat can't escape.	[1]Simple diagram of the greenhouse effect
Just turning on the air conditioner won't help much. If you want to cool your hot car as quickly as possible, what you need to do is follow these steps.	Text on screen: Follow these steps.
First, open the car windows. Even if it's hot outside, it will be even hotter inside the car. It's the hotter air inside that's the problem, so you need to let it out.	Driver opening car windows, looking relieved.
Next, push the button on the air conditioner that brings fresh air from the outside into the car.	[2]Close-up of 'outside air' button
If you recycle the hot air inside the car it will take a lot longer to cool down.	[3]Close-up of 'recycle air' button with X through it
And now, at long last, you can turn on the air conditioner.	Driver turning on air conditioner
It's only when the air inside the car is cooler than the air outside the car that you want to press the air recycle button.	[4]Close-up of 'recycle air' button
And that's it. So when the weather is hot, just remember this rule: Put windows down first – it's the fastest way to cool.	When the weather is hot, just remember this rule, Put the windows down first – it's the fast way to cool.

SPEAKING

1 Work in pairs. Discuss the questions.
1 When did you last go online to learn how to do something? What did you learn how to do?
2 A 'life hack' is a strategy or technique for doing something better or more efficiently, or for solving a problem, sometimes in a clever or unexpected way. Can you think of an example of a useful life hack you've found online?

READING FOR WRITING

2 Read the video brief. Discuss the questions.
1 Have you ever had the problem described in the brief?
2 What is the name of the scientific concept described in the brief?
3 How could this principle be applied to other situations, for example a hot room in a house?

3 Read the Writing skill box. Then match the images (a–d) with the descriptions of the visuals (1–4) in the video brief.

WRITING SKILL
Supporting a text with images

When writing a video brief, decide what type of image will best support your message in each part. Ask yourself:
- Is the idea easier to show than tell? Will an image help make my message clearer?
- What type of image will be the most useful to the viewer? Photo or illustration? A still or series of stills or a moving image? A table or diagram?
- Is it important to connect with the viewer? Would a presenter talking directly to camera be the most effective way to do this?

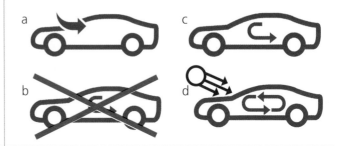

Top life hacks

1 Clean out an old sun cream bottle.

2 When you lend something to a friend, take a photo of them with it.

3 When you leave your house and lock the front door before a trip, do something unusual.

4 When you're having your picture taken, close your eyes a bit, as though you're looking at a bright light.

5 Tie a small knot in your earphone cable, near the left ear piece.

6 Put your phone cables in a glasses case.

4 Match each hack (1–6) above with the reason why it's useful (a–f). Work in pairs. Have you tried any of these hacks? Or would you? Why? / Why not?

a That way, you'll remember who borrowed what.

b When you go to the beach, you can hide your money and keys inside.

c Then you'll definitely remember having done it.

d Then you'll always be able to tell the left from the right, just by feeling it.

e That way, they will stay neat and tidy in your bag.

f This will make your smile appear more genuine.

5 Think of something that people do in everyday life that they could do better. Choose something you feel you can make some suggestions about. Use one of these ideas or your own idea. Make some notes about the problem.

- Sleep, fitness, well-being
- Kitchen work, food preparation
- Computers, phones or other gadgets
- Staying organized at home
- Studying English
- A sport or hobby you know about

6 Make notes about hacks or steps in a process to deal with the problem you chose in Exercise 5.

EXPLORE MORE!

Search online for 'science life hacks'. Choose three that you find useful.

WRITING TASK

7 **WRITE** Create a blank video brief with two columns. Fill in the two columns with the words you will say and the images you will show. Write 250–300 words. Follow these steps:

- Use your notes from Exercise 5 to write the introduction.
- Use the video brief model, the sentences in Exercise 4 and your notes from Exercise 6 to write about the hack (or hacks).
- Write a sentence or two to conclude the script.

8 **CHECK** Use the checklist. I have …

☐ provided an introduction.

☐ explained what the problem is.

☐ given a clear solution.

☐ supported the text with visuals.

☐ included a conclusion.

9 **REVIEW** Work in pairs. Read your partner's video script. Tell your partner whether or not you think their life hack is useful.

Go to page 132 for the Reflect and review.

A school of fish are attracted to the *Duane* coastguard ship, sunk intentionally off the coast of Florida, US, to be repurposed as an artificial reef.

6

Redesigning our world

GOALS

- Summarize an article using concept maps
- Discuss representation using conditional structures
- Talk about good and bad design
- Learn new words and phrases while listening
- Accommodate your conversation partner
- Write a report

1 **Work in pairs. Discuss the questions.**
   1 Look at the photo. What are the benefits of using the ship in this way?
   2 Can you think of other ways an old ship might be repurposed?

WATCH ▶

2 ▶ 6.1 Watch the video. How have Rebecca or Alec repurposed the following things?

NATIONAL GEOGRAPHIC EXPLORERS

REBECCA WOLFF   ALEC JACOBSON

1 pillows
2 socks
3 fisherman's bag
4 scraps of paper

3 **Make connections.** What objects have you repurposed for a different job to the one they were designed for? Do you tend to buy new things or try to 'make do' with what you have?

LESSON GOALS
- Summarize an article with a visual concept map
- Identify a writer's opinions
- Discuss how to create your own map

City lights on a map of the Arabian peninsula

READING

1 Work in pairs. Discuss the questions.

1 When was the last time you consulted a map?
2 Do you find it easy to read maps? Does anything frustrate you about them?
3 Have you seen a map that you thought was particularly interesting or beautiful?

2 Read the article on page 73. Which of the following aspects of maps are discussed?

1 essential features of maps
2 how maps are made
3 the future of maps
4 the origins of maps
5 the lost art of reading maps
6 the purposes of maps
7 types of map
8 what maps can teach us

3 Look at the Reading skill box. Then read the article again and create a concept map about it. Use the example concept map as a starting point. Then compare your map with a complete version on page 166.

READING SKILL
Summarizing with a visual concept map

A concept map helps you prioritize and organize your notes and can be more memorable than written notes.

Start designing a concept map with the main topic in the middle. Around this, note down the main ideas that the text covers and, from these, add key details, examples, new words, etc.

Link and organize ideas using arrows, icons and boxes. You don't have to use drawings, but lines, symbols and diagrams can help show relationships between ideas clearly.

4 Work in pairs. Imagine your partner has not read the article. Take turns to describe the article, referring only to your concept map.

EXPLORE MORE!

5 Work in pairs. Look at the Critical thinking box. Then read the article again and discuss what you think the writer's opinion is about these things.

maps in general   Google maps   Toby Lester's maps
Daniele Quercia's research   creative maps   cartograms
the future   any other aspects of maps

CRITICAL THINKING SKILL
Identifying the writer's opinions

In certain types of text, such as autobiographies, reviews and blog posts, we expect to read the writer's opinions. In other, less personal, types of writings, such as reports and some articles, the writer's views may not be so clear. However, there are often clues about their opinions, and identifying these may lead to a better understanding of the text. Ask yourself:

- What information does the writer include about the topic? What do they leave out? Why?
- What words or ways of expressing ideas suggest support for an idea or criticism of it?
- Do they identify with or sympathize with particular people or ideas in the text?
- How much of the article do they spend on certain topics or ideas? How often do they mention them?

SPEAKING

6 Work in groups. Agree on something to map. Choose one of these ideas or create your own.

- a real or imagined place, e.g. somewhere you once lived, or your childhood neighbourhood
- something abstract, e.g. a fun map of your brain, or of a social media platform
- a map with a specific purpose, e.g. showing the places you'd show a visitor in your town
- a guide map for the future, e.g. a map of a school in the year 2100

7 Design and create your map, then present it to the class.

Find a cartogram on a subject that interests you Search online for 'cartogram + [key words]'.

Redrawing the map

1 Like the earliest maps drawn by sailors during the age of exploration, most of the maps we consult these days are designed for just one thing: navigation. A street map can tell you how to get to
5 the post office, but not which route is the safest. A relief map, showing height above sea level, indicates how hard it might be to climb that hill, but not how many trees you'll see on the way. Map making means filtering out – ignoring everything
10 but the one thing being mapped.

If maps were designed to fulfil all possible roles, they'd end up impossible to read and therefore useless. Despite the dominance of Google maps, there will always be a need for variety: maps that
15 show tourists the homes of Hollywood stars; that describe the migratory patterns of birds; that reveal to pirates where to dig for the treasure; 'X' can mark the spot for almost anything. Both the science and the art of map making are developing
20 at incredible speed; as new and surprising uses for maps are being found, so the limits of form are also being explored in exciting and playful ways.

Toby Lester decided to map the sounds in his environment. In his new office, he'd found himself
25 harmonizing and humming along with the sound of his noisy heater. His computer played a different note and he realized that together they made a rather tuneful major chord; he wondered whether this music was affecting his attitude to his work.

30 Toby started noticing similar sounds and the effects they were having on him in other places, such as at home. What was the noise of the fridge doing to his emotions, for example?

Daniele Quercia and team's light-hearted project
35 'Smelly Maps', mapping common city smells – from 'dusty subway to 'baked food' – is another example of maps that don't just provide practical information, but also explore the world around us in more creative ways. In fact maps need not be
40 limited to the geographical sphere at all; almost anything can be mapped: music genres, light pollution, the internet, even the human heart.

Maps also provide us with a chance to view the world from perspectives we wouldn't normally
45 consider and as such can be great tools to raise awareness. Maps can compare places over time, showing changes such as global heating and deforestation. 'Cartograms' are maps that alter the physical size of places to depict information which
50 is not normally visible. A cartogram showing carbon emissions, for example, makes countries bigger the more greenhouse gases they emit.

For centuries, maps have helped us to navigate our world; could they now also help us find our way
55 around the complexities of the future? Map makers are already using design and technology to map our future world. Let's hope their creativity and imagination reveal a clear way forward for us.

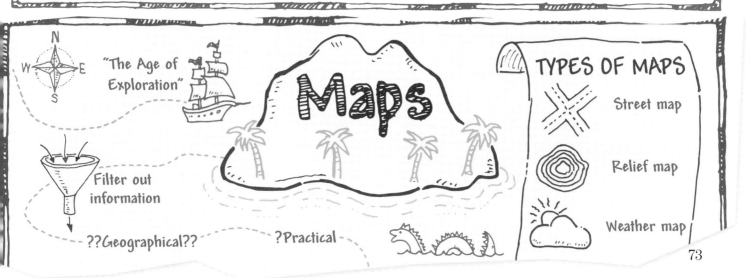

6B
Representation by design

LESSON GOALS
• Learn some alternative conditional structures
• Use the correct stress on words with suffixes
• Discuss how to design a logo to represent a group

SPEAKING

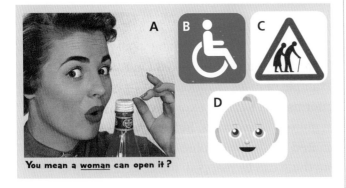

You mean a **woman** can open it?

1 Look at the images and symbols. Work in pairs to discuss the questions.

1 Who do these images represent? Where might you see them?
2 Why might some of the people represented by each of these images not be happy with them?
3 Can you suggest how they could be improved?
4 Turn to page 165 to see alternatives to each symbol. Do these solve any of the problems that you identified?

LISTENING AND VOCABULARY

2 🎧 **6.1** Listen to an interview with a designer. Check your ideas about the images in Exercise 1.

3 Read the sentences. Check you understand the meaning of any words in **bold** that are new to you.

1 Two important principles are **diversity** and **inclusivity** – design that **represents** everybody.
2 The problem with this symbol is that it **highlights** certain **negative stereotypes**.
3 The most **prominent** feature is the wheelchair, which is **unrepresentative of** most disabled people.
4 Giving these symbols **a makeover** helps **change people's perceptions** about the issues.
5 We need a more dynamic image that **emphasizes** the idea that older people can still be active, not one in which they **resemble** tortoises!

4 Use the correct form of a word from Exercise 3 to complete each sentence.

1 Our aim is to create a fairer, more _____ society.
2 Most stereotypes of my country are completely _____ of what we're really like.
3 Spelling mistakes are _____ in green.
4 Even though he had a _____ role in the team, his efforts were never recognized.
5 The company logo has had a _____ and now looks modern and dynamic.
6 I can't _____ enough how important it is to consider people with hearing difficulties.
7 The logo _____ a seashell to symbolize the sea.
8 Photographs of the accident affected people's _____ of the technology forever.

Go to page 140 for the Vocabulary reference.

LISTENING AND GRAMMAR

5 🎧 **6.1** Match the sentence beginnings (1–4) with the endings (a–d) to make sentences from the interview. Listen again to check.

1 Design is good design ...
2 Supposing there were no disabled toilets or lifts in a school, ...
3 You're going to feel represented ...
4 I don't think design would have started to progress ...

a as long as you recognize people like you in the world around you.
b could a disabled person get the same educational opportunities as a non-disabled person?
c provided it represents the whole of society.
d unless rights groups had campaigned for better representation.

6 Answer the questions about the sentences in Exercise 5.

1 Which sentences describe general truths?
2 Which express ideas that are imagined, not real?
3 Which words replace *if* in each of the sentences?
4 Find an example of a) first b) second c) third d) zero conditionals?

7 Read the Grammar box and check your answers to Exercise 6.

> **GRAMMAR** Alternative conditional forms
>
> Conditional sentences usually have a main clause and a subordinate clause. The subordinate clause may be introduced by *if*, *unless*, *as long as*, *supposing*, *assuming* or *provided*. Four main types – zero, first, second and third – are commonly used, but there are many alternative forms.
>
> **Zero conditional:** *Design is good design* ***provided*** *it represents the whole of society.*
>
> **First conditional:** *You're going to feel represented* ***as long as*** *you recognize people like you.*
>
> **Second conditional:** ***Supposing*** *there were no disabled facilities in a school, could a disabled person get the same educational opportunities as a non-disabled person?*
>
> **Third conditional:** *I don't think design would have started to progress* ***unless*** *rights groups had campaigned for better representation.*
>
> **Go to page 154 for the Grammar reference.**

8 Work in pairs. Look at the sentences. Discuss in what way each sentence is a variation on the 'typical' conditional structure, as they are often taught.

1 In those days, if something was designed for 'people', that often meant men. (zero)

2 If you haven't asked the communities you are representing, don't assume your design is inclusive. (first)

3 You might be shocked if you were to see certain adverts from just fifty years ago. (second)

4 If people hadn't fought for change, we wouldn't be seeing all these creative new ideas! (third)

9 Work in pairs. Choose the correct option. Sometimes more than one answer is possible. Add two questions about possible changes in another area of design. Then ask and answer all the questions.

1 If you *would design* / *redesigned* / *were to redesign* the 'elderly people' road sign, what would it look like?

2 In Curitiba in Brazil, the crossing time for pedestrians *was* / *is* / *would be* increased for older people if they use their senior citizen cards at the traffic lights. Would that be useful where you live?

3 If society *had been* / *was* / *were* run by the most elderly members of the community, what advantages might there be?

4 Would older people be better or worse off if the computer technology of the last thirty years *didn't happen* / *hadn't happened* / *might not have happened*? Why?

5 *Assuming* / *As long as* / *Unless* you reach ninety years old, do you think your attitude towards young people will have changed? How?

PRONUNCIATION

10 🎧 **6.2** Look at the Clear voice box. Mark the stress on these words, then divide them into two groups according to their word stress. Listen, check and repeat.

---

complexity   disparity   diversity   grammatical
impossible   inclusivity   independence   invisible
performance   population   professional   representation
simplicity   technological   uncomfortable

> **CLEAR VOICE**
> **Using the correct stress on words with suffixes**
>
> Words with multiple syllables can be difficult to say if you are not sure of the main stress.
>
> However, word stress follows patterns for certain types of words, especially words with suffixes. For example, words ending in *–nce*, e.g. re***sem***blance. and *-tion*, e.g. organi***za***tion usually have the main stress on the second syllable from the end.
>
> Many other long words have the stress on the third syllable from the end, e.g. tech***no***logy.

SPEAKING

11 Work in pairs. You are going to design a logo, emoji or sign. Follow the steps.

1 Choose a group or community that you belong to, e.g. industry, college, club or organization. You could also choose your age group, social group or a hobby you do with others.

2 Discuss which aspects of the group you want to highlight and what kind of image or symbol you want to use to represent it.

12 Present your designs to other groups. How inclusive and representative are your designs?

EXPLORE MORE!

Find an image from a campaign and decide how effective it is. Do an image search online using 'awareness-raising + campaign'.

Design fails

LESSON GOALS
• Learn new words and phrases while listening
• Talk about good and bad design
• Use compound adjectives

SPEAKING

1 Match the photos of design fails (A–D) on page 77 with the online comments (1–4) that people left under each. What is wrong with each design? Add your own comments to one or more of the photos.

1 Great! Now I can use them in the summer.
2 At least I'm not wasting water any more …
3 Much safer – so long as I don't plan to eat anything.
4 My vision is so much sharper now!

2 Work in pairs. Tell each other about …

• an object, product or service whose design annoys you or frustrates you.
• an object, product or service whose design you really appreciate.

LISTENING

NATIONAL GEOGRAPHIC EXPLORERS

3 🎧 6.3 Listen to Rebecca Wolff and Alec Jacobson talking to each other about design in their lives. Complete the extracts with the six things they discuss. What are the British equivalents of the American words in sentences 1 and 4?

1 Seems like it's time for somebody to design women's pants with proper _____.
2 And it was like they expect you to buy a new _____ every couple of months or something …
3 My _____ lasts for years and years and years and does everything I need it to.
4 You get the bag of _____ and it's mostly air.
5 The thing that we like the most is our _____. It's stylish, it's practical and we use it every single day.
6 … if you have nice _____, whatever you eat, all of a sudden becomes just a little bit more exciting.

4 🎧 6.4 Look at the Listening skill box. Then listen to three extracts and follow the steps outlined in the box to identify words and expressions you hear that describe design.

LISTENING SKILL
Learning new words and phrases while listening

It is easy to identify interesting new words and expressions that you might want to learn when reading, but much harder when listening.

• Listen first to get the general meaning. This can help by giving context to the new words.
• Pause and replay sentences which contain useful vocabulary. Write the new word or phrase in context – copy out the full sentence.
• Try to focus on words that are related in some way. For example, if you are listening to a football match commentary, you might only note down the words related to football.

5 🎧 6.3 Listen to the conversation in Exercise 3 again and write other words and expressions you hear related to design. Write whole expressions or sentences if you can.

VOCABULARY AND SPEAKING

6 Work in pairs. Read more comments about problems with design. Discuss what they might refer to. Use a dictionary to help you.

1 I didn't buy it for its **looks**, but it's the only one that's **compatible** with my phone.
2 It's **pointless** choosing anything unless they're **functional** as well as stylish. It's got to do the job you bought it for.
3 I know they're **artificial**, but they look so real. And the colours are very **striking**.
4 The old system was **illogical** and **unreliable**. The latest version is much more **user-friendly**.
5 Where they've put this is completely **impractical** – it'll just get **in the way**.
6 I agree it's pretty, but it's too **fragile** for **everyday** use. It's too small for my needs, anyway.

Go to page 140 for the Vocabulary reference.

7 Read the Focus on box. Then match 1–10 with a–j to make ten common compound adjectives that can be used to describe products and designs. In pairs, discuss what the adjectives might describe.

FOCUS ON Compound adjectives

Compound adjectives consist of two or more words and are usually written with hyphens when they are used in front of the noun they describe, but not if they come afterwards.

*It's such a **well-recognized** logo. / The logo is so **well recognized**.*

Hyphens are not used when the compound is made up of a *-ly* adverb + adjective.

*It's a **badly made** chair.*

With compound adjectives made up of a number + a noun, the noun remains singular.

*It comes with a **two-year** guarantee.*

Sometimes a hyphen is essential to avoid confusion. Compare, for example: *small-business owners* and *small business owners*!

Go to page 155 for the Focus on reference.

1	brightly_____	a	catching
2	user-_____	b	cold
3	eye-_____	c	date
4	full-_____	d	looking
5	ice-_____	e	free
6	long-_____	f	friendly
7	modern-_____	g	lasting
8	sugar-_____	h	length
9	two-_____	i	lit
10	up-to-_____	j	week

8 Complete the questions with a word from Exercise 6 or 7. Sometimes more than one answer is possible.

1 When was the last time you bought something completely _____, just for fun?

2 Are you comfortable handling _____ cups and glasses, or do you tend to break things?

3 Do you try to have the most _____ designs, e.g. of phones, bags and trainers?

4 Would you buy a car more for its _____ or performance? What else would be important to you when deciding what car to buy?

5 Do you believe the theory that many products are not built to be _____, but to break after a couple of years?

6 Are there any drinks you prefer at room-temperature to _____?

7 Are there any websites you visit that aren't very _____? Why?

8 What design problems annoy you in your _____ life such as on your way to work or school?

9 Write two or three more questions about the design of things. In pairs, take turns to ask and answer the questions in Exercise 8 and your own.

A: If there was one thing you'd change about the design of your house, what would it be? Why?

B: I would love a lighter living room and more modern-looking furniture. Everything is quite old-fashioned. If I could paint the walls, I would use more striking colours.

A

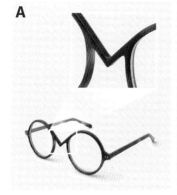

B

C

D

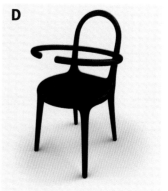

EXPLORE MORE!

Find more examples of 'design fails' online.

Accommodating your conversation partner

LESSON GOALS

- Learn about different situations where accommodation is necessary
- Practise accommodating your conversation partner
- Practise stressing key words and using pauses

SPEAKING

1 Work in pairs. Have you ever been in a conversation in your own language where the following happened? Why do you think there was a problem?

- You found someone hard to understand.
- Someone found what you were saying hard to understand.

2 🎧 **6.5** Listen to the conversation between Stefan, Jameela and Lorenzo – an extreme example of someone not accommodating their conversation partner. Then in pairs, try to reconstruct what Stefan said about the work he'd done to his new house.

3 Work in pairs. Discuss the questions.

1 What are the differences between the ways Jameela and Lorenzo reacted during the conversation? How do you think they might each have been feeling?

2 Do you think Stefan, Jameela and Lorenzo should have behaved differently during the conversation? What could they have done differently?

3 How did you feel when listening to the conversation? What was going through your mind?

MY VOICE ▶

4 ▶ **6.2** Watch the video. Answer the questions. Then compare your answers in pairs.

1 What are some reasons Chia gives for not being able to follow a conversation?

2 What are two reasons it's a good idea to accommodate our conversation partner?

3 If Stefan had paid attention to Lorenzo's responses and reflected on what he knew about Lorenzo, what might he have realized?

4 When accommodating someone, what should we a) avoid doing?; b) not assume?

5 Look at the Communication skill box. Which of these strategies do you already use?

COMMUNICATION SKILL
Accommodating your conversation partner

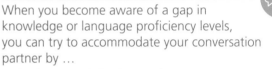

When you become aware of a gap in knowledge or language proficiency levels, you can try to accommodate your conversation partner by …

- thinking carefully about what you want to say and avoiding talking too much or jumping from one topic to another.
- explaining, paraphrasing, simplifying and giving examples where necessary.
- stressing key words and using pauses.
- not assuming they'll understand everything you say.

6 🎧 **6.6** Listen to this alternative conversation between Stefan, Jameela and Lorenzo. In pairs, discuss these questions.

1 Which of the strategies in Exercise 5 did Stefan use? How did he do this?

2 Why does Stefan say 'I don't know how interested you are in (rather than 'how much you know about …') home improvement'?

7 Look at the Useful language box on page 79. Which of these ways of accommodating do you use when speaking in your first language? Do you do this as often in English? Why? / Why not?

Useful language Accommodating your conversation partner

Acknowledging potential gaps
I don't know if you're interested in (home improvement), but …
Let me know if this doesn't make sense, but …

Making clear what the main point is
The thing is …
What I'm trying to say is …

Paraphrasing, simplifying and clarifying
It's a kind of (material).
It's a bit like (wood).
It's the opposite of (dry).
Let me give an example.

PRONUNCIATION AND SPEAKING

8 🎧 **6.7** Look at the Clear voice box. Listen to how the key words are stressed in the example sentence and notice what happens after each group of words.

CLEAR VOICE
Stressing key words and using pauses

When accommodating someone who doesn't share your knowledge or who speaks English differently from you, it can help to emphasize key words and to take frequent pauses after groups of words e.g. fixed phrases, clauses and sometimes even grammar structures.

In this **living** room || for **example**, || I **wanted** to || **repaint** all the **walls,** || but I had to **prep** the walls || **first**.

9 🎧 **6.8** Work in pairs. Look at sentences 1–3. Decide which words you would stress and where you would pause when trying to be extra clear. Then listen to one way of doing this. Practise the sentences. Note that there is no one correct way.

1 In my opinion, the red looks better than the blue.
2 This lamp is beautiful, but, to be honest, it's too big for this room.
3 A mood board is a collection of pictures, colours and materials and it gives you a feeling, an idea of how you would like the room to look.

10 OWN IT! Look at the scenarios (1–4). Then work in pairs and discuss which people might need to accommodate their conversation partner. Then suggest what they can do to accommodate.

1 Jay designs product packaging and is presenting his latest design to a client. He noticed looks of confusion when he spoke about PP bottles and Tetra Paks and was surprised that the client doesn't know the differences between recyclable packaging and packaging using recycled content.

2 Vera doesn't know much about computers, but recently got herself a smartphone. Ani is talking to Vera on the phone and helping her work out how to use her new social media account, but Vera is finding it difficult to understand what Ani is saying.

3 Darius is on a walking tour holiday, but has got lost. He has a map, but the street signs are in the local language. He stops someone in the street to ask them if they can give him directions in English, but soon notices they have very limited understanding of English.

4 Tania's son brought his friend Windson home for dinner. Tania is trying to get to know Windson, but has noticed that, although his English is fluent, he speaks a very different variety of English from what she's familiar with. Windson seems to use words and phrases that Tania has never heard before and is struggling to understand him.

11 Work in pairs. Choose two scenarios from Exercise 10 to roleplay, taking turns to be the person who needs to accommodate. Use the Communication skill tips and the Useful language to help you.

12 Work in small groups. Discuss the questions.
1 What might be the reasons why some people don't accommodate others in conversation?
2 How do you think gestures, images and translation devices can help us get our message across more effectively?

6E

A better user experience

LESSON GOALS
* Describe visual data
* Refer to different aspects of a subject
* Write a report

SPEAKING

1 Work in pairs. Discuss your experience of shopping online. Which of these issues would put you off buying something?
* lack of photos or information about the product
* extra cost for postage
* an old-fashioned looking website
* difficulty navigating the site
* poor language use, e.g. spelling
* concerns about the ethics of the company

2 Look at the icons. What do they refer to?

A   B   C   D

READING FOR WRITING

3 Look at the information about SOS Swifts! What kind of organization is it?

SOS Swifts! is a charity that protects the common swift, a bird whose population has fallen by almost a half in less than 20 years.

4 Read the report. Are the statements true (T) or false (F)?
1 The report was written to point out problems with the charity's online shop.
2 It was written by someone who works for the charity.
3 The report was written before changes were made to the website.
4 It shows the results of a survey the website's visitors completed.
5 The report makes further recommendations.

5 Work in pairs. Look again at the list of potential problems of online shops in Exercise 1. Which were problems for the SOS Swifts! website? Have all of them been solved now?

Report on the SOS Swifts! online shop

Introduction

The purpose of this report is to evaluate the success of improvements made to our online shop. It is based on feedback from a survey whose respondents included visitors to the shop. The information is summarized in figures 1 and 2 on page 81.

General points regarding the makeover

The general feedback on the shop was positive. As can be seen from the comparison table, the results show that visits to the shop have increased by 13%. More than one in ten visitors now buy at least one item. With respect to user experience, respondents appreciated the more eye-catching navigation buttons and more prominent search box on the homepage. Many people had highlighted poor-quality product photos as an issue, so we can assume that the more appealing images are helping.

Ongoing user experience issues

Regarding user-friendliness on mobile devices, feedback indicates that this is still an issue. Each page is quite long, making it impractical when scrolling through to locate a product. On the subject of payment, several respondents pointed out the high postage costs and that these are only added to the total cost at the final stage. This conclusion is supported by the number of baskets abandoned at the payment stage.

Other problems

Respondents expressed a desire to see more information about how and where products are made and where the materials are sourced on product-specific pages. Also, a significant number of visitors had been put off because of simple mistakes in grammar and spelling. These have been corrected.

Conclusion and further recommendations

It's clear that the makeover has been a success. When it comes to overall user experience, our ratings and sales have increased significantly. However, to improve this even more, we recommend fewer items per page to reduce scrolling. As far as postage costs are concerned, which represent a significant addition to overall cost, we suggest including some of this cost in the basic price of each item.

Fig. 1 – Comparison of visits & sales before and after makeover

	VISITS & SALES	
	YEAR 8	YEAR 9
Visits/month	12,500	13,560 ↑13%
Conversion rate*	7%	11%
Sales (dollars)	$8,750	$14,916 ↑70%

*Percentage of people visiting the site who made a purchase

Fig. 2 – Year 9: Feature approval rating

I can find what I'm looking for easily 84% (↑12%)

The search function helped 64% (↑9%)

The photos accurately reflected the product I received 92% (↑19%)

There is sufficient information about each product 51% (↑2%)

There were no bad surprises at the checkout 32% (↑4%)

Pages on my mobile phone were easy to navigate 48% (↑4%)

The shop represents good value for money 68% (↑1%)

The website is well-written and clear to read 93% (↑15%)

6 Look at the Writing skill box. Then find where the information in the visual data is mentioned in the report. How else does the report refer to the information from the survey?

WRITING SKILL
Writing from visual data

In reports we often present information in both written and graphic form. If your writing is accompanied by the visual data it describes there is usually no need to repeat numerical data. You can …

- vary the expressions you use to refer to the graphic information in the report, e.g. as *shown in the table, A surprising result from the survey is …*
- use alternative ways to refer to numbers and amounts in the report, e.g. *One widespread perception was …, feedback was mixed, a significant number, etc.*
- use more subjective language when interpreting the information, e.g. *Surprisingly, …, the standout finding is …, etc.*

7 Change the expressions in bold to avoid referring to numbers.

1 **7% of** visitors to the shop bought something. *Surprisingly few visitors …*
2 Sales **increased by 70%**.
3 **84% of visitors** can now find what they are looking for easily.
4 **19% more people** believe the product photos accurately reflect the products.
5 **32% of** shoppers received a bad surprise at the checkout.

8 Read the report again. Underline expressions used to refer to the different aspects in Figure 2. *With respect to user experience …*

WRITING TASK

9 Work in pairs. Read the writing task below. Decide what the online company sells. Write at least five questions that would be asked in the survey. Use what you know about your chosen industry to invent the survey results, then represent that data visually in a table or graph.

> You work for an online company. Your manager has noticed a drop in sales and has asked you to carry out a survey to find out where the problems lie.
>
> Your report should explain what items are currently popular, summarize customers' opinions, and suggest what action if any should be made in light of the information.

10 **WRITE** Write a 250–300-word report based on your visual data.

11 **CHECK** Use the checklist. I have …

☐ organized the report into logical paragraphs.
☐ referred to different aspects of the survey.
☐ used alternative expressions to express numerical information.
☐ commented on the numerical information.

12 **REVIEW** Work in pairs. Exchange reports and compare the written and visual information. How accurately has your partner described the information?

Go to page 132 for the Reflect and review.

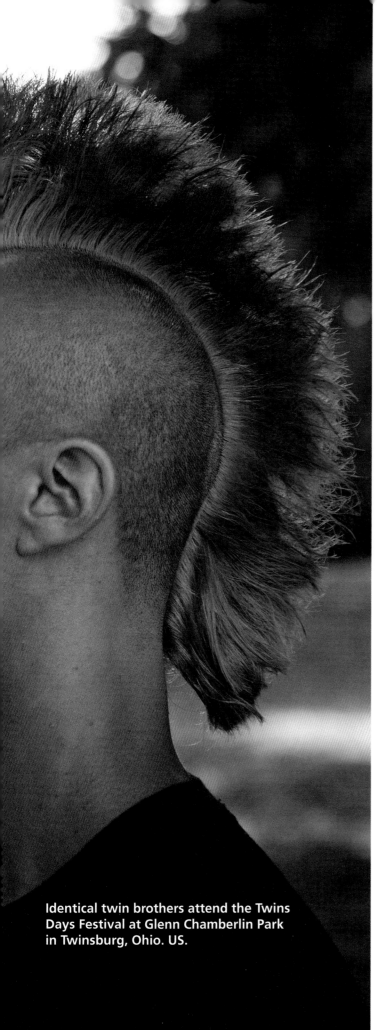

7

Same but different

GOALS

- Deal with unknown words in a literary extract
- Talk about changes and trends using the continuous aspect
- Use collocations to talk about work; discuss different ways to use the voice
- Deal with non-linguistic listening challenges
- Practise finding your voice in English
- Write an opinion essay

1 **Work in pairs. Discuss the questions.**

1 Look at the photo. Why might the two men have adopted such different styles?

2 How similar are you to your friends and family?

3 To what extent do you think people in other parts of the world are similar or different to each other?

WATCH ▶

2 ▶ 7.1 Watch the video. Answer the questions.

NATIONAL GEOGRAPHIC EXPLORERS

CAROLINA CHONG MONTENEGRO

GABBY SALAZAR

1 In what ways have Carolina and Gabby changed over the years?

2 In what ways are they similar to how they were as children?

3 **Make connections.** How much do you feel you have changed and how much you have stayed the same over the years?

Identical twin brothers attend the Twins Days Festival at Glenn Chamberlin Park in Twinsburg, Ohio. US.

7A
A different country

LESSON GOALS
* Deal with unknown words in a literary text
* Understand analogies in literature
* Talk about the pros and cons of emigration

READING

1 Work in pairs. Discuss the questions.

1 Are you someone who likes trying different things or do you like things to stay the same?

2 Have you ever lived or would you like to live in a different town or country? Why? / Why not?

2 Read the extract from the first chapter of the memoir *Lost In Translation* by Eva Hoffman on page 85. Where is Eva moving to? What does she fear she will miss about her home country?

3 Look at the Reading skill box. Work out the meaning of the underlined words in sentences 1 and 2 below, taken from the extract. What helped you work out the meaning?

READING SKILL
Dealing with unknown words in literary texts

To work out the meaning of new words ...

• try to relate the word to another word in the family that you know.

• consider if the word is made up of other words you know.

• use the context to understand a word by looking at the information around it.

• look for synonyms: if you don't know a word, is the word explained in other words elsewhere?

• consider if you have a similar word in your first language.

1 My sister, four years younger than I, is <u>clutching</u> my hand <u>wordlessly</u>; she hardly understands where we are, or what is happening to us.

2 I am <u>pierced</u> by a youthful <u>sorrow</u> so powerful that I suddenly stop crying and try to hold still against the pain.

4 Find five more words in the extract that you'd like to know the meaning of. Use the suggestions in the Reading skill box to help. Check in a dictionary. Then discuss the words with a partner.

5 Read the extract again. Are the sentences true (T) or false (F)?

1 The main character feels completely separated from the crowd below.

2 She sees her emigration as only temporary.

3 It's the only time she will feel *tęsknota*.

4 Her future looks uncertain and unknown.

5 She believes she has a better chance of becoming a pianist in Canada.

6 Look at the Critical thinking box. Then find and underline the analogies in lines 6, 14, 20–21 and 26. In pairs, discuss why you think the author chose these analogies. Can you find any others?

CRITICAL THINKING SKILL
Understanding analogies in literature

Analogies show similarities between two things that on the surface might seem completely different, in order to illustrate a larger point in the story. Writers tend to use them to evoke certain feelings or images, create unexpected comparisons, or say something in a more abstract way, which encourages the reader to think more deeply. Ask yourself:

• What two things are being compared, and how similar and different are they in real life?

• How does the analogy help you picture the scene?

• What feelings and unexpected thoughts does this comparison create?

LISTENING AND SPEAKING

NATIONAL GEOGRAPHIC EXPLORER

7 🎧 **7.1** Listen to Carolina Chong Montenegro talk about her reaction to the text. How similar or different was it to your own?

8 Work in pairs. Discuss the questions.

1 In what situations have you felt or would you feel homesick? What have you missed / would you miss the most (e.g. people, food, etc.)?

2 To what extent can living abroad for some time also be a positive experience? Why?

EXPLORE MORE!

Search online for more information about Eva Hoffman's work and life.

Part 1 PARADISE
From *Lost in Translation* by Eva Hoffman

1   IT IS APRIL 1959, I'm standing at the railing of the *Batory*'s upper deck, and I feel that my life is
ending. I'm looking out at the crowd that has gathered on the shore to see the ship's departure from
Gdynia – a crowd that, all of a sudden, is irrevocably on the other side – and I want to break out, run
back, run toward the familiar excitement, the waving hands, the exclamations. We can't be leaving all
5   this behind – but we are. I am thirteen years old, and we are emigrating. It's a notion of such crushing,
definitive finality that to me it might as well mean the end of the world.

My sister, four years younger than I, is clutching my hand wordlessly; she hardly understands where
we are, or what is happening to us. […]

When the brass band on the shore strikes up the jaunty mazurka rhythms of the Polish anthem, I am
10 pierced by a youthful sorrow so powerful that I suddenly stop crying and try to hold still against the
pain. I desperately want time to stop, to hold the ship still with the force of my will. I am suffering my
first, severe attack of nostalgia, or *tęsknota* – a word that adds to nostalgia the tonalities of sadness and
longing. It is a feeling whose shades and degrees I'm destined to know intimately, but at this hovering
moment, it comes upon me like a visitation from a whole new geography of emotions, an annunciation
15 of how much an absence can hurt. Or a premonition of absence, because at this divide, I'm filled
to the brim with what I'm about to lose – images of Cracow, which I loved as one loves a person, of
the sun-baked villages where we had taken summer vacations, of the hours I
spent poring over passages of music with my piano teacher, of conversations
and escapades with friends. Looking ahead, I come across an enormous, cold
20 blankness – a darkening, an erasure, of the imagination, as if a camera eye has
snapped shut, or as if a heavy curtain has been pulled over the future. Of the
place where we're going – Canada – I know nothing. There are vague outlines
of half a continent, a sense of vast spaces and little habitation. My father had a
book with him called *Canada Fragrant with Resin* […], which spoke to him
25 of majestic wilderness, of animals roaming without being pursued, of freedom.
But to me, the word 'Canada' has ominous echoes of the 'Sahara'. No, my
mind rejects the idea of being taken there, I don't want to be pried out of my
childhood, my pleasures, my safety, my hopes for becoming a pianist. The
Batory pulls away, the foghorn emits its lowing, shofar sound, but my being is
30 engaged in a stubborn refusal to move.

GLOSSARY:

Mazurka – traditional Polish music popularized abroad by the Polish composer, Fryderyk Chopin
Shofar – a traditional Jewish instrument made from ram's horn

7B
Working differently

LESSON GOALS
- Talk about similarities and differences at work
- Understand /ʌ/, /əʊ/ and /aɪ/ across accents
- Discuss present, past and future changes in the workplace

Changes at work around the world

Average commuting time 2020

 Mexico City
150 minutes

 Tokyo
49 minutes

Foreign workers

Singapore
1970s: 3.2%
2010s: 35+%

Minimum hourly wage

 Costa Rica
2001: $2.9
2019: $3.5

 Turkey
2001: $3.0
2019: $6.7

Percentage of women in the workforce

 Thailand
2000: 64%
2020: 59%

Average work hours per year

 Germany
1990: 1,583
2017: 1,354

 United States
1990: 1,796
2017: 1,757

SPEAKING AND VOCABULARY

1 Work in pairs. How important are the following for you in an ideal job? Why?

colleagues	commuting time	salary
work-life balance		your own ideas

2 Look at the infographic. In pairs discuss which of the presented changes surprise you most and least.

3 Add these adjectives and adverbs to sentences 1–4 to complete the collocations with a similar meaning to the collocations in bold. There are two words you do not need. Can you find and correct the two sentences that are not true, according to the infographic?

approximate	broadly	marginally
notable	strikingly	subtle

1 People in Germany still work _____ / **roughly the same** number of hours now as they did in the 1990s.
2 The average commuting times in Mexico City and Tokyo are _____ / **radically different**.
3 The average wage in Costa Rica in 2001 was only **slightly** / _____ **lower** than that in Turkey.
4 There was a **dramatic** / _____ **increase** in the number of women in the Thai workforce between 2000 and 2020.

4 Work in pairs. Use the phrases from Exercise 3, to discuss the changes over time in different aspects of work, such as commuting times, pay, equal opportunities or average work time, in your country or other countries you know.

Go to page 141 for the Vocabulary reference.

PRONUNCIATION

5 🔊 **7.2** Listen to speakers of different nationalities pronouncing sentences 1–3. Which pronunciation is the closest to yours? Look at the Clear Voice box to learn more.

CLEAR VOICE
Understanding /ʌ/, /əʊ/ and /aɪ/ across accents

The sounds /ʌ/, as in r**ou**ghly, /əʊ/, as in n**o**tably, and /aɪ/, as in str**i**king, can vary across accents, both among first and second language English users. The different pronunciations are equally 'correct'. Whichever you choose, try to maintain the same pronunciation for all words with that sound, as this makes it easier for other people to understand you.

1 We have r**ou**ghly similar responsibilities at work.
2 There are some n**o**table differences in our work hours.
3 The difference in salary is str**i**king.

LISTENING AND GRAMMAR

6 🔊 **7.3** Listen to two people working at the same company. What do you think their jobs might be? What's the most notable difference between them with regards to their attitude to work?

7 🔊 **7.3** Complete the sentences with the continuous forms of the verbs in brackets that you heard in Exercise 6. Listen again to check.

1 So how long _____ you _____ (work) here?
2 I _____ constantly _____ (change) jobs.
3 … I _____ (not / progress) at all.
4 I _____ (do) this same job for several years …
5 So, do you think you _____ still _____ (work) here when you're, let's say, 65?

8 Look at the sentences in Exercise 7 again. Answer the questions (a–c) about them. Which sentences …

a describe i) the past; ii) the present and iii) the future?
b refer to trends or things that are temporary?
c show how long an action has been in progress?

EXPLORE MORE!

9 Read the Grammar box to learn more about the continuous aspect.

GRAMMAR   The continuous aspect

The continuous aspect in English can be used in many situations to refer to the past, present and future. The continuous aspect can be used …
- to show an action continuing for some time or to distinguish a shorter action from a longer one.
  *When I started, I **was** work**ing** really long hours*
- to show something that starts at an earlier point and continues until a later one
  *I**'d been** do**ing** this same job for several years..*
- to talk about trends, and temporary or changing things.
  *I**'m** always look**ing** for new challenges.*
- to describe a repeated action, especially if the speaker finds it surprising or annoying.
  *It **was** becom**ing** slightly repetitive.*
- It can sometimes also be used with state verbs.
  *I**'m** lov**ing** it!*

Go to page 156 for the Grammar reference.

10 Choose the most appropriate verb form to complete the sentences.

1 It's quite clear that the way we work *changes / is changing* rapidly.
2 We won't *even be using / even use* the same computer systems in five years' time.
3 My previous boss *was continuously criticizing / continuously criticized* my work.
4 Over the last decade I've *worked / been working* in three different countries.

11 Use the prompts to form questions about work. Then write at least three more questions you'd like to ask people. Consider: commuting, likes and dislikes, changes over time.

1 how long / work / current / job
2 there / anything annoying / someone / constantly / do
3 what / situations / you / feel / most / ease / at work

SPEAKING

12 Ask and answer the questions from Exercise 11 with as many classmates as possible. Ask follow-up questions. At the end, work in pairs to compare what you learned about your classmates.

Search online for more information about 'jobs for the next decade'. Which attracts you the most and least? Why?

LESSON GOALS
• Feel comfortable with your accent in English
• Talk about different ways to use the voice
• Deal with non-linguistic listening challenges
• Recognize homophones and homographs

7C
Different voices

SPEAKING AND PRONUNCIATION

1 Look at the quotation. Do you agree? Then work in pairs to discuss questions 1 and 2 below.

'Words mean more than what is set down on paper. It takes the human voice to infuse them with deeper meaning' – Maya Angelou, poet

1 In what different ways do you use your voice? Do you sing or act or speak in public?
2 How do people's voices change a) on a phone or video call? b) in different regions of your country? c) among people of different ages?

NATIONAL GEOGRAPHIC EXPLORERS

2 🎧 7.4 Listen to Carolina Chong Montenegro and Gabby Salazar talk about their accents in a foreign language they speak and in their mother tongue. Answer the questions.

1 How does Carolina feel about her English accent?
2 Why did Gabby lose her Southern US accent?
3 What problems did Gabby have with Spanish?

3 Look at the Clear Voice box. Work in pairs. Discuss questions 1–3.

CLEAR VOICE
Feeling comfortable with your accent

English is used by approximately 2.3 billion people all over the world, all of whom speak it slightly differently. Although some accents are often thought to be 'standard', it's worth remembering no accent is 'better' or more 'correct' than another. It's as important a part of your identity and heritage as where you come from and you have every reason to own it and be proud of it. Aim to speak clearly, but not to change your accent.

1 Do you agree with Carolina and Gabby that it's OK to have an accent in your second language? How do you feel about your accent in English?
2 What do you think about the fact that Gabby was told to change her accent at school?
3 Carolina says that our accents make us unique and are part of who we are. Do you agree? Why? / Why not?

VOCABULARY

4 Work in pairs. Look at the phrases below. Which refer to …

1 the manner of speaking?
2 the loudness of the voice?
3 voice and technology?
4 expressing an opinion?

give someone a voice	speak at the top of your voice
lower your voice	speak out
moan about	speak up
mumble	voice recognition
raise your voice	you're breaking up

5 Work in small groups. Discuss the questions.

1 In what situations might you lower your voice?
2 What do you moan about sometimes?
3 Which groups of people need to be given a greater voice or to speak out more in society? Why? How?
4 Do you know anyone who tends to mumble or needs to speak up more?
5 Have you ever tried any voice recognition software? How easy or difficult was it to use?

Go to page 141 for the Vocabulary reference.

LISTENING

6 🎧 **7.5** Listen to the three recordings. Work in pairs to discuss what the main topic of each one is and what is causing problems with understanding.

7 Look at the Listening skill box. Discuss which tips you think are the most and least helpful.

LISTENING SKILL
Dealing with non-linguistic listening challenges

Speech can be hard to understand because of background noises, poor phone/internet connection, an unfamiliar accent, or the way the person uses their voice. To help yourself, you can …

• listen for key words – often you don't need to understand every word.

• use non-linguistic cues such as gestures or visuals and signs to help you understand.

• notice the differences – pay attention to how a speaker says certain sounds, words or phrases, so you can understand them more easily next time.

EXPLORE MORE!

Search online for 'English accents video' to learn more about how English is spoken around the world.

8 🎧 **7.5** Listen to the recordings from Exercise 6 again and choose the best option based on what you hear.

1 In conversation 1 Joe would like to have *an active / a warm / a mountain* holiday.
2 In conversation 2, the speakers use voice recognition to ask about *Apollo missions / a 'Mrs Polo' / a pole that's missing*.
3 The voice coach in conversation 3 says a powerful tool is speaking *louder / with pauses / faster*.

9 Read the Focus on box. Then look at phrases 1 and 2. Can you think of any homophones or homographs for the words in bold?

FOCUS ON Homophones and homographs

Homophones: In English many words sound the same, but are spelled differently and mean something different. Some examples include: *tail/tale, knew/new, steal/steel, they're/their*

Homographs: Other words are spelled the same but have a different meaning, and, sometimes, a different pronunciation. Some examples include: *bow /bəʊ, baʊ/, minute /maɪnjuːt, mɪnɪt/, wound / wuːnd, waʊnd/*

Go to page 156 for the Focus on reference.

1 you're **breaking** up
2 I **knew** it's not just

10 Student A: go to page 166. Student B: go to page 167. Check how to pronounce the words in bold. Read the sentences to each other and write down the ones your partner said. Who spelled more homophones and homographs correctly?

SPEAKING

11 Work in pairs. Choose one of these topics. Make some notes.

an experience you've had of a misunderstanding
a person you admire
an experience you've had related to sport or entertainment

12 Work in pairs. Sit opposite your partner. Take turns to talk about your topic for three minutes. Ask each other three follow-up questions. Try to understand each other despite the distraction of people talking around you.

7D
Finding your voice in English

LESSON GOALS
• Explore ways to make your voice heard in English
• Identify ways to change how people might see you
• Practise managing the impression you make in English

SPEAKING

1 Work in pairs. Discuss the questions.

1 Think of three adjectives to describe how you see yourself.

2 Would you use the same adjectives to describe how you see yourself when you're interacting in English? Why? / Why not?

3 Do you think people sometimes take on a different personality when speaking another language?

2 Look at Marta's story. Then in pairs, answer questions 1–3.

> Marta has been learning English for many years and is one of the top students in the Advanced English class at her community college. She's usually confident and sociable when speaking in her first language, but feels less confident when she interacts with people in English outside the classroom. Last week, for example, her American colleague made references to an American television game show and acted really surprised when Marta said she had never heard of it. Marta felt uncomfortable and as if she ought to know this show, which made her feel less confident about her English.

1 Do you think Marta's feelings come from her inability to speak English well? Why? / Why not?

2 How could Marta's colleague make her feel less uncomfortable about not understanding cultural references?

3 How could Marta assert herself in such an interaction?

MY VOICE ▶

3 🎧 7.2 Watch the video. In pairs, answer the questions.

1 How is *identity* defined in the video?

2 Do most people have one fixed identity? Why? / Why not?

3 What example is given of people having more positive experiences of speaking English?

4 How does Marta change how the others see her without seeming arrogant?

5 How do you think expressing other aspects of her identity helped Marta feel more confident when speaking English?

4 Look at the Communication skill box. In pairs, discuss how Marta puts into practice the tips (1–3) from the box in the video. Would you do it in a different way from Marta? Why? / Why not?

COMMUNICATION SKILL
Finding your voice in English

Sometimes, we might feel like other people are not seeing us the way we want to be seen. Consider these tips:

• Be aware of how the situation is making you feel.

• Consider how you want others to see you and the impression you want to make.

• Alter how other people might see you in that context by ...

1 talking about an area of expertise you want them to know you for.

2 sharing stories about yourself in roles that you want them to see you in.

3 sharing your knowledge with them.

5 OWN IT! Look at these situations. In pairs, discuss why you think Kazumi, Stasia and Güven are having a problem in each situation. Decide what advice you would give each person. What would *you* do?

1 Kazumi feels confident about his ability to read and write in English and enjoys using English to interact with people from different parts of the world. He doesn't like making mistakes in English but the thing that makes him most uncomfortable is having to speak English in front of other Japanese people. He worries that they might speak better English than him and judge him based on his English ability. So he becomes extra self-conscious when there are other Japanese people in the group and avoids talking in English.

2 Stasia goes to a volleyball club, where she has got to know several English-speaking friends. She likes their company, but thinks that they only see her as someone who speaks English as a second language and are unaware that Stasia used to be a business owner. She wants them to know that side of her, but doesn't know how to bring up the topic. During their last meet, one of her friends was talking about starting a new business – something Stasia knows a lot about. The conversation moved very quickly and nobody asked Stasia for her opinion. Stasia felt frustrated that her professional identity was not being recognized, but she didn't know how to make them aware of this.

3 Güven sees himself as the funny one and he always makes his friends and colleagues laugh when speaking in his first language. He enjoys being quick-witted and always having an opinion about everything. Recently, Güven had a group conversation in English with his new international colleagues and hoped he was coming across as confident and charming. Afterwards, though, he felt worried because they hadn't seemed as amused as his friends usually were and he felt a bit exhausted from trying to entertain them.

6 Look at Situations A and B. Make some notes. In pairs, discuss the questions (1–3) in relation to each situation.

Situation A: Think of a time when you were speaking English and you felt that people did not see you the way you wanted to be seen.

Situation B: Think of a time when you felt confident speaking English and you felt that you were able to successfully make the impression you wanted to.

1 Describe the situation.
2 How do you think your conversation partner saw you?
3 Do you feel you were able to assert your identity? If so, how? If not, how could you have done?

7 Look at the Useful language box. Substitute the words in brackets with information appropriate to your own life. Practise saying these phrases to your partner.

> **Useful language** Managing the impression you make
>
> **Sharing your expertise**
> After (ten) years of being (a parent/a teacher/in sales), I've learned that …
> I actually did some research/reading on (this).
>
> **Sharing your knowledge about something**
> Did you know that (there are three different ways to say rice in Chinese)?
> You'd probably be surprised to hear that (in Spanish, a librería is actually a bookshop)!
>
> **Sharing stories about yourself**
> I've got a (funny/interesting) story about (that)!
> When I was (working as a biologist), …

8 Work in groups of three. Taking turns, explain the context you described in Situation A from Exercise 6. Then roleplay that situation with your group, remembering to use the Communication skill tips and the Useful language in your roleplay.

9 Work in your groups from Exercise 8. Discuss the questions and give your group members feedback on how they dealt with the situations.

1 What strategies did you use to assert your identity and increase your confidence? How helpful were those strategies?
2 What would you do differently in the future when confronted with situations like Situation A?

EXPLORE MORE!

The way we try to influence how others see us and manage the impressions others might have of us can cover a wide range of strategies. Search online for 'impression management' to find out more.

A more equal society

LESSON GOALS
- Structure an argument in an essay
- Express opinions in an impersonal way
- Write an opinion essay

SPEAKING

1 What do you know about universal basic income? Read two extracts from different newspapers and the first paragraph of the essay to find out. Then discuss questions 1 and 2 below.

> **This free cash plan would pay you $1,320 per month and wouldn't cost the government a cent.**

> *Universal basic income may sound attractive, but would be more likely to increase poverty than reduce it.*

1 What positive and negative consequences of Universal basic income (UBI) can you see? Think about …
- people who are poor, rich, unemployed and elderly.
- the economy.
- people's motivation to work.
2 Should UBI be implemented? Why? / Why not?

READING FOR WRITING

2 Read the essay. What is the writer's position on UBI? Are you convinced by their arguments? Why? / Why not? Discuss in pairs.

3 Read the essay again. Complete the outline with the writers' arguments in paragraphs 2–4.
1 Writer's main position: _____
2 Paragraph 2
 a Main argument: _____
 b Evidence: _____
3 Paragraph 3
 a Main argument: _____
 b Evidence: _____
4 Paragraph 4
 a Main argument: _____
 b Evidence: _____

Universal basic income (UBI) refers to the idea of offering a monthly allowance to all citizens regardless of their age, income or employment status. While this proposition has been heavily criticized by some, it is argued here that UBI could have a very positive effect both on individuals and the economy of the countries involved.

UBI has received criticism for two main reasons. Firstly, its critics argue that receiving this income is likely to discourage people from working and secondly, its implementation is widely considered to be prohibitively expensive. However, it is questionable whether most citizens would leave their jobs, since it is generally true that many people enjoy their jobs and want to make a contribution to society. The costs of UBI could also be fully covered, for example, through additional taxes on companies.

In fact, it is worth pointing out that UBI could stimulate the economy; experts estimate that a UBI of $1000 would grow the US economy by $2.48 trillion in eight years. Similarly, in an ongoing UBI project in Kenya it is predicted that for every dollar invested, its economy will grow by $2.61. This is largely due to the increased spending and investment capacity of the citizens receiving UBI. Therefore, it is clear that the economic benefits of implementing UBI are far greater than its potential costs.

Moreover, it has been shown that UBI can have a positive social impact. One reason for this is that the mental health of citizens receiving UBI tends to improve thanks to their having fewer concerns about their financial situation. Additionally, in some parts of the world it is common for children to work in order to help support the family, and therefore UBI could help increase school attendance. This was indeed the result of a randomized trial in India. Finally, it has also been reported that UBI can reduce racial inequalities by addressing the notable pay gap found in some places.

Although UBI has been tested in approximately 130 countries on all continents, from Namibia, through the Netherlands, to Brazil and Japan, it still has its critics, who claim that the scheme would discourage people from working and be too costly to implement. Nevertheless, the evidence clearly suggests that UBI can not only have a significant positive impact on the economy, but also trigger important social change, thus potentially contributing to a more equal society.

4 Look at the Writing skill and read the essay again. Then work in pairs to discuss questions 1 and 2.

WRITING SKILL
Structuring an argument in an opinion essay

An opinion essay aims to present and justify a writer's position on a topic. However, it is important that you acknowledge the opposing point of view and then show why you believe your viewpoint has more validity.

In each of the following two paragraphs, present one argument in favour of your opinion and support it with evidence. Avoid giving personal or subjective examples. Present facts and expert opinions whenever possible.

1 Which paragraph of the essay gives an opposing opinion to the rest of the essay?
2 Do opinion essays use personal examples and the pronoun *I*?

5 Look at the three essay topics below. Choose one and decide what your opinion on it is. List arguments to support your opinion, providing some evidence or examples and 2 or 3 reasons some people might put forward against your opinion. Then think of reasons why you believe these counterarguments are not valid.

1 The rich should pay much higher taxes.
2 Space exploration is a waste of money.
3 The world would be a better place if the internet had not been invented.

6 Work with people who chose the same topic. Using your notes from Exercise 5, present your argument. Whose argument is more convincing? Why?

7 Look at the Useful language box and learn more about expressing opinions in an impersonal way in essays. Go back to the argument you presented in Exercise 6 and write at least three sentences using the Useful language.

> **Useful language** Expressing opinions in an impersonal way
>
> It is worth noting that …
> It is questionable/debatable whether …
> It has been shown/proven that …
> It is important to observe that …
> It should be noted that …
> It could be / is (thus) argued here / in this essay that …
> It is widely thought/believed that …

WRITING TASK

8 **WRITE** Write an opinion essay on one of the topics from Exercise 5 or another topic of your choice. Write between 300 and 350 words.

9 **CHECK** Use the checklist. I have …

☐ presented a clear opinion in the introduction.
☐ organized the text into 4–5 paragraphs.
☐ acknowledged the opposing point of view and shown why it isn't valid.
☐ presented several objective reasons and examples to support my opinion.
☐ expressed my opinion in an impersonal way.

10 **REVIEW** Work with someone who chose the same topic. Read each other's essay and discuss the questions.
- How is your partner's argument similar/different from yours?
- Which arguments are the strongest/weakest?
- How could you improve your arguments based on your partner's ideas?

Go to page 133 for the Reflect and review.

Scott Mason trains a rescued Egyptian vulture to fly using a paraglider, as part of the Parahawking Project, which rescues, rehabilitates and releases birds, Nepal, Asia.

Nature

GOALS

- Summarize texts with an outline
- Use dependent prepositions
- Talk about natural wonders and natural talents
- Understand common patterns in fast speech
- Practise ways of confronting difficult issues
- Write an essay suggesting solutions to problems

1 Work in pairs. Discuss the questions.
1 Look at the photo. What relationship between humans and nature does it show? How would you describe your relationship with nature?
2 Which do you enjoy more: being in the natural world or being in a busy city?

WATCH ▶

2 ▶ 8.1 Watch the video. Answer the questions.

NATIONAL GEOGRAPHIC EXPLORERS

JEFF KERBY   MARIA FADIMAN

1 How would you describe Jeff's and Maria's relationships with nature? Why?
2 Why does Jeff think humans need to find better ways to coexist with nature?
3 What important lesson has Maria learned from animals that used to scare her?

3 Make connections. What have you learned from spending time in nature?

8A
Naturally created?

LESSON GOALS
- Summarize texts with an outline
- Understand and avoid personal biases
- Debate opinions on modifying or re-creating food

READING

1 Look at these foods. Work in pairs. Put them in order according to how natural (5) or artificial (1) they seem to you. Give reasons.

purple carrots	lab-grown meat
tomatoes	chicken nuggets
wheat	genetically modified crops

2 Skim the opinion article. What is the author's main point? Do you agree? Why? / Why not?

3 Look at the Reading skill box. Then complete the gaps in the summary below with one word.

READING SKILL
Creating an outline of a text

When reading longer and more complex texts, it might be worth summarizing the main points in an outline. When creating an outline …

- focus on the main points first – these are typically listed in the introduction and mentioned in the first sentence of each paragraph.
- include supporting examples – note down the arguments, stories or examples the writer uses.
- use bullet points and headings to organize ideas.
- use abbreviations and symbols – this will help you write faster (people ➔ ppl, for example ➔ e.g.).

Title: Long ¹_____ of modifying
        nature
A Selective ²_____ of wheat and
    carrots:
    i modern wheat has larger ³_____
    ii ⁴_____ carrots are not
    natural: created by the Dutch
B GM crops:
    i rice yields ↓ bc of ⁵_____ change
    ii GM rice ➔ ⁶_____ to droughts
        and floods
C Current developments:
    i ⁷_____ designed DNA
    ii virus resistant bacteria to
        ⁸_____ illnesses

4 Look at the Critical thinking box and apply the steps to the topic of lab-grown meat and genetically modified (GM) crops. Discuss in pairs.

CRITICAL THINKING SKILL
Understanding and avoiding biases

We all have unconscious biases and fixed assumptions. When reading a text, these might lead us to have a strong and immediate response before we have properly evaluated the writer's claims. To understand and avoid your own biases you can do the following:

- Ask yourself what your immediate reaction to a topic is and what it is based on (e.g. emotions or facts).
- Give sufficient time to evaluate the writer's position objectively, listing the arguments they make and identifying those that are objectively sound.
- Re-evaluate your own position in the light of the writer's arguments.

Applying these steps doesn't mean you need to change your position, but it allows you to have a better understanding of your initial biases before you form your opinion of the writer's claims.

SPEAKING

5 You are going to take part in a debate on the topic *Can modifying or recreating food help save the planet?* Follow the steps:

- Divide into As and Bs. Student A: you agree, Student B: you disagree.
- Work with someone who has the same opinion (Student A with another A, Student B with another B) to list arguments and examples to support your opinion. Note down at least one counterargument and your response to it.

6 Work with another pair who has the opposing point of view. Present your arguments and respond to the other pair's points.

7 Reflect whose arguments were the …

- strongest?
- most objective?
- most different/similar to yours?

OPINION

How natural is our food?

1 Singapore has become one of the first countries in the world to approve the sale of lab-grown meat. Chicken nuggets entirely produced in a laboratory will soon be available for purchase. While this may seem extraordinary
5 to some people, it is merely the most recent example of a thousand-year history of humans modifying and designing nature to suit their own purposes.

Wheat cultivation is a prime example of human intervention in natural processes. The wheat we eat
10 today is vastly different from wild wheat, which was first collected by humans around 23,000 years ago. By deliberately selecting and breeding wheat for millennia, farmers created wheat with significantly larger grains, thus increasing productivity and yield. In essence, the
15 same principle underlines genetically modified (GM) food: selecting specific genes that code for a desirable trait.

A striking example of selective breeding is orange carrots. Interestingly, up until the 17th century, orange carrots were incredibly rare, and the most common colours
20 were white, purple and yellow. It was the Dutch who first created an orange variety and then promoted it widely (allegedly in honour of the royal house of Orange), leading to a near extinction of the other types. Similar human-driven modifications have completely changed countless
25 other fruits and vegetables, from corn, through pineapple, to bananas.

While previously these modifications took decades of patient crossbreeding to obtain the desired colour, size or taste, now they can happen almost instantaneously in a
30 lab through genetic modification. For example, scientists are currently working on creating GM rice varieties that will be flood- and drought-resistant. This is important since rice is a staple crop throughout Asia for billions of people. Currently, climate changes make it increasingly
35 challenging to produce sufficient yields due to excessive flooding or heat. While finding naturally occurring flood- and drought-resistant varieties might be possible, this

would be likely to take decades rather than just the few years it should take by applying genetic technology.

40 In this context, lab-grown meat might start to appear less artificial and increasingly natural – as a logical and inevitable step in our thousand-year-old quest for more nutritious, easier-to-produce food. It also has important advantages for the climate since no land or feed is needed
45 to produce it. Moreover, no animals are killed in the process, making it a potentially attractive alternative to the ever-growing consumption of 'natural' meat.

Thus, it is likely that scientists might soon be able to artificially create DNA and simple organisms – in the lab.
50 In fact, early steps are being taken in Cambridge, UK, where a team have designed the first synthetic bacteria. According to researchers, such bacteria hold enormous potential for medicine, as they would be virus-resistant, and could be used to treat numerous diseases.

55 Taking into account the long history of humans modifying food and nature to suit their purposes and the potential benefits for the environment of GM food, it seems clear that our definition of what is natural will carry on evolving as we gain more knowledge and continue to alter our
60 environment to suit our purposes.

WHAT DO YOU THINK?

GLOSSARY:

chicken nuggets – small pieces of chicken coated in breadcrumbs and fried

8B
Natural talent

LESSON GOAL
• Talk about skills and talents using dependent prepositions
• Talk about success
• Say /dʒ/, /tʃ/ and /ʃ/

SPEAKING

1 Work in pairs. Look at the photo. Do you know anything about this bird? Look at the animal talents (1–5) and match them with the animals (a–e).

1 It can shake 70% of its fur dry in just four seconds.
2 It can eat up to ten times its mass in one meal.
3 Its skin releases a natural sunscreen that prevents it from getting sunburned.
4 It can completely change its colour in less than a second.
5 It is said to be able to perfectly reproduce almost any sound in the environment.

a black swallower fish
b lyrebird
c cuttlefish
d hippo
e dog

2 Discuss which of the talents in Exercise 1 you find the most and least impressive. Which talents would be useful to have as a human?

LISTENING AND GRAMMAR

3 🎧 8.1 Listen to the talk. What have Judit Polgar and Stephen Wiltshire achieved? To what extent are their achievements due to natural talent or to hard work in your opinion?

4 🎧 8.1 Complete the sentences from the talk in Exercise 3 with the correct prepositions. Then listen again to check.

1 So how did they become so good _____ chess?
2 … and having long-term commitment _____ becoming the best
3 So from very early on, they were focused _____ the game and practised every single day.
4 Where do his amazing abilities stem _____?
5 But already as a child Stephen had a natural talent and a passion _____ drawing.

A lyrebird.

98

5 Read the Grammar box. Then choose the correct preposition to complete sentences 1–5.

> **GRAMMAR** Dependent prepositions
>
> In English many words are followed by dependent prepositions. These can be nouns (*talent for*), adjectives (*skilled at*) and verbs (*focus on*). To know which preposition to use, you need to memorize the word + preposition combinations as there are no fixed rules. However, it is useful to learn them thematically (e.g. words related to talent).
>
> Remember that when a preposition is followed by a verb, you should use the verb in the *-ing* form (even if the preposition is *to*).
> *They were committed **to being** the best.*

Go to page 157 for the Grammar reference.

1 Complete mastery *of / on / at* any skill takes thousands of hours of deliberate practice.

2 In order to succeed *for / to / in* music or art or sport, etc., you need innate talent.

3 If you can focus intensely *in / on / for* practising a particular skill for a long period of time, you're bound to become an expert at it.

4 You can commit yourself *to / for / at* being the best as much as you want, but if you don't have talent, there's no way you'll succeed.

5 If a child lacks a flair *in / on / for* languages, there's little a teacher can do to help them.

6 Look at the sentences in Exercise 5 again. Work in pairs to discuss to what extent you agree or disagree with them. Give reasons and examples.

VOCABULARY

7 Look at these phrases. Which four suggest someone works hard for their success?

be a born (tennis player)	(it/music) is in the genes
(not) be cut out for	have drive
be deeply committed to	have flair
be driven	have a flair for
be persistent	have natural/innate talent
be a first-rate (singer)	have a natural / an innate
be an accomplished (painter)	talent for

8 Write at least five sentences about yourself or people you know using the phrases in Exercise 7. Make some of them true and some false.

9 Work in pairs. Show each other the sentences you wrote in Exercise 8. Try to work out which of your partner's sentences are false by asking questions to find out more information.

Go to page 142 for the Vocabulary reference.

SPEAKING AND PRONUNCIATION

10 **8.2** Look at the Clear voice box. Student A: go to page 166. Student B: go to page 167. Individually, practise your sentences, paying attention to the underlined words. Then listen to check your pronunciation.

> **CLEAR VOICE**
> **Saying /dʒ/, /tʃ/ and /ʃ/**
>
> All three sounds: /dʒ/ as in *langua**ge***, /tʃ/ as in *na**t**ure* and /ʃ/ as in *accompli**sh**ed* are pronounced in the same place with the tongue behind your teeth. However, when saying /dʒ/ and /tʃ/, you need to stop the air (unlike in /ʃ/). In addition, /dʒ/ should be voiced. This will help make your pronunciation clearer.

11 Student A work with Student B. Read the sentences you practised in Exercise 10 and write down what your partner says. If necessary, ask your partner to repeat more clearly. Were you correct? Check the difficult sentences.

SPEAKING

12 Follow the instructions.

- Individually, choose a person you know something about who is successful in a particular discipline (e.g. sports, maths, business, singing, etc.).
- Consider what has enabled them to become successful and prepare to talk for a couple of minutes about them.
- Work in groups of three. Take turns to talk about the person you chose.
- Ask questions to learn more. Then discuss …

1 whose success story is the most inspiring.

2 which person relies the most/least on their innate talent.

3 what lessons you could apply to your own life to become more successful.

EXPLORE MORE!

Search online for 'deliberate practice + Ericsson + video' to learn more about becoming an expert through hard work.

8C
Moments in nature

LESSON GOALS
* Talk about natural wonders
* Adapt your pronunciation to say /w/, /v/, and /b/
* Understand merging and disappearing sounds in fast speech

SPEAKING AND GRAMMAR

1 Think about the landscape in your area or country. Work in pairs to discuss the questions.

1 Which landscape features (e.g. mountains, rivers, beaches) do you enjoy spending time in or near the most? Why?

2 What are the top three natural spots you know that you would recommend to a visitor?

2 Think again about the names of the natural features you discussed in Exercise 1. Which use a definite article? Read the Focus on box to check how you say these in English.

> **FOCUS ON** Using the definite article with natural features
>
> The definite article is used before names of mountain ranges (*the Andes*), island chains (the Pacific Islands), geographical areas (*the Middle East*), forests (*the Black Forest*), and rivers, seas and oceans (*the Atlantic*). You can also use *the* with a singular noun to refer to an animal species as a whole.
>
> *The tiger is the largest cat species.*
>
> Do not use *the* before names of individual mountains or islands (BUT *the Isle of Wight*), continents, waterfalls or lakes. Also, do not use it with a plural noun to refer to animals or people in general.
>
> *Tigers live in Asia.*

Go to page 158 for the Focus on reference.

3 Choose the correct option, *the* or no article (–), to complete the sentences.

1 Arriving at the top of *the* / – Mount Kilimanjaro was one of the most inspiring experiences of my life.

2 The flora and fauna found on *the* / – Madagascar is completely unique because it has been separated from *the* / – mainland Africa for millions of years.

3 *The* / – snow leopard is a critically endangered species that can be found in *the* / – Himalayas.

4 I love *the* / – polar bears, but they are threatened with extinction because temperatures in *the* / – Arctic are rising at least twice as fast as the global average.

5 I have friends in *the* / – Canada with a small cabin on *the* / – Lake Healey, which you can only reach by boat.

VOCABULARY

4 Read the sentences. Check the meaning of any new words and phrases in a dictionary. Change three or four of the sentences to make them true for places you know. Compare your sentences in pairs.

1 From the **summit** of Tomaree Mountain you'll see views of **unspoiled** beaches and **crystal clear** ocean water.

2 One of the most **impressive landmarks** in my region are these interestingly shaped **rocky cliffs**. I love watching the waves **crashing** against them.

3 There are some **scenic routes** around where I live that take you through **tranquil woods** and **picturesque valleys**.

4 I will never forget the **lush green vegetation** of the Amazon; it made you feel completely **immersed** in the natural world.

5 **Witnessing** the sunrise over the Sahara and seeing the **vastness** of its **untouched** dunes was one of the most **memorable moments** for me.

Go to page 142 for the Vocabulary reference.

PRONUNCIATION

5 🎧 8.3 Listen to the two short conversations. Write down the word that causes problems in each conversation. How should it be pronounced? Read the Clear voice box to learn more.

> **CLEAR VOICE**
> **Adapting your pronunciation to say /w/, /v/, and /b/**
>
> The sound /w/, as in *wild*, can often be mispronounced as /v/. Some speakers also say /v/ as /b/, which can make their meaning less clear. If these sounds are challenging for you, try to adapt your pronunciation. You can also add an explanation or a synonym to clarify further.

6 Work in pairs. Practise saying these sentences.

1 I would love to see that very rare berry.

2 We visited vast wild areas with no vegetation.

3 There were beautiful views over the valley and the woods to the west.

Jeff Kerby photographs gelada monkeys in Ethiopia.

LISTENING

7 🎧 8.4 Listen to Jeff Kerby and Maria Fadiman discuss their experiences in nature. What did they experience?

8 🎧 8.5 Look at the Listening skill box, then listen to some phrases said by Jeff and Maria. Write down what you hear.

LISTENING SKILL
Understanding fast speech (2): merging and disappearing sounds

In fast speech, words often sound differently from how they're pronounced individually. For example:

• some sounds: might disappear from the word: *perhaps* ➔ /præps/

• Two or more words can also merge together. *Th* might not be pronounced at all: *And then* ➔ /ənen/.

• The last consonant might get attached to the next word if it begins with a vowel: *hold its* ➔ /hɒldis/.

Paying attention to these processes can help you understand fast speech better.

9 🎧 8.4 Listen to Jeff and Maria's experiences in Exercise 7 again and answer the questions below.

1 Why is Jeff passionate about the natural world?
2 Why did he follow the gelada monkey and what did he see?
3 What reflections did the event cause Jeff to have?
4 What did Maria do at the waterfall?
5 What made the moment special for her?

SPEAKING

10 Work individually. Think about a memorable experience you had in nature. Prepare to describe it to a classmate. You can use Jeff and Maria's stories as inspiration and the words and phrases from Exercise 4 to help you.

11 Work in pairs. Describe the experience to one another. Whose experience is more …

a exciting?
b inspiring?
c relaxing?

EXPLORE MORE!

Search online for 'natural wonders of the world' to learn more. Find inspiring photos to share with your classmates next time.

LESSON GOALS
- Learn about the importance of managing conflict
- Identify effective ways of having a conversation to resolve conflict
- Practise having a conversation to confront a difficult issue

8D
Confronting difficult issues

SPEAKING

1 Look at the situations (1–3). What is your natural tendency when dealing with each of these situations? Choose a, b, or c below. Work in pairs and give reasons for your choices.

1 A good friend has done something to upset you. They've never done it before.
2 A work colleague has an annoying habit that is upsetting everyone in the office.
3 A family member has consistently behaved in a way that has annoyed you.

a Ignore it and avoid confrontation.
b Have a conversation with that person about it.
c Complain to someone else and hope they'll resolve it for you.

2 🎧 8.6 Listen to Ayana, Dimitri and Hardi talking about difficult situations they've been in. Then read the statements and label them A (Ayana), D (Dimitri) or H (Hardi).

1 I thought I was approaching the situation in a nice and friendly way.
2 I thought it was best that I didn't confront the situation.
3 I thought being firm about how I felt was the best way to deal with the situation.
4 The talk worsened our working relationship.
5 Since then, we've been very careful around each other. It's not a nice way to be.
6 We're no longer friends.

3 Work in pairs. Discuss the questions.

1 What do you think went wrong in the three scenarios in Exercise 2? What do you think Ayana, Dimitri and Hardi should or shouldn't have done?
2 Have you ever dealt with a difficult situation in the same way as Ayana, Dimitri and/or Hardi? What happened as a result?

MY VOICE ▶

4 ▶ 8.2 Watch the video. Answer the questions. Work in pairs to compare your answers.

1 When faced with conflict, what do many people naturally do instead of confronting the issue?
2 What two things can we achieve by effectively managing conflict?
3 What is the purpose of having a conversation about the problem?

5 According to the video, there are things we should avoid in a difficult conversation. Match the labels (1–4) with the examples of what might be said (a–d).

1 Blaming
2 Being defensive
3 Overgeneralizing
4 Making judgements on their personality

a 'You never ever help anyone. You always put yourself first.'
b 'You're a selfish person and you're very narrow-minded.'
c 'This is your fault. None of this would have happened if it wasn't for you!'
d 'I didn't do that! What on earth are you talking about? Why don't you look at yourself?'

6 Look at the Communication skill box. In pairs, discuss if you've ever prepared what you wanted to say before having a difficult conversation. Why might preparing your opening be a good thing?

COMMUNICATION SKILL
Confronting difficult issues

When faced with conflict, it could help to have a conversation about the issue to try and resolve the conflict. We can make these conversations more effective by preparing how we intend to start them. In your opening …

1 describe the problem.
2 give examples and say how you feel about the issue.
3 highlight the impact and say why it's important.

Then, listen in order to understand.

WRITING AND SPEAKING

7 Look at the Useful language box. Then choose one of the situations (1, 2 or 3) and write an opening to that conversation. Compare your opening with your partner's.

> **Useful language** Confronting difficult issues
>
> **Starting the conversation**
> I wanted to talk to you about …
> I've noticed that …
>
> **Saying how you feel about the issue**
> I feel that …
> It seems to me that …
>
> **Highlighting the impact**
> I fear that if this continues …
> As a result, …
>
> **Inviting a response**
> I'd really like to find out how you feel and resolve this.
> I hope you can help me see things from your point of view.

1 You live with someone who has a very different approach to tidying. You prefer tidying and cleaning as you go along, putting things away straight after you use them. Your housemate Ewa prefers to leave everything and then do a big clean-up every few days. You find yourself doing most of the tidying and cleaning in the house and this is really bothering you.

2 When deciding where to go on your group holidays, you mentioned your preference for a more cultural holiday, but Dante continued to talk about a beach holiday. You feel that Dante has consistently been ignoring what you say and this is not the first time he has done that. This has been upsetting you for some time.

3 Choose a real-life conflict that you wish to address.

8 **OWN IT!** Work in groups of three. Take turns to roleplay Students A, B and C. Remember to use the Communication skill tips and the Useful language.

Student A: Open the conversation using what you've prepared in Exercise 7 and try to resolve the conflict you have with Student B.

Student B: Take on the role of the person that Student A has a conflict with.

Student C: Observe the conversation between Student A and B. After their roleplay, provide them with feedback on how you felt the conversation went and what could be improved.

9 Work in small groups. Discuss the questions.
  1 What do you think makes such conversations difficult? Why do you think some people prefer to avoid having these kinds of conversations?
  2 Do you think the conversation is enough to resolve the conflict? What do you think needs to be done after such a conversation?
  3 Are there situations where confrontation conversations are best avoided? What kind of situations might they be?

8E

One possible solution is . . .

LESSON GOALS
• Use cautious language in essays
• Talk formally about effects and solutions
• Write an essay suggesting solutions to problems

SPEAKING AND LISTENING

NATIONAL GEOGRAPHIC EXPLORERS

1 **8.7** Work in pairs. Look at the list of environmental issues and potential solutions. Which issues are the most serious? Which solutions could be most effective? Then listen to Jeff and Maria. Which issues and solutions do they mention?

Environmental issues	Potential solutions
Decline in animal populations	Sustainable use of forest resources
Increase in droughts	Banning trade in rare animals
Rising sea levels	Raising people's awareness and educating them
Habitat loss	
Plastic pollution	Reducing plastic waste
More floods	Purchasing sustainably produced products
Melting ice caps	

2 Look at the Useful language box. Match these words and phrases with the words in bold in the box. Some synonyms can be matched with more than one bold word.

---
make smaller   strong   do   small   not complete
cheap   bad   for a long time   complete   doable

Useful language Discussing effects and solutions

Have a(n) **adverse/devastating/detrimental/profound** impact/effect on
Have a **cumulative/lasting/far-reaching** impact/effect on
Have a **negligible/minimal/marginal** impact/effect on
Exert/produce/create an impact/effect on
Lessen/minimize/reduce the effect/impact on
Propose a **comprehensive/radical/partial** solution to (a problem)
Reach a **viable/workable/cost-effective** solution for (solving)

3 Work in pairs. Discuss what environmental problems there are in your city, area or country. How could they be solved? How important do you think they are? Use the Useful language to help.

READING FOR WRITING

4 Read the essay on page 105 about one of the problems Jeff described. List the three main types of solutions proposed in the essay. Then discuss which would in your opinion be the most and least …
1 lasting?
2 comprehensive?
3 cost-effective?

5 Compare sentences 1 and 2. Which is more appropriate for formal writing? Why? Read more about cautious language in the Writing skill box. Then underline other examples in the essay.

WRITING SKILL
Using cautious language in essays

When writing formal texts, it is important to be careful about your claims. Your claims will sound more objective and will be more difficult to disprove if you use cautious language, such as:
• modifying adjectives and adverbs: *potential(ly), possible, probably, (un)likely, virtually, practically*
• modal verbs: *might, can, could, may*
• introductory verbs: *suggest, indicate, seem*
• quantifiers: *some, sometimes, most, to some extent, one, rather, somewhat*

1 This will definitely have a devastating effect on everyone around the world.
2 This could have a potentially devastating effect for many around the world.

6 Rewrite the sentences using cautious language.
1 Flooding will affect coastal cities.
2 Wider use of electric cars is a solution to global heating.
3 A solution to saving endangered species is banning the trade in rare animals.

One potentially devastating impact of global heating is rising sea levels. Numerous megacities around the world, which are home to hundreds of millions of people, are situated on the coast. It is therefore likely that many of these could be almost completely flooded.

A possible solution to rising sea levels is to lessen the effect of global heating by emitting fewer greenhouse gases. One way this could be achieved is through switching to greener energy sources and electric vehicles. A substantial reduction in meat consumption could also bring lasting effects. Nevertheless, green technologies could potentially still take decades to become financially viable solutions. The sustainability of the production of ion batteries, essential for electric cars, might also be questioned. Additionally, it seems somewhat unlikely that sufficient numbers of meat-eaters could be persuaded to give up their steaks or burgers. It is fair to conclude, therefore, that these two options do not seem to provide workable solutions to the problem of the rising sea levels, at least in the short term.

A mangrove forest in Thailand.

Another set of solutions would involve rethinking the design of our cities. For example, by constructing sea walls, the impact of flooding could be lessened. Although funds would be required for regular maintenance, this would still be a cost-effective solution when compared with repairing the destruction caused by flooding. Artificial beaches might also serve the same purpose, acting as a barrier against flooding while exerting a minimal impact on the environment. It is also possible to raise the level of existing roads and build more effective drainage systems. All of these interventions could be implemented with existing technology in a short timeframe.

An alternative means of addressing the problem of rising sea levels is to harness the power of mother nature. It has been suggested that planting mangrove forests could provide a natural barrier to rising flood waters and reduce the erosion of coastal areas. Moreover, this could have a lasting beneficial effect on the local ecosystem, providing a habitat for numerous species. Since mangroves are also known to absorb substantial quantities of CO_2 (carbon dioxide) from the atmosphere, this solution may have a cumulative impact on global heating.

To sum up, rising sea levels are likely to have an adverse effect on millions of city dwellers. Although reducing CO_2 emissions could provide a lasting solution, redesigning cities and planting mangroves appear to be more workable and cost-effective alternatives.

7 Read the essay again. Notice how it is structured. Answer the questions. Then use the framework to plan an essay on a topic from Exercise 1 or another topic you are interested in.
  1 What two things does the writer do in the first paragraph?
  2 What is the purpose of the first sentence in paragraphs 2–4? What about the last sentence in paragraphs 2 and 3?
  3 How are the ideas in the paragraphs linked? Give at least five example words or phrases.

WRITING TASK

8 WRITE Write an essay describing the problem from Exercise 7 and suggesting solutions to the problem.

9 CHECK Use the checklist. I have …
  ☐ introduced the problem in the first paragraph.
  ☐ organized the text into 4 or 5 paragraphs.
  ☐ used cautious language when appropriate.
  ☐ used a variety of collocations with *impact*, *effect* and *solution*.
  ☐ summarized my arguments and written a conclusion.

10 REVIEW Exchange essays with a partner. Then discuss how important the problems you've written about are for your country and how feasible the suggested solutions would be.

Go to page 133 for the Reflect and review.

EXPLORE MORE!

Find out more about the solutions currently being implemented to deal with one of the problems in Exercise 1. Search online for '[name of problem] + solution'.

Three students of fashion pose at the launch of the Junk Kouture Recycled Fashion competition in Ireland, dressed (from left to right) as 'Lady Data', a knight and a dancer.

Fashion and trends

GOALS

- Use topic sentences
- Use ellipsis and substitution in conversation
- Talk about fashion; discuss green business trends
- Understand hedging
- Learn strategies to increase your trustworthiness
- Write an anecdote

1 Work in pairs. Look at the photo and discuss the questions.
  1 What different elements of fashion and style can you see?
  2 What would you say inspires these styles and ideas? Where do they come from?

WATCH ▶

2 ▶ 9.1 Watch the video and answer the questions.

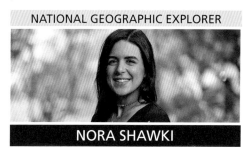

NATIONAL GEOGRAPHIC EXPLORER

NORA SHAWKI

  1 What three trends in Nora's field of research does she describe?
  2 What are the benefits of these trends to Nora's field?

3 Make connections. What field of study or work are you in, or would you like to be? What trends are happening at the moment in this area?

9A
Never out of fashion

LESSON GOALS
• Use topic sentences
• Identify commercial interests
• Discuss and justify choices

READING

1 Work in pairs. Discuss the questions.

1 Look at the photos on page 109. Did you use to play any of these games?

2 What toys and games do you remember from your school days? Were any of them *crazes*, (i.e. very popular for a short time)?

3 Did you use to *improvise* any games (i.e. invent them while you played). Can you describe one?

2 Read the blog post on page 109. Why does the author think that some games have stood the test of time?

3 Read the blog post again. What point does the author want to make by mentioning each of the following?

a 'toothpaste', 'snake eyes' and 'jumbos' (lines 1–2)
b Egypt three millennia ago (lines 6–7)
c video/computer games (lines 11, 23 and 25)
d cognitive growth (line 19)
e *In the attic* (line 29)
f rules and structure (line 34)

4 Look at the Reading skill box. Identify the topic sentence in paragraphs 1–5 of the article. What is each topic sentence doing? Then in pairs, choose a 'pull quote' from the post for the empty box in the blog post.

READING SKILL
Using topic sentences

Paragraphs in more formal texts such as articles and essays often include topic sentences. Most topic sentences are at the beginning or end of the paragraph. They summarize the paragraph in some way: by stating the argument, asking a key question or establishing the structure or content of the paragraph.

It may be useful to identify topic sentences, such as when you need to summarize a text. Some topic sentences may sum up the message of the entire text, so one use of topic sentences in articles is as 'pull quotes'. These are short quotes from the text that are displayed on the same page in larger writing to encourage people to read the article.

EXPLORE MORE!

Find an article or video that discusses the benefits of video games for children's development.
Search online for 'effects + video games + child development'.

5 Work in pairs. Look at the Critical thinking box and answer questions 1–3 in the box with reference to the blog post.

CRITICAL THINKING SKILL
Recognizing commercial interests

Many articles, blog posts, etc. that look like unbiased journalism are in fact advertisements in disguise. Look for clues to tell you who wrote the text, such as links to online shops, logos, and so on. When you are reading, ask yourself:

1 Does the message of the article promote particular products, services or ideas?

2 Who might have paid to have this written and published?

3 Is the argument supported with scientific or anecdotal evidence that may or may not be true?

6 Identify where in the blog post you could add each expression (a–d) to make the commercial interests clearer.

a … judging by our sales, …
b … some of which you can find on our website.
c … which explains why our ropes are consistently one of our best sellers .
d … which is why we don't include the instructions with our toys.

SPEAKING

7 Work in pairs. You are going to design a 'play pack', a box of things to entertain children. Think about what is discussed in the text and your own ideas. Choose an age range to design for and decide which of these criteria are important. Then make a list of ten toys or objects for your play pack. Justify your choices.

cheap   develop motor skills   educational   fun
no need for batteries / power supply
objects adaptable for many uses   plastic-free
promote physical exercise   safe for children
stimulate creativity   other (what?)

A celebration of improvised play

1 ❶ My seven-year old niece showed off her marble collection to me the other day. I spotted 'toothpaste' marbles, 'snake eyes' and 'jumbos', and though she didn't refer to the different types by these names, which I used to use, it was great to share a moment of shared fascination for these timeless objects. My grandfather was able to join in too, with his own memories of playing marbles as a child. In fact, marbles have been enjoyed for thousands of years, but
5 seem to be as popular as ever.

❷ Marbles are not the only toys and games that have enjoyed a long history. Spinning tops were all the rage in Egypt three millennia ago; they came back in a few years ago, and though the modern tops have LEDs, which light up when they spin, you still start them off with the string wrapped tightly around and a flick of the wrist. While sometimes more, sometimes less popular, skipping has also stood the test of time.

marbles

10 ❸ So what is it about traditional games that keeps them popular despite the modern distractions of today's video games? My niece and nephew provide us with a possible explanation. As soon as the TV is switched off, they complain they're bored. But it only takes a few screen-free minutes for them to invent something fun to do with everyday objects. The simpler the object, the more
15 their creative minds can transform it into something fantastical. I've seen a skipping rope transformed into a tail, a bridge, a dog lead, a prison and a snake, to name a few.

❹ Importantly, there is a growing body of evidence to suggest that improvised games lead to cognitive, social and academic growth. High-quality pretend play
20 prompts children to adopt different perspectives, think abstract thoughts, solve problems and develop their linguistic skills. Children are constantly improvising, not only in play, but in language, music, movement and art.

spinning top

❺ Contrast this with video games. These come with very clearly defined pathways for players to follow; the rules are written long before the child gets their hands
25 on the game. While computer games can help develop motor skills and are undoubtedly entertaining, children are not in control in the same way. With true play, children collaborate to decide on the rules, the storyline and the characters; nothing is planned, and the game continues to develop until the players are forced to stop. A favourite story book of my niece's, *In the attic*,
30 contains the line: 'My friend and I found a game that could go on forever … but it was time for dinner'. In other words, it never gets boring.

❻ It's curious to reflect that in a world where such a lot of ready-made entertainment is available, children derive so much benefit from opportunities to play without the support of technology, rules and structure, precisely
35 because they can invent and re-invent their worlds of imagination for themselves.

Disclaimer: this post contains sponsored content.

skipping

9B
A passing fad?

LESSON GOALS
• Speak concisely using ellipsis and substitution
• Say elided expressions with the correct stress.
• Describe fashions

READING AND SPEAKING

1 Work in pairs. Read the information. Then look at the photo and discuss whether, in your opinion, the boots are fads, trends or classics.

A fad
• Style is extreme, e.g. bright fluorescent colours, huge collars, oversized clothes
• Doesn't suit many body types
• Poor quality – usually only worn for a few months
• This season's 'must-have'?

A trend
• Colours, materials and cuts quite normal e.g. cargo pants, large jumpers, skinny jeans
• Suits many people
• Trend lasts up to 5 years, but styles might change during that time

A classic
• Standard style that changes very little over time, e.g. the stripy Breton top, the little black dress, a trench coat
• Looks good on most people
• Good quality – designed to last
• Forms the basis of an outfit and goes well with many styles, colours and accessories

2 Work in pairs. Tell each other about one classic you own, one current trend and one current fad.

LISTENING AND GRAMMAR

NATIONAL GEOGRAPHIC EXPLORER

3 🎧 **9.1** Listen to Nora Shawki. Make notes on a) her attitude to fashion; b) her two favourite things to wear; and c) how she dressed when younger.

4 Complete each extract with one word if there is a gap. If there isn't a gap, cross out any words that aren't necessary in spoken English.

1 'And have you always been the same?' 'No, I don't think _____.'
2 'I used to be more focused on what I looked like rather than comfort, but I shifted towards more practical clothes.'
3 'I love to wear cargo pants. I love the khaki green colour and army-style outfits.'
4 'My colleagues have always commented on how I look trendy. I definitely try _____.'
5 'I like clothes I can wear again and again rather than clothes which are designed for one specific occasion.'
6 'There must have been some fads you bought and now you look back on with horror, were there?' 'Oh, yes, there _____.'
7 'There isn't a photo I can see is there?' 'I hope _____!'

5 🎧 **9.1** Read the Grammar box and make any changes to Exercise 4. Then listen again to the interview in Exercise 3 to check your answers.

GRAMMAR Ellipsis and substitution

Ellipsis: You can leave out words and expressions, especially in spoken English, when the meaning is clear without them. Use ellipsis …
• after linkers: *I used to be more focused on what I looked like, **but I shifted** towards more practical clothes.*
• after auxiliary verbs: *Oh, yes, there **were.***
• with infinitives: *I definitely try **to.***
• with relative clauses: *I like clothes I can wear again and again rather than ~~for one specific occasion or~~ ~~which are~~ worn in one specific way..*

In informal spoken English you can often omit the subject.
*~~I~~ **Love** the khaki green colour*

Substitution: To avoid repeating whole clauses after verbs of thinking, you can replace them with the auxiliary verb, with pronouns and with *so* and with *not*. *It can **do** / The red **ones**? / I don't think **so** / I hope **not**.*

Go to page 158 for the Grammar reference.

6 🔊 **9.2** Read the conversation between Ayla (A) and Disha (D). Make the conversation more concise by deleting unnecessary words and expressions or substituting them. How many possible changes can you find? Listen to check.

A: Disha, you study fashion, don't you?

D: Yes, I study fashion.

A: Would you say flares are back in fashion again?

D: I think they're back in fashion, yes. I don't have any myself, but I'd like to have some.

A: Well, I found these gorgeous flared trousers, which are for sale at a second-hand store near me.

D: Get them! It doesn't matter if they're in fashion or they aren't in fashion. But will you wear them?

A: I'm sure I'll wear them. They're classic seventies fashion.

D: They are classic seventies fashion, but actually, they've been around since the 18th century.

A: Are you joking?

D: I'm not joking at all. Sailors in the navy wore wide-legged trousers. The hippies rejected mainstream fashion, so they went to the second-hand supply shops …

A: … And they found some old sailors' trousers which were just waiting to be turned into fashion!

D: I bet you don't want to buy them now!

PRONUNCIATION

7 🔊 **9.3** Look at the Clear voice box. Listen and repeat the example sentences.

CLEAR VOICE
Saying elided expressions with the correct stress

Auxiliary verbs, prepositions and other grammatical words are not usually stressed, but this may change when used for ellipsis and substitution. Listen to how the words in bold are pronounced in these expressions.

I'd **love to**. / *I* **suppose so**.
I **hope not**. / *I Who* **would**?

8 Write four questions or suggestions that could be answered by one of the following: *I'd love to, I suppose so, I hope so/not, Who would/ wouldn't?* Work in pairs. Take turns to ask and answer your questions.

EXPLORE MORE!

Find a photo or video online of the latest fashions, e.g. from a fashion show. Describe them in writing or commentate over the image.

VOCABULARY

9 Complete the sentences (1–5) with the correct form of these words or expressions. Write three more sentences that are true for you using some of the words and expressions that are new to you.

be back in (fashion)	dress code
flattering	formal	glamorous	outfit
practical	scruffy	see better days
smart casual	trendy	unconventional

1 I wear a lot of black because it is _____ for my body shape, quite _____ because it doesn't show the dirt, and still comes across as _____.

2 I work from home now, so I love an occasion to get out of my _____ everyday clothes and dress up in something more _____.

3 On Fridays we don't have to wear a suit, but the _____ in the office is still _____.

4 My friend Dani is very _____. The _____ she wears are really _____, but she has such a great sense of style, she gets away with it.

5 Most of my clothes have _____, to be honest. Some of them are so old, they're _____ again.

10 Work in pairs. Talk about …

a what, in your opinion, *smart casual* means
  a) for women; b) for men.

b advice you have heard for making outfits more flattering.

c someone you think is very glamorous/scruffy/ trendy/unconventional.

d the most formal clothes you've worn and why.

e a fad that you're glad has gone out of fashion.

Go to page 143 for the Vocabulary reference.

SPEAKING

11 Work in pairs. Write down the three questions (a–c) Nora is asked in Exercise 3. Then write three more questions about fashion to ask your classmates.

12 Work in pairs to ask and answer the questions from Exercise 11.

9C Green business trends

LESSON GOALS
- Talk about sustainability
- Learn to describe changes and trends
- Understand hedging
- Practise a useful technique to help stress long words

The Smartflower POP, the word's first all-in-one solar system, in Edinburgh, UK.

SPEAKING

1 Work in pairs. Discuss the questions.

1 How do you think the technology in the photo might be used?

2 Do you know of any companies that are changing to more environmentally-friendly practices?

VOCABULARY

2 Read about the trends in business practices (1–6). Work in pairs. Which words and phrases in bold are related to …

a environmental issues?

b business and economics?

c change?

1 **Refillable bottles** will never **catch on**. Most consumers will refuse to use them. We need companies to invest in the development of **biodegradable** plastics instead.

2 The big **energy companies** haven't been ambitious enough in **switching** to **renewable energy**.

3 More and more companies are working towards sustainable practices even if it is costing their **investors** money.

4 Businesses, governments and society must freeze **fossil fuel** extraction immediately if they hope to bring an end to **carbon emissions** in time.

5 The **upward trend** in electric vehicles is as problematic as sticking with petrol because the battery storage needed requires precious **natural resources** such as lithium and cobalt.

6 It isn't realistic to expect big companies to transform their working practices if it means becoming less **competitive** in the markets. They need to be forced, either by law or **consumer demand**.

Go to page 143 for the Vocabulary reference.

3 Work in pairs. Which do you think are the most optimistic and the most pessimistic statements in Exercise 2? To what extent do you agree with the statements?

4 Read the Focus on box. Then underline all the words and expressions in Exercise 2 that describe change in addition to the words in bold.

> **FOCUS ON** Expressing change and trends
>
> Change and trends can be expressed …
> - using the continuous verb structures.
>   *They're switching to renewables.*
> - with the verb *become* or *get*.
>   *As weather events become more and more common, business is likely to be disrupted.*
> - using verbs with specific meanings to do with change, e.g. *adapt*.
> - using certain nouns.
>   *there was an increase in … a sharp fall*
>
> Go to page 159 for the Grammar reference.

LISTENING

5 🎧 **9.4** Listen to a news report about business trends. Is it optimistic or pessimistic about what is happening?

6 🎧 **9.4** Listen again. Make notes on 1–6 and how they are changing to become more green (or helping others become more green).

1 Earth shampoo
2 The car industry
3 Wrap
4 Ørsted
5 Microsoft
6 Unilever

7 🎧 **9.5** Look at the Listening skill box. Then listen to five extracts from the report and note how they differ from sentences a–e. What words and expressions are used in the report to hedge?

LISTENING SKILL
Understanding hedging

Speakers may want to indicate uncertainty when they are not entirely sure of the ideas they are expressing, or when they are aware that other people may have differing opinions on the subject. Indicating uncertainty can show that you are open to alternative ideas.

Verbs: *appear, indicate, seem, suggest, tend to*
The passive voice: *It's been claimed that …*
'That' clauses: *It's possible that …*
Modal verbs: *They may have …*
Vague expressions: *sort of, just, somewhat*

a Beyond Burgers taste better than meat.
b The market for eco-friendly products will continue to grow for decades.
c Ørsted is the second most sustainable company in the world.
d Some companies are aiming to be carbon neutral by 2050, which will be too late.
e Replacing plastics isn't a money saver.

PRONUNCIATION AND SPEAKING

8 🎧 **9.6** Work in pairs. Look at the Clear voice box and listen to the technique. Then practise the technique with these words. What long words or expressions do you find difficult to say?

> e**co**logy   e**co**nomist   eco**no**mics
> environ**men**tally-**friend**ly **prac**tices   re**new**able **e**nergy

CLEAR VOICE
Stressing polysyllabic words and expressions correctly

It can be hard to stress long words or expressions containing multiple syllables correctly, even when you know the correct stress. A useful technique is to say the word or expression from the final stressed syllable, and then gradually add syllables: **lo**gically – co**lo**gically – eco**lo**gically **za**tions – gani**za**tions – organi**za**tions – **cha**ritable – **cha**ritable organi**za**tions

9 Work in pairs. Do you think the world is getting better or worse or neither? Discuss your opinion with regard to three of these topics.

> health   education   entertainment   the environment
> equality   food and drink   standard of living

EXPLORE MORE!

Find examples of other companies that are making 'green' changes. Search for 'greenest + companies'.

Increasing your trustworthiness

LESSON GOALS
- Learn about what makes a person trustworthy
- Identify ways to enhance your trustworthiness
- Practise building trust in relationships

SPEAKING

1 Work in pairs. Discuss what type of people need to be trustworthy. Think about specific jobs.

2 Look at the infographic. Discuss the questions.
1 Which are the most trusted professions?
2 What are the most important things to consider when deciding how trustworthy someone is?
3 What element of the trust equation has the biggest impact on our trustworthiness?

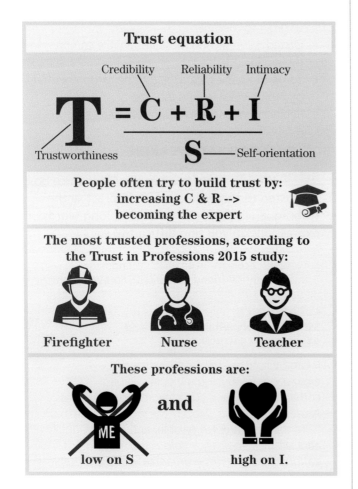

MY VOICE ▶

3 ▶ 9.2 Watch the video. Answer the questions.
1 How can getting to know someone improve their perception of our reliability?
2 Why is it not always a good idea to increase our credibility by talking about what we know?
3 What do we need to try and balance when building a relationship?

4 Think about someone you know and like. Consider your interactions with them and how they might see you. Using the questions below as a guide, give yourself scores for Credibility, Reliability, Intimacy and Self-Orientation, where 1 means you show the lowest amount of the characteristic and 10 the highest.

1 **Credibility** – For someone from work, how competent and capable do they think you are? For a friend, how much confidence do they have in you? Do they feel that you tell the truth?
C SCORE: _____

2 **Reliability** – Do they feel that they can depend on you? Do they think you are consistent and do what you say you'll do?
R SCORE: _____

3 **Intimacy** – Do they feel emotionally safe with you? Are they happy to share their hopes and fears with you?
I SCORE: _____

4 **Self-orientation** – To what extent might they feel that you think about yourself before others? Think back to your interactions with them. Are your conversations usually about you? Are you often focused on sharing your problems and your points of view?
S SCORE: _____

5 Look at the Communication skill box. In pairs, discuss which of these you find easy / more difficult to do.

COMMUNICATION SKILL
Increasing your trustworthiness

In order to have strong and lasting relationships, we need to build trust. We can do that by focusing on these four areas:

Enhancing credibility

Be transparent, honest and open. Demonstrate your capabilities through actions rather than by talking too much about them.

Enhancing reliability

Keep the promises and commitments you make.
Get to know the other person.

Enhancing intimacy

Open up about your hopes and fears, your successes and failures and allow yourself to be vulnerable.
React emotionally to what the other person says.

Lowering self-orientation

Ask questions and show that you care about the other person and pay attention to what they say.
Avoid talking at length about yourself too frequently.

6 **OWN IT!** Look at these situations. What do you think might be happening and what advice might you give Pasha, Özlem and Saif?

1 Wanda and Pasha were childhood friends and reconnected a year ago. Wanda really enjoys Pasha's company and finds his relaxed attitude inspiring. However, she recently found out that he told a few other people something she specifically told him not to tell anyone. She continues to hang out with Pasha but refrains from telling him anything of importance. Pasha knows Wanda doesn't trust him, but he thinks it's because she thinks he's not competent.

2 Özlem worries a lot and always seems to be concerned about how people see her. She likes to confide in Gabriel and often talks extensively about the people she thinks don't like her. Gabriel wants to be there for Özlem, but he finds these conversations exhausting. He starts to make excuses when Özlem wants to meet.

3 Saif is admired by everyone at work. He seems to know everything and has a solution to every problem. He never shows any emotions and doesn't like to appear weak. Saif has noticed that his colleague Drina regularly organizes social events with others in the office and wonders why he never gets invited.

7 Look at the Useful language box. Which score in the Trust Equation could these four categories of phrases increase/decrease?

Useful language Increasing trustworthiness

Being transparent
I'm going to be completely transparent with you about this …
I only know this because …

Reassuring someone
You can count on me.
I promise I won't let you down.

Reacting sensitively
Oh dear. That sounds (awful).
Would you like to talk about this? Is there anything I can do to help?

Moving the topic from you to others
Enough about me, I want to know (what you think).
I don't want to bore you with (my problems/stories). Tell me about …

8 Work in pairs. Building on the scenarios 2 and 3 from Exercise 6, take turns to take the role of Student A. Remember to use the Communication skill tips and the Useful language in your roleplay.
Student A: Turn to page 166.
Student B: Turn to page 167.

9 Work in small groups. Discuss the questions.
1 Think of someone you find hard to trust. What is it about them that you don't trust? What would they have to do to gain/re-gain your trust?
2 How do you think culture might play a part in the way we build trust?

EXPLORE MORE!

Find out more about the Trust Equation by searching online for 'The Trust Equation'.

9E
The lost shirt

LESSON GOALS
- Choose an effective opening for a story
- Describe problems with clothes
- Write an anecdote

SPEAKING

1 Work in pairs. Look at the photos of clothing on page 117 and discuss how you think each item (A–D) ended up in the situation or state it is in.

2 Look at the Useful language box. Which sentences describe the four photos? What items of clothing could the other sentences describe? Use a dictionary to help.

> **Useful language** Describing problems with clothes, shoes and accessories
>
> **I heard it rip** as I was reaching up to change a lightbulb.
>
> His pen leaked and **the stain was very noticeable** on the white fabric.
>
> **I'd left it somewhere** on the way. And that was the last I saw of it, or so I thought.
>
> **They looked faded,** as if they had been in the sun a long time.
>
> **It must have fallen off** as they were getting her in the car.
>
> When he didn't give it back after the game, **I thought I'd lost it for good.**
>
> **It shrank in the wash** and only fit my four-year old sister after that.

3 Work in pairs. Tell each other about an item of clothing of yours that …
- you once lost (and maybe found again).
- you made yourself, or someone made for you.
- got ripped, stained, shrunk or spoiled in some other way.
- you borrowed from someone else but never gave back.
- you spent a lot of (or very little) money on.
- went on a journey without you!
- you wore only once, or never at all.

READING FOR WRITING

4 Read the anecdote. Which phrase from the Useful language box could refer to this story? Do you think the story is a) a true anecdote, b) fiction, or c) partially true, but exaggerated?

The gang of friends I hung out with at school called ourselves *Los Chavales*. We did everything together. We had nicknames for each other like Maz, Edu and Pob, which are what we still call each other. Most of all we loved playing tricks on each other. One of our many traditions was 'borrowing' items of clothing from each other without asking. Consequently, our mothers were often confused by all the unfamiliar t-shirts and jumpers appearing in the wash.

My Argentinian grandfather sent me an Argentina rugby shirt for my birthday. The blue-and-white-striped top even had my name written on the back and I loved it. This was definitely not for borrowing. But one day, Pob asked to borrow it. He and Gregory, a Uruguayan friend of ours, had tickets to watch Uruguay and Argentina play at rugby. Pob wanted to annoy Grego, so I let him wear it. The game came and went, but my top didn't make it back. Pob mentioned that he might have left it on the train. I was disappointed to say the least.

After school, we went off to different cities to work or study, but we stayed in touch, often by sharing photos online. One day I noticed Edu wearing a top identical to my old one in a photo of him on a beach in Chile. A few weeks later, Maz was wearing one at university. This time you could see my name on the back! After that, it kept turning up all over the place: on Simón on a motorbike in Europe; on Tavi playing football with his nephews; even on a statue in the park once.

Then, on my 23rd birthday, we had a party. It was great to be together again, but the best moment was when I opened their gift to me. A bit faded and scruffy-looking – it was my rugby shirt! And on top was a photo album with pictures of everyone who'd ever worn it. Even though it had definitely seen better days, I was thrilled to have it back.

That was years ago, but ever since then, I've always worn it for photos of special moments to share with the *Chavales*. A few weeks ago I put it on for my first photo with my baby daughter.

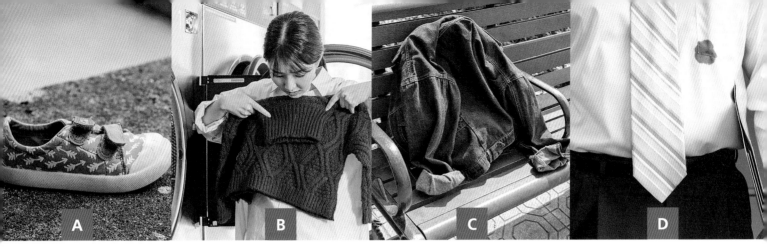

A   B   C   D

5 Look at the Writing skill box. Then read three alternative opening sentences for the story. Which approach does each adopt, and which do you prefer? Why?

WRITING SKILL
Starting a story

When writing a story of any kind, an obvious place to start is at the chronological beginning. However, choosing a different opening may make the story funnier, more exciting, or more mysterious. Consider the following opening styles and choose one that makes the reader want to continue reading:

• State something true that suggests the story that follows will illustrate this message.

• Start the story at the end or somewhere in the middle, so that the reader wonders what happened beforehand.

• Start with a description with details that make the reader want to know more about it.

1 My favourite item of clothing is without a doubt a blue-and-white-striped rugby shirt with a yellow puma emblem on the front and my name written on the back.

2 How was it that an old rugby shirt of mine that had been lost for years kept appearing in photos from around the world?

3 While many possessions lose their value as they get used and broken, others grow in significance through experience.

6 Choose three of the items of clothing that you talked about in Exercise 3. Write the first sentence for an anecdote about each of them. Decide which of the ways outlined in the Writing skill box will work well for your anecdote, or choose your own style of opening.

WRITING TASK

7 WRITE Read the invitation to submit an anecdote to a website. Decide how you will respond.

• Will you develop one of the anecdotes you started in Exercise 6?

• Will you add invented details to make it funnier or more exciting?

• Will you invent a story?

x

We at CuriousLives love stories that are funny, terrible, true, invented, personal ... interesting!

For this month's story challenge we want you to write an anecdote about a problem related to an item of clothing. A shopping mistake? A day you wore the wrong outfit? A ruined jacket? A horrible scarf your grandmother made you wear?

Tell your story in no more than 300 words. The best entries will appear in a featured article. Include a photograph if possible.

SUBMIT

8 CHECK Use the checklist. I have ...

☐ told an interesting, engaging story.

☐ written a suitable opening to engage the reader.

☐ included a description of the item of clothing.

☐ organized the anecdote into paragraphs.

9 REVIEW Read a few of your classmates' anecdotes. Give feedback using the checklist in Exercise 8. Whose anecdote is the most interesting to you?

Go to page 134 for the Reflect and review.

Stephen Wilkes's photo of the Regata Storica, an annual event in Venice, Italy, is made up of thousands of single photos and edited into a composite image to show the passage of time over one day.

10

Time

GOALS

- Use definitions in a text to understand new words
- Talk about the future from the perspective of the past
- Synthesize information from multiple sources
- Use expressions with *time* and talk about different perceptions of time
- Manage turn-taking in group conversations
- Write a letter to your younger self

1 Work in pairs. Discuss the questions.
  1 Look at the photo. Which part was taken in the morning and which, later in the day?
  2 Think of a place you know. How does it look at different times of the day or year?

WATCH

2 ▶ 10.1 Watch the video. Answer the questions.

NATIONAL GEOGRAPHIC EXPLORER

ALISON WRIGHT

  1 Why does Alison think it's important to remind herself of what she's done during the day?
  2 How does she try to be 'fully present' with people?
  3 What does she not like spending time on?

3 Make connections. Discuss the questions.
  1 Do you often procrastinate? What kind of tasks do you often find yourself putting off until later?
  2 What do you always try to make time for?
  3 What do you hate spending time on?

10A
Keeping time

LESSON GOALS
- Use definitions to understand new words
- Evaluate the degree of a writer's certainty
- Talk about rhythm

READING

1 Work in pairs. Do you think you have a good sense of rhythm? Why? / Why not?

2 🎧 10.1 Can you keep time? Listen and clap the rhythms you hear.

3 Look quickly at the photo and headings in the article on page 121. What types of information do you think it will provide? Then skim the article and check your answers.

4 Read the article. Complete the notes.

1 The fastest rhythm a human can hear: _____

2 The language skill that children with a natural sense of rhythm are good at: _____

3 The typical rhythm of the sea hitting the beach: _____

4 What kinds of rhythm people with no musical training choose to create a song: _____

5 The suggested maximum beats per minute for people who want to do a fast workout: _____

5 Look at the Reading skill box. How are 1–5 defined in the article?

READING SKILL
Finding meaning: using definitions

Sometimes the definition of a word
– particularly a technical word or an abbreviation – appears in the text. A definition may ...
- come directly before the word.
- be signalled by expressions such as *in other words, that is,* and *which is to say.*
- be introduced by certain punctuation, including dashes — , parentheses (brackets), commas, a colon or quotation marks.

1 tempo
2 bpm
3 hardwired
4 synchronizes
5 move in time

6 Look at the Critical thinking box. Then read sentences 1–6. Which ones express facts? Which ones express ideas that may be open to discussion? Which words indicate uncertainty?

CRITICAL THINKING SKILL
Evaluating the degree of certainty

Factual texts sometimes include information that is probably true, but not quite certain or that is open to debate. When evaluating the degree of certainty, ask yourself:

- Has the statement been proven or observed to be true? Is it the result of accurate measurements? Expressions such as *has/have shown, has/have found* and *has/have proven* may indicate that something is a fact unless there are words that specifically show uncertainty.

- Are there any words that indicate uncertainty? Words and expressions such as *suggests, it's possible that, there's some evidence that, some (people) believe* can signal that the statement isn't being offered as a pure fact.

1 Studies have found that when people are asked to tap a rhythm, they tend to choose a rhythm of about 120 bpm.

2 Some researchers believe that rhythm is hardwired in humans.

3 When you hear a musical rhythm, it's not unusual to move in time with it.

4 Scientists have found that rhythm and language are closely connected.

5 Some research shows that exercising to a steady rhythm may help coordinate the body's movements and make them more efficient.

6 Resting adult human heart: 60–100

SPEAKING

7 Work in pairs. Discuss the questions.

1 What's your 24-hour rhythm like, e.g. do you feel you think more clearly at a certain time of day?

2 What activities bring rhythm to your day? Are there things you do at the same time each day?

3 Is your rhythm different at weekends? How?

Traditional Taiko drummers at a competition, Tokyo, Japan.

The **power** of rhythm

1 Rhythm is all around us and even inside us. It's in our heartbeat, the music we listen to, the waves breaking on the beach and the clackety-clack of a passing train. Here's what you need to know about rhythm.

The rhythm of life

Humans can perceive a tempo – the speed or rhythm
5 of a piece of music – between 40 and 300 bpm
(beats per minute). Below that and it's too slow for
us to notice the pattern. Above and it turns into a
continuous buzzing sound. Studies have found that
when people are asked to tap a rhythm, they tend
10 to choose a rhythm of about 120 bpm. This is also a
very common beat in popular music.

A universal phenomenon

Poet Henry Wadsworth Longfellow described music
as humanity's 'universal language.' And science
15 supports that view. Analysis of music around the
world shows that almost all music – from hip-hop to
classical – shares common features including a strong
rhythm. In addition, people without any musical
training use predictable beats when asked to create
20 a song, which makes some researchers believe that
rhythm is hardwired in humans. In other words,
rhythm may be in your genes, almost like a sense.

A language teacher

Scientists have found that rhythm and language
25 are closely connected. As children learn to speak
and understand language, they also develop their
sense of rhythm. What's more, listening to music
can improve kids' language development. Those
with a strong sense of rhythm have shown a higher
30 level of reading ability than those with less natural
rhythm. And in any language, the stress and
rhythm of speech can make the difference between
understanding and a breakdown in communication.

Social glue

35 Rhythm unites people. Researcher Dr Thomas Currie says, 'the
most common features seen in music around the world relate
to things that allow people to coordinate their actions, and
suggest that the main function of music is to bring people
together and bond social groups – it can be a kind of social
40 glue.' Rhythm makes it easier for people to interact because
it synchronizes – that is, coordinates – their brain waves and
makes it easier to process language.

A call to move

When you hear a musical rhythm, it's not unusual to move
45 in time with it: nod your head, tap your foot or get up and
dance. Listening to a fast song with a strong beat really
makes you want to move – and that can help to motivate
exercise. What's more, some research shows that exercising to
a steady rhythm may help coordinate the body's movements
50 and make them more efficient. 120 bpm is a comfortable
rhythm for walking, while runners in the gym typically prefer
music with an average of 160 bpm. Some exercise websites
recommend songs as fast as 180 bpm for people who
are trying to run fast, but research shows that above 145
55 bpm there is no further improvement in pace or increase in
motivation.

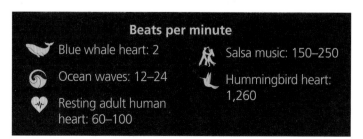

Beats per minute

Blue whale heart: 2

Ocean waves: 12–24

Resting adult human heart: 60–100

Salsa music: 150–250

Hummingbird heart: 1,260

10B
A matter of time

LESSON GOALS
- Share opinions using expressions with *time*
- Talk about the future from the perspective of the past
- Pronounce /r/ vs /l/ at the end of words
- Talk about time travel

VOCABULARY

1 Work in pairs. Discuss the questions.
1 Do you think time travel will ever be possible? Why? / Why not?
2 If time travel were possible, what good things could come from it?
3 What problems could time travel cause?

2 Read the sentences. Work in pairs. Try to write definitions for the words and phrases in bold. Then discuss which of the sentences are true for you.
1 Some people think it's impossible, but I think it's **only a matter of time** until someone finds a way to travel between the past, present and future.
2 I'm a **long-time** fan of science fiction books and films.
3 There are some things I didn't do when I was younger that I wish I'd done, so I want to **make up for lost time** by doing them now.
4 Eventually I'd like to move, but **for the time being** I'm happy where I am.
5 Preparing a good meal is **time-consuming**, but it's worth it.
6 My hair's too long. **It's about time** I had it cut.
7 If you choose the right recipe, you can make a delicious meal **in no time**.
8 Some people say multi-tasking works for them, but I prefer to **take things one at a time**.

Go to page 144 for the Vocabulary reference.

READING AND GRAMMAR

3 Read the story about a party for time travellers and answer questions 1–3.
1 Where did Hawking think people would travel from to attend his party?
2 When did Hawking send out the invitations?
3 Who attended the party?

Stephen Hawking's time-traveller party

In 2009, the world-famous physicist Stephen Hawking thought it was about time someone properly investigated the possibility of time travel. He set up an experiment that would be remembered as one of his more entertaining investigations – a reception for time travellers. 'I like simple experiments', Hawking said of the event. According to the invitations, the party was going to take place at noon on 28 June; however, the invitations weren't to be sent out until 29 June so that anyone showing up to the party on time was bound to be a time traveller. Hawking believed that at least some of the invitations were likely to survive for thousands of years and eventually be seen by someone who could travel back through time to attend. 'My time traveller guests could be arriving at any moment now,' Hawking said as the party was about to officially begin. But midday came but no guests. So, for the time being, the question of whether time travel is possible remains unanswered.

Stephen Hawking.

4 Read the Grammar box. Match 1–6 with a form in bold from the box.

1 means that something had been planned
2 means that something almost certainly would happen
3 shows a prediction in the past
4 means *probably would*
5 means *was at the point of*
6 is another way of saying *wasn't going to* or *wouldn't*

> **GRAMMAR**   The future in the past
>
> Use these forms to talk about the future from the perspective of the past:
>
> *The experiment **would** be remembered as one of his more entertaining investigations.*
>
> *The party **was going to** take place at noon on 28 June.*
>
> *The invitations **weren't to** be sent out until 29 June.*
>
> *Anyone showing up to the party on time **was bound to** be a time traveller.*
>
> *Hawking believed some of the invitations **were likely to** survive for thousands of years.*
>
> *The party **was about to** officially begin.*
>
> Go to page 161 for the Grammar reference.

5 Choose the correct options to complete the first part of a story about time travel.

The man from the future

In 2011, João, a physicist, was the head of an important scientific project in Brazil. However, his angry and eccentric behaviour at work meant that he ¹*would / will* soon lose his job. It was only a matter of time. Then one day, while conducting an experiment, he unintentionally ²*travelled / was going to travel* twenty years into the past to the moment when his relationship with his girlfriend Helena was ³*ended / about to end*. João realized that if he said the right thing to Helena at that moment he ⁴*could / was likely to* be able to stop the events that would lead to the break-up. That's what he ⁵*did / was going to do* and, in no time, the relationship was restored. However, …

---

6 Work in pairs. Discuss how you think the story ends. Then turn to page 167 and check. Choose the correct options to finish the story.

PRONUNCIATION

7 🔊 **10.2** Look at the Clear voice box. Listen and circle the word you hear in sentences 1–4.

> **CLEAR VOICE**
> **Saying /r/ vs /l/ at the end of words**
>
> In some accents, /r/ is not pronounced at the end of a word (e.g. *more*), so *more* and *mall* may sound similar. Try to make the /l/ sound clear or say the /r/ sound when clarifying: I didn't say *mall*, I said *more*.
> To practise the /l/ and /r/ sounds, first isolate them.
> • Say *la la la*. Then slow it down and leave out the *a* so you're only saying the *l* sound.
> • Say *rrr*
> • Build the words up from the two sounds. *Rrrrr – more. La – l – mall.*

1 What do you *feel / fear* when you think about time travel?
2 Was he able to *heal / hear* after the accident?
3 They weren't able to *steal / steer* the time machine.
4 How did the time traveller *appeal / appear* to you?

8 Practise saying the four pairs of words in Exercise 7, making the difference between the /l/ and /r/ sounds as clear as you can.

SPEAKING

9 Work in pairs. Discuss the questions. Give reasons.

1 If you could time travel, would you choose to go back in time or forward? Who would you like to meet from the past/future?
2 If you went backwards, would you like to meet any of your ancestors or perhaps meet your parents as young children?
3 If you could change anything in the past, would you?
4 If you went forwards in time, would you like to meet members of your family who haven't been born yet?
5 When you were young, what did you think your future life would be like? Where did you think you'd live? What did you think you'd do for a living? Where did you think you'd travel and so on? What else did you think life had in store for you?

Time flies!

LESSON GOALS
Talk about perceptions of time
Synthesize information from multiple sources
Use expressions with *take*
Practise saying voiceless consonants in stressed syllables

VOCABULARY AND SPEAKING

1 Work in pairs. Discuss the questions about time.

1 When you're meeting someone, do you usually arrive early, on time or late?

2 Where you live, how important is punctuality?

2 Read the short texts A–E. Match the words in bold (1–8) with their meanings (a–h).

a boring and taking a long time

b movement at a slower speed than normal

c the way you think (about something)

d as late as possible

e passed

f earlier than necessary

g the movement of minutes, hours, days, etc.

h quickly

Go to page 144 for the Vocabulary reference.

3 Complete the sentences with the words in bold from the texts in Exercise 2.

1 I really notice _____ when I look at old photos and see my younger self.

2 Everyone's _____ of the world is informed by their life experiences.

3 Time seems to pass more _____ when you feel you don't have much of it.

4 After another hour had _____ with no news from him, they began to get anxious.

5 You can relax more if you arrive _____.

6 We were late because I decided to change clothes _____.

7 It's an interesting subject, but unfortunately his lecture was rather _____.

8 When the waiter dropped everyone's food, it seemed to happen in _____.

Five things science tells us about how we experience time

A There is wide variation around the world in ideas of what it means to be on time and to be late. In some cultures, it might be considered a bit rude – or at least odd – to arrive at exactly the agreed time or slightly ¹**ahead of schedule**, while in others, it's impolite not to.

B People who are routinely late tend to misjudge how long it will take them to get to their destination. In addition, multi-taskers – people who do more than one thing at a time – often arrive ²**at the last minute** or late because they lose track of time.

C Psychologists believe that our ³**perception** of time is linked to attention. If it's taken up with something that interests us, we don't notice how much time has ⁴**elapsed**. However, when we're doing something ⁵**tedious**, requiring little attention, we notice time passing.

D Our sense of time may change based on the amount of information we have to process. Children are constantly having new experiences, which causes ⁶**the passage of time** to seem slower to them compared with adults, who generally have fewer new experiences.

E More than 70% of people who have some kind of accident say that time seemed to slow down. They believe that this sense of ⁷**slow motion** is the body's 'fight or flight' instinct taking over and giving us the opportunity to react ⁸**swiftly**.

LISTENING

4 🎧 **10.3** Look at the Listening skill box. Then listen to five conversations. Match each conversation (1–5) with the texts (A–E) from Exercise 2. Then check your answers in pairs.

LISTENING SKILL
Synthesizing information from multiple sources

Synthesizing occurs when you think critically about a topic using information from two or more sources such as reading, conversation and images. By comparing information, you can gain new ideas or insights into the topic. When you synthesize, ask:

- What does each source of information say about the topic?
- How is the information in each source similar or different?
- How does the information relate to things I've learned about the topic or my own experience?

5 🎧 **10.4** Work in pairs. Listen again to part of Conversation 3 and re-read text D. Discuss the questions.

1 What is the experience that both Conversation 3 and text D explain?
2 What two explanations do they give?
3 Which explanation do you think is more likely to be correct?

6 Read the Focus on box. Work in pairs. Look at the sentences in the box from Exercises 2 and 4. Discuss what you think the verbs in bold mean.

FOCUS ON   Expressions with *take*

Take is a common verb, which is frequently combined with other words to form expressions. In some cases, it's not easy to work out the meaning of the expression from the words that make it up and the expression just has to be learned.

*If our attention **is taken up with** something that interests us, we don't notice the time.*

*The body's 'fight or flight' instinct **takes over**.*

***Take your time**, Lea. We're supposed to take regular breaks.*

*She never **takes into account** the time it takes to get ready.*

*Don't **take my word for it**.*

Go to page 161 for the Focus on reference.

7 Use the expressions from the Focus on box to write possible answers to questions 1–5.

1 Do I need to hurry up?
   No, don't worry. Take your time.
2 Do you think we should check that information she gave us?
3 Why are you so busy at the moment?
4 Do you think the traffic will be bad on the way to the airport?
5 Who will be in charge while you are away?

PRONUNCIATION AND SPEAKING

8 🎧 **10.5** Look at the Clear voice box. Then listen and circle the words you hear in 1–6.

CLEAR VOICE
Saying voiceless consonants in stressed syllables

When you say /p/, /t/ and /k/ there is no voice from the throat and air comes out of your mouth. When these sounds are at the beginning of a word or stressed syllable, the air is an important part of the sound. Without it, *poor* might sound like *bore*, *town* like *down* and *could* like *good*. This can cause communication problems.
Try to make sure /p/, /t/ and /k/ include a little puff of air and say /b/, /d/ and /g/ with little or no air.

1 May I have the *bill / pill*?
2 I need to *try / dry* that.
3 He can't find the *clue / glue*.
4 Was it *pouring / boring*?
5 Look at the *train / drain*.
6 It was *cold / gold*.

9 Work in pairs. Take turns to read the sentences in Exercise 8 out loud. Is it clear to your partner which of the two words you're saying?

10 Think of some situations when your perception of time has changed or has been different from other people's. Use some of the ideas from Exercise 2. Make notes.

1 When did time seem to pass swiftly? Why do you think it seemed that way?
2 When did time seem to pass more slowly? Why?

11 In small groups, discuss your answers from Exercise 10.

EXPLORE MORE!

Search online to find out more about 'How we experience time'.

10D
Managing turn-taking in group conversations

LESSON GOALS
- Learn about our own preferences for turn-taking
- Identify strategies for holding the floor and interrupting
- Manage turn-taking in a group conversation

SPEAKING

1 Work in pairs. Discuss the questions.

1 Do you sometimes not get to say what you want to in a group conversation? Why?

2 Think of someone you know who often holds the floor, i.e. speaks for a long time without letting anyone else speak. How do they do this?

2 Look at the quiz. Think about conversations you have in your own language. Circle a or b for each question.

3 Do the quiz again, this time thinking about conversations you have in English.

MY VOICE ▶

4 ▶ 10.2 Watch the video. Answer the questions. Work in pairs to compare your answers.

1 Why are some people more comfortable with holding the floor and interrupting than others?

2 Why is the ability to manage turn-taking in conversations especially important in intercultural communication?

3 How can useful phrases help you?

4 What should you be confident about?

Quiz

Which of the two statements do you agree with more?

1 In a group conversation, ...
   a I find it hard to get a turn to speak.
   b I find it easy to get a turn to speak.

2 When I'm speaking for a long time, ...
   a I often get interrupted.
   b I'm comfortable holding the floor.

3 When people interrupt me, ...
   a I just let them take over the conversation.
   b I get them to wait for their turn to speak.

4 When someone is speaking, ...
   a I never interrupt them.
   b I feel comfortable interrupting them.

5 If I'm waiting to say something and the topic changes, ...
   a I drop what I wanted to say.
   b I try to bring the conversation back to the previous topic.

6 When I finish what I'm saying, ...
   a people often know that I'm finished and take their turn naturally.
   b there is often a silence before someone else says something.

5 Look at the Communication skill box. Work in pairs to discuss which strategies you might use to manage a conversation in your first language.

COMMUNICATION SKILL
Managing turn-taking in group conversations

Here are some strategies to help you manage turn-taking in group conversations:

Interrupting someone and taking your turn
Wait for a pause, say the other person's name and comment on what they've said. Then continue with what you want to say.

Holding the floor
Use a rising intonation before pausing and fill the silences with phrases to show you're not finished.

Dealing with interruptions
Slow your pace down, look at them, smile and raise your hand slightly, indicating they should wait.

6 🎧 **10.6** Listen to four different examples of people managing a group conversation. Match the extracts (1–4) with the descriptions (a–d) below. What strategies do the speakers use?

a Interrupting someone to change the topic
b Holding the floor so others don't interrupt
c Dealing with an interruption
d Bringing the conversation back to a previous topic

7 Look at the Useful language box. Work in pairs. Discuss if you would use similar phrases to manage conversations in your first language.

Useful language Managing turn-taking

Interrupting to add to the topic
(Ahmed) is absolutely right. I think …
(Pavel), that's so interesting. I had a similar
  experience …

Interrupting to change the topic
Speaking of (skydiving), I …
On a slightly different note, I wanted to (ask/say) …

Stopping someone from interrupting
Sorry, if I could just finish …
Sorry, just to finish my point …

Bringing things back to a previous topic
Earlier you were saying …,
Sorry, but if I could just go back to what we were
  talking about earlier …

SPEAKING

8 OWN IT! Look at these situations. Work in pairs. Discuss what you would do if you were Zeki, Karin and Huifang.

1 Zeki gets together with his friends every week and, most weeks, Nik tends to dominate the conversation with his stories. Zeki doesn't usually mind, but this week, he's got some big news to tell his friends: he's going to propose to his girlfriend. He wants to talk about how he's going to propose, but he's afraid Nik might take over the conversation again.

2 Karin started working in this company a year ago and, although she has a lot of previous experience, she feels she hasn't been able to contribute much during meetings. Her colleagues are always interrupting her and, although Karin thinks interrupting is rude, she has noticed that everyone there seems to interrupt each other with ease.

3 Huifang goes to an English club. She really likes the international friends she's met there, but she finds it difficult to keep up with the conversation. She feels insecure about her English and likes to plan what she wants to say, but by the time she's ready to participate, they've already moved on to a different topic.

9 Work in groups of three. Choose two scenarios from Exercise 8. Take turns to be Student A. Remember to use the Communication skill tips and the Useful language in your roleplay.

Student A: Turn to page 165.
Student B: Turn to page 166.
Student C: Turn to page 167.

10 Work in small groups. Discuss the questions.

1 What strategies did each of you use to achieve your objectives? Were you successful?
2 How well do you think your strategies might work in a real-life scenario? In what type of scenarios will they be more useful?
3 What can you do to improve how you manage group conversations?

EXPLORE MORE!

Turn-taking in conversations is an important skill. Learn more about how people take turns by searching the 'turn-taking + conversations' online.

10E
Dear younger me

LESSON GOALS
- Write a personal timeline
- Think of advice to give your younger self
- Write a letter to your younger self

SPEAKING

1 Work in pairs. Discuss the questions.

1 Ten years ago, what did you expect you would be doing now?

2 What are some things that you know now that you didn't know ten years ago?

3 Have your goals, dreams and interests changed a lot since you were a child, or have they stayed the same?

READING FOR WRITING

NATIONAL GEOGRAPHIC EXPLORER

2 Read Alison Wright's timeline. Answer the questions.

1 When did she get her first job in journalism?

2 In what two years did she have books published?

3 What year was she hurt badly?

3 Look at the Writing skill box. Follow the steps in the box and make a personal timeline. Only include things that you're happy to share with the class.

WRITING SKILL
Making a personal timeline

It can sometimes be useful to look at the past in an organized way. Reflecting on our experiences can help us to understand events in our life that have shaped us and show us how we've changed and ways in which we've remained the same through time. When you make a timeline:

- Think of 8–10 of the most important events in your life and make a note of when they happened.
- Use present tenses.
- Organize them on the timeline.
- Write positive events above the timeline and label them *Ups*.
- Write challenging or difficult events below the timeline and label them *Downs*.

4 Work in pairs. Tell your partner about two or three of the experiences on your timeline.

5 Read Alison's letter to her younger self on page 129. Answer the questions.

1 What does Alison tell her younger self not to a) worry about?; b) not to be afraid of?; c) not to lose?

2 How do you think the younger Alison would feel about older Alison's life? Proud? Worried? Excited?

6 What verb tense does Alison use to talk about a) her younger self; b) the future?

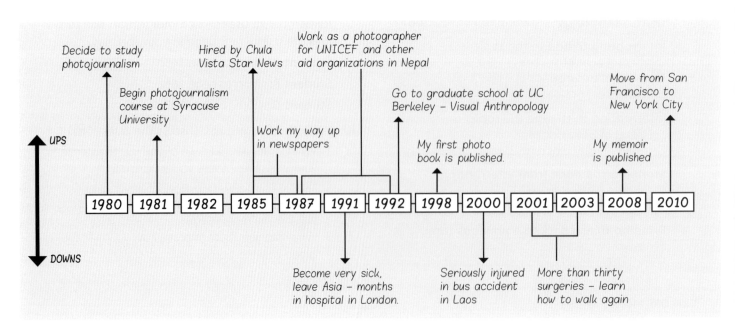

UPS

Decide to study photojournalism

Begin photojournalism course at Syracuse University

Hired by Chula Vista Star News

Work as a photographer for UNICEF and other aid organizations in Nepal

Work my way up in newspapers

Go to graduate school at UC Berkeley – Visual Anthropology

My first photo book is published.

Move from San Francisco to New York City

My memoir is published

| 1980 | 1981 | 1982 | 1985 | 1987 | 1991 | 1992 | 1998 | 2000 | 2001 | 2003 | 2008 | 2010 |

DOWNS

Become very sick, leave Asia – months in hospital in London.

Seriously injured in bus accident in Laos

More than thirty surgeries – learn how to walk again

Dear Alison

I remember how excited you were to receive your first little Kodak Instamatic camera for your tenth birthday. Who knew that it would be so life defining? You loved taking photos of your friends and the life around you, especially when travelling with the family. In high school you enjoyed taking photos for the yearbook and school newspaper. When Mr Lee, your English teacher, took you aside and told you that you could actually make a living as a photographer, it set you on an unwavering path. You were fifteen years old. It was the first time you ever heard the word 'photojournalist'.

You ran home and told Mom and Dad that's what you wanted to be, someone who travelled the world, documenting the lives of those whom you'd meet along the way. I remember how great your desire was to help others. Mom was a flight attendant for Pan Am Airlines so you already had the wanderlust. Dad wanted you to be a doctor, but he was so happy that you found your passion that he always supported your dream, giving you the wings to fly. You loved reading books so much, all you ever wanted to do was to publish your own.

Well, your dreams will come true, so don't worry about the future. You're going to go to 160 countries. You're going to publish eleven books. Your life will turn out to be interesting enough to even write a memoir.

You will have some major setbacks including illnesses from your travels that will require many hospital stays. A devastating bus accident while on assignment in Laos will be the most difficult to recover from. But don't fear the challenges – bad things will turn into good things and you will learn from difficult experiences. This close call will help you appreciate your own mortality – the reality of death, the fragility of life and the desire to live life to its fullest. All the past challenges in your life will help you to find the strength and resiliency to overcome this setback, enduring over 30 surgeries and learning how to walk again. In the end it is your undying curiosity that will keep you going to see how your wonderful life unfolds and turns out. Don't ever lose that sense of awe.

Go, girl!

Alison

7 Underline examples of how Alison gives herself advice in the letter. Compare with a partner. Then look again at your timeline. What advice would you give your younger self about things that are going to happen in your life? Write a sentence using each of the expressions you underlined.

WRITING TASK

8 WRITE Write a letter to your younger self.
- Using past tenses, tell your younger self what you remember doing.
- Using future tenses, explain some things that will happen in the younger self's future.
- Include the advice you thought of in Exercise 7.

9 CHECK Use the checklist. I have ...
- [ ] included important events from my timeline.
- [ ] used the correct verb tenses.
- [ ] used appropriate language for giving advice.

10 REVIEW Work in pairs. Read your partner's letter. Discuss the questions.
1 What part of their letter do you find interesting or surprising?
2 What did you think of the exercise of writing a letter to your younger self? Was it challenging? Enjoyable? Something else?

Go to page 134 for the Reflect and review.

Reflect and review

1 Encounters Pages 10–21

1 Look at the goals from Unit 1. How easy are they for you to achieve? Order them from 1 (easiest) to 6 (most difficult).

Use a dictionary to understand a literary extract

Use the perfect aspect to talk about events as seen from a later point

Talk about encounters; describe finds and possessions

Use mindmaps to help predict what you might hear

Learn to adapt to different personality types

Write a follow-up email

2 Work in pairs. Discuss the questions.

1 Which goal do you most want to improve on? Why?

2 What do you think you did well in this unit?

3 Which goal will be the most useful outside the classroom? Why?

3 Read the ideas for working on the Unit 1 goals. Choose the three ideas that are the most useful for you. Then add one more idea of your own.

Read short stories and use a dictionary to check unknown words.

Discuss interesting past events with a friend.

Read online articles about unusual ways people have met.

Find podcasts about subjects that interest me and make mindmaps to predict their content.

Do some online personality quizzes.

Practise adjusting my conversation according to my partner's personality traits.

Practise writing emails to people I have met and would like to see again.

My idea: _____

2 Fresh ideas Pages 22–33

1 Look at the goals from Unit 2. How confident do you feel about them? Write the letters a–f on the scale.

a Create a timeline to understand a biography

b Use multi-word verbs to talk about innovation

c Explain features and benefits; use noun suffixes

d Understand consonant sounds in English

e Encourage creative problem-solving

f Write a formal proposal

very confident   **not at all confident**

⟵————————————————⟶

2 Choose one of these topics and make a mind map:

• words and expressions to talk about innovation

• strategies to solve problems creatively

3 Look at the goals in Exercise 1. Choose the two goals that you feel least confident about. Make a plan for how you will work on them. For each goal think about …

• where you can find more resources to help you.

• how you can work together on these goals with others.

• how often you will work on practising these goals.

• by when you aim to have achieved the goals.

3 On the move *Pages 34–45*

1 Look at the goals from Unit 3. How confident do you feel about them? Write the letters (a–f) in the table.
a Identify connections between cause and effect
b Practise ways to interpret and speculate about events
c Describe ways of moving; talk about life moves
d Infer a speaker's opinions
e Support others through change
f Write an email to confirm arrangements

Goals I feel confident about	Goals I need more practice on

2 Work in pairs. Write a short description of your language-learning experience in this unit. Include two things you would like to improve on. Then exchange descriptions and offer suggestions for what your partner could do to improve.

3 Work in pairs. Discuss these questions.
1 Where can you find interesting texts about the history of migration? How can you analyse them to identify connections between cause and effect?
2 Where can you find audio recordings of different speakers talking about their personal experiences. How can you practise inferring their opinions?
3 Are there any new communication strategies from this unit that you want to use in the future?

4 The arts *Pages 46–57*

1 Look at the goals from Unit 4. Use these words and phrases to say how you feel about each goal. You can use the words and phrases more than once.

feel quite confident	find … rather difficult
don't quite understand	need more practice
… is/isn't a prioritywill/won't be useful	

• Analyse arguments in a forum thread
• Use discourse markers
• Talk about music and oral traditions
• Understand final consonants in fast speech
• Use humour in international communication
• Write a film review

2 Choose a topic and write a short paragraph about it.
• a traditional tale from my country
• the music I love to listen to
• a disappointing film
• something that made me laugh

3 Look at the goals in Exercise 1. Think about how you might achieve them. Compare your ideas with a partner.
• To improve my skills at analysing arguments, I can …
• To practise using discourse markers, I can …
• To practise talking about music and oral traditions, I can …
• To practise understanding final consonants in fast speech, I can …
• To improve my understanding of using humour in international communications, I can …
• To practise writing film reviews, I can …

Reflect and review

5 Sciences *Pages 58–69*

1 Look at the goals from Unit 5. Which goals are the most important to you? Order them from 1 (very important) to 6 (not a priority).

Summarize ideas using a Venn diagram
Learn how to add emphasis with cleft sentences
Talk about health benefits; learn to build words related to research
Use abbreviations when taking notes
Convince someone who questions the evidence
Write a video brief

2 Write down …
1 three reasons why we laugh.
2 three ways to convince someone in an argument.
3 three life hacks you have learned from this unit.

3 Think about the two Unit 5 goals that you decided were the most important. Write three things you would like to do to improve these goals. Use some of these ideas or your own. Then share your ideas with a partner.
- read texts and make Venn diagrams to summarize their ideas
- listen to humorous podcasts
- find infographics about scientific subjects and note down new vocabulary
- practise rewriting sentences to add emphasis
- watch science videos and take notes of the key information
- join and participate in online discussion groups
- watch some life hack videos and analyse the images used

Three things I plan to do to improve are …

_____

_____

_____

6 Redesigning our world *Pages 70–81*

1 Look at the goals from Unit 6. Tick (✓) the two that are the most important for you to achieve. Think about why they are important.

Summarize an article using concept maps
Discuss representation using conditional structures
Talk about good and bad design
Learn new words and phrases while listening
Accommodate your conversation partner
Write a report

2 Complete the sentences with your own ideas. Then compare with a partner.
1 … is an example of good design because …
2 One way I can help my conversation partner if they don't understand me is …
3 …., unless they see more people who look like them in the media.

3 Read the ideas for working on the Unit 6 goals. Choose the three ideas that are the most useful to you and make notes about how you will put them into practice. Then share your ideas with a partner.

Read online articles and create concept maps to summarize them.
Write questions using conditional structures, exchange them with a partner and answer their questions.
Watch videos and documentaries about successful and unsuccessful design ideas.
Listen to podcasts and focus on learning new words and phrases.
Practise thinking about my conversation partner and accommodating what I say when we speak.
Practise writing reports using visual data like tables, charts, graphs and maps.

7 Same but different Pages 82–93

1 Look at the goals from Unit 7. How confident are you with them? (1 = very confident, 4 = not at all confident).

Deal with unknown words in a literary extract
Talk about changes and trends using the continuous aspect
Use collocations to talk about work; discuss different ways to use the voice
Deal with non-linguistic listening challenges
Practise finding your voice in English
Write an opinion essay

2 Think about the Unit 7 goals. Complete the sentences with your own ideas.
1 … is still difficult for me.
2 … is something I enjoy and feel confident about.
3 … is something I can improve.

3 Read the ideas for working on the Unit 7 goals. Order them from 1 (very helpful) to 6 (not helpful). Then write notes about how you will work on the goals you feel least confident about.

Read short stories or extracts from longer books and identify the important unknown words.
Find infographics about changes and use the continuous aspect to summarize the information
Listen to different speakers and then describe how they use their voices.
Watch videos and listen to podcasts of speakers with a range of accents.
Use English to share knowledge or a skill you have with others.
Write a short article expressing your opinion about a recent event.

8 Nature Pages 94–105

1 Look at the goals from Unit 8. Rank them in order of how confident you feel about them from 1 (very confident) to 6 (needs more practice).

Summarize texts with an outline
Use dependent prepositions
Talk about natural wonders and natural talents
Understand common patterns in fast speech
Practise ways of confronting difficult issues
Write an essay suggesting solutions to problems

2 Work in pairs. Write down …
- two nouns, two adjectives and two verbs that are followed by dependent prepositions.
- three words to describe natural wonders.
- two ways to start a difficult conversation.

3 Choose three goals from Unit 8. Discuss with a partner different ways you can achieve them. Think of at least one idea for each goal.

To practise summarizing texts with an outline, we could look back through the Student's Book and write outlines of reading texts from previous units.

Reflect and review

9 Fashion and trends <small>Pages 106–117</small>

1 **Look at the goals from Unit 9. How confident do you feel about them? Rank them from 1 (the easiest) to 6 (the most difficult).**
   Use topic sentences
   Use ellipsis and substitution in conversation
   Talk about fashion; discuss green business trends
   Understand hedging
   Learn strategies to increase your trustworthiness
   Write an anecdote

2 **Choose a topic and write a paragraph.**
   • my favourite outfit when I was a child
   • my worst fashion disaster
   • how to make businesses greener
   • a time when I lost trust in a friend

3 **Think about the goals from Unit 9 that you are least confident about. Which of the ideas below can help you work towards those goals? Add one more idea of your own. Then share your ideas with a partner.**
   • Read blog posts about clothes, toys or games and identify the topic sentences.
   • Make a mind map for fashion-related words.
   • Talk to a friend about fashion and try to avoid repeating unnecessary words.
   • Listen to online interviews and identify how the speakers use ellipsis and substitution.
   • Find online articles about green business ideas.
   • Watch news programmes and interviews and note how the speakers express uncertainty.
   • Think about ways to show that I am credible, reliable and can be trusted.
   • Keep a diary with anecdotes about my daily experiences.
   • My idea: _____

10 Time <small>Pages 118–129</small>

1 **Look at the goals from Unit 10. Tick (✓) the two that you feel least confident about. Make notes about what you find difficult and why.**
   Use definitions in a text to understand new words
   Talk about the future from the perspective of the past
   Synthesize information from multiple sources
   Use expressions with *time* and talk about different perceptions of time
   Manage turn-taking in group conversations
   Write a letter to your younger self

2 **Work in pairs. Discuss the questions.**
   1 What phrases can you remember to describe perceptions of time?
   2 How can you manage and participate in group conversations?
   3 What two pieces of advice would you give your younger self?

3 **Work in pairs. Ask your partner which goals from Unit 10 they feel least confident about. Use the ideas to give some advice. Then ask your partner for advice.**
   • Read texts about popular science and identify how new words and phrases are defined.
   • Watch videos about time travel and note down new vocabulary.
   • Practise describing how people in the past made plans for the future.
   • Use multiple sources to research a topic and summarize the information in a mind map.
   • Join in group discussions and use strategies to participate fully.
   • Search online to find letters written by successful people to their younger selves.

Vocabulary reference

UNIT 1B

approachable (adj) /əˈprəʊtʃəbl/   *You can always ask my sister for help – she's very approachable.*

bump into (phr v) / bʌmp ˈɪntuː/   *She bumped into her teacher at the supermarket.*

come across as (phr) /kʌm əˈkrɒs æz/   *He certainly doesn't come across as shy!*

distant (adj) /ˈdɪstənt/   *She can seem a bit distant when you first meet her, but she's actually very kind.*

flow (v) /fləʊ/   *The conversation flowed all evening.*

get thrown together (phr v) /get θrəʊn təˈgeðə/   *They got thrown together at an evening class they both took.*

happen to (phr v) /ˈhæpən tuː/   *I happened to be in the library when he was returning a book.*

not think much of (phr) /nɒt θɪŋk mʌtʃ ɒv/   *He doesn't think much of his new manager.*

strike up (phr v) /straɪk ʌp/   *They joined the choir at the same time and soon struck up a friendship.*

take someone under one's wing (phr) /teɪk ˈsʌmwʌn ˈʌndə wʌnz wɪŋ/   *Sue took me under her wing in Rome.*

turn out (phr v) /tɜːn aʊt/   *It turns out that he used to work with my brother.*

1 Complete the conversation with the correct form of the words and phrases from the word list.
   A: Vera told me that she ¹_____ you yesterday at the sports centre.
   B: That's right! I ²_____ be at reception and she walked in. How did you first meet her?
   A: Oh, we ³_____ when we were both working on the same research project last year. To be honest, I ⁴_____ her at first.
   B: Really? That's hard to believe. She's so ⁵_____ and outgoing.
   A: Yes, I know! But she was very ⁶_____ when I first met her. In fact, she ⁷_____ as quite unfriendly!
   B: So, what made you change your mind?
   A: We ⁸_____ a conversation one day and discovered that we both loved sport.
   B: And the conversation ⁹_____ after that?
   A: Yes! And, it ¹⁰_____ she was working part-time as a tennis coach, which was great because I was trying to improve my tennis.
   B: So she gave you tennis lessons?
   A: Yes, she did. She ¹¹_____ and really encouraged me.

2 Work in pairs. Describe the last time you were thrown together with some people you didn't know well.

UNIT 1C

aesthetically pleasing (phr) /esˈθɛtɪk(ə)li ˈpliːzɪŋ/   *The large, bright room was very aesthetically pleasing.*

evoke (emotions) (phr) /ɪˈvəʊk (ɪˈməʊʃənz)/   *This music evokes memories of the first time I visited Paris.*

feel (emotionally) attached (phr) /fiːl (ɪˈməʊʃənli) əˈtætʃt/   *She felt deeply attached to the blanket her grandmother made.*

have sentimental value (phr) /hæv ˌsentɪˈmɛntl ˈvæljuː/   *This picture may not be worth much, but it has great sentimental value to me.*

it takes me back to (phr) /ɪt teɪks miː bæk tuː/   *The smell of bread baking takes me back to my aunt's house.*

all shapes and sizes (phr) /ɔːl ʃeɪps ənd ˈsaɪzɪz/   *She has a large collection of dolls of all shapes and sizes.*

serve as / be a manifestation of (phr) /sɜːv æz / biː ə ˌmænɪfɛsˈteɪʃən ɒv/   *His strange behaviour was a manifestation of his mixed emotions.*

stumble across/upon (phr v) /ˈstʌmbl əˈkrɒs/əˈpɒn/   *I stumbled across this old photograph of my great grandparents.*

a vague/vivid recollection (phr) /ə veɪg/ˈvɪvɪd ˌrekəˈlekʃən/   *He had a vivid memory of his first day at school.*

1 Complete the sentences with the correct form of the words or phrases from the word list.
   1 Although I can't recall any of the details, I have a _____ of going to Berlin with my family when I was just three years old.
   2 Hearing her talk about that wonderful day back in June _____ some strong emotions.
   3 While he was walking the dog, he _____ the ruins of an old building.
   4 My uncle gave me this dictionary when I was ten years old, so it has great _____.
   5 Watching this film always _____ my first week at university.
   6 Joe's neat and tidy room _____ his need for order and structure in his life.
   7 It's true that it's a very _____ sofa, but it's also really uncomfortable!
   8 Dogs come in _____, from a 1.5 kg Chihuahua to an 80 kg Great Dane.
   9 She felt very _____ to that little park, where she had spent many happy hours as a child.

2 Write a short description of something that has sentimental value to you. Try to use at least four expressions from the word list.

Vocabulary reference

UNIT 2B

adaptation (n) /ˌædæpˈteɪʃ(ə)n/   *They made several adaptations to their home after the accident.*

affordable (adj) /əˈfɔːdəbl/   *This is a basic, affordable laptop, perfect for students.*

corporation (n) /ˌkɔːpəˈreɪʃn/   *He works for a large corporation based in the city centre.*

cutting-edge (adj) /ˈkʌtɪŋ-edʒ/   *The company is known for its use of cutting-edge technology.*

emerging (adj) /ɪˈmɜːdʒɪŋ/   *We believe that this product will be very successful in some of the emerging economies around the world.*

infrastructure (n) /ˈɪnfrəˌstrʌktʃə/   *This area does not have the infrastructure to support so much new building.*

luxury (n) /ˈlʌkʃəri/   *We couldn't afford luxuries like holidays abroad when I was a child.*

market (n) /ˈmɑːkɪt/   *There is a very big market for these kinds of products at the moment.*

reverse (adj) /rɪˈvɜːs/   *You can reverse engineer a product by taking it apart to find out how it works.*

1 Complete the sentences with the correct words from the word list.
   1 In some sectors, _____ markets are growing faster than the more mature markets.
   2 The flat didn't have many _____, but at least it was very inexpensive.
   3 This model is an _____ of our original product, designed for younger children.
   4 We hoped the new advertising campaign would increase sales, but it had the _____ effect.
   5 The _____ for this industry is still at an early stage of development.
   6 Our company is way ahead of its competitors in its use of the latest, _____ design.
   7 This phone is too expensive – I'm looking for something much more _____.
   8 This multinational _____ has offices in major cities around the world.
   9 We need to develop our _____ before we get any bigger.

2 Complete the sentences with your own ideas. Then compare with a partner.
   1 Although … is a luxury, I …
   2 I wish more people had access to affordable …
   3 I think that the market for … will grow in the next twenty years.
   4 I'd like to find out more about emerging technologies like …

UNIT 2C

awareness (n) /əˈweənəs/   *Children usually start to develop an awareness of themselves by the age of two.*

boredom (n) /ˈbɔːdəm/   *Sometimes you can have your best ideas at times of extreme boredom.*

collaboration (n) /kəˌlæbəˈreɪʃən/   *This project is a collaboration between local artists and businesses.*

commitment (n) /kəˈmɪtmənt/   *He's ready to make a commitment to the business.*

freedom (n) /ˈfriːdəm/   *You have the freedom to make your own choices.*

involvement (n) /ɪnˈvɒlvmənt/   *There was a lot of active involvement from the community.*

likelihood (n) /ˈlaɪklɪhʊd/   *The likelihood is that it will take some time before we can develop a better product.*

partnership (n) /ˈpɑːtnəʃɪp/   *We decided to form a partnership and share our ideas.*

probability (n) /ˌprɒbəˈbɪlɪti/   *I think there's a good probability that this will be a very successful business.*

1 Choose the correct words from the word list to complete the article. Sometimes more than one option may be possible.
   How can we increase the ¹_____ that we will enjoy our work, when so many of us complain about ²_____ in the office? One possible solution might be to bring nature into the workplace. Studies have shown that ³_____ and interaction with the natural world can lead to better mental health and a general sense of well-being. Local firm Greener Growth, has a strong ⁴_____ to developing and improving green spaces within buildings. It has recently formed a ⁵_____ with recruitment company Open Doors and is now looking for ⁶_____ from local businesses and community groups to help raise ⁷_____ of the importance of nature in our daily lives. 'We strongly believe that everyone should have the ⁸_____ to explore some of the wonderful green spaces in our area,' said a spokesperson for Greener Growth. 'There is a strong ⁹_____ that spending time in nature leads to improved health and happiness.'

2 Work in pairs. Discuss the questions.
   1 Do you have any involvement in your community?
   2 The philosopher Slavoj Žižek said 'Without boredom there is no creativity.' Do you agree?
   3 In what ways is collaboration important in the workplace, at school and in your social life?

UNIT 3B

be in no rush (phr) /biː ɪn nəʊ rʌʃ/   *I'm in no rush, so you can go ahead of me if you like.*

creep past (phr) /kriːp pɑːst/   *He tried to creep past the security guard, but was spotted immediately.*

dash around (phr) /dæʃ əˈraʊnd/   *I'm not surprised she's exhausted, she's always dashing around.*

go for a leisurely stroll (phr) /gəʊ fər ə ˈleʒəli strəʊl/ *Let's go for a leisurely stroll around the park after lunch.*

make a flying visit (phr) /meɪk ə ˈflaɪɪŋ ˈvɪzɪt/   *I'm afraid I'm just making a flying visit today.*

race against the clock (phr) /reɪs əˈgenst ðə klɒk/ *It was a race against the clock to get the project in on time.*

take your time (phr) /teɪk jɔː taɪm/   *I'd rather not rush this – let's take our time and get it right.*

trek through (the mountains) (phr) /trek θruː/   *I'd love to trek through the Andes one day.*

(walk) at an unhurried pace (phr) /ət ən ʌnˈhʌrɪd peɪs/   *They explored the town at an unhurried pace.*

wander around (phr) /ˈwɒndər əˈraʊnd/   *I live near the museum, so I often wander around it for an hour or so.*

1 Match the beginnings of the sentences (1–10) with the endings (a–j).
  1 We crept past the sleeping dog
  2 I suggest that you take your time with the exam
  3 We spent the afternoon
  4 If you want to trek through the mountains,
  5 After lunch we took a leisurely stroll
  6 Mikel made a flying visit to his grandmother
  7 You can take the book on holiday if you like –
  8 It'll be a race against the clock
  9 I prefer to walk at an unhurried pace
  10 Don't just dash around

  a make sure you have all the right equipment.
  b on his way home from the supermarket.
  c to get this article written in time.
  d and hurried round to the back of the house.
  e there's no rush to return it.
  f wandering around the old part of town.
  g trying to see all the sights – enjoy it!
  h rather than rush around all the time.
  I and read the questions carefully.
  j around the castle and its grounds.

2 Work in pairs. Describe a recent trip that you have made using at least four expressions from the word list.

UNIT 3C

at a crossroads (phr) /æt ə ˈkrɒsˌrəʊdz/   *I'm at a crossroads – I don't know what I want to do next.*

backward step (phr) /ˈbækwəd step/   *Taking this job would actually be a backward step for me.*

bright future (phr) /braɪt ˈfjuːtʃə/   *If she continues to work hard, she has a bright future ahead of her.*

do one's own thing (phr) /duː wʌnz əʊn θɪŋ/   *I'd prefer to do my own thing for a few months.*

embark on (v) /ɪmˈbɑːk ɒn/   *My parents are about to embark on a big trip to Europe.*

fall through (phr v) /fɔːl θruː/   *His plans fell through.*

feel stuck (phr) /fiːl stʌk/   *She feels stuck in her job.*

follow the crowd (phr) /ˈfɒləʊ ðə kraʊd/   *You don't need to follow the crowd – make up your own mind.*

further (v) /ˈfɜːðə/   *If he wants to further his career, he should do some more training.*

get away (phr v) /get əˈweɪ/   *I'd love to get away for a few months and leave all this behind.*

settle down (phr v) /ˈsetl daʊn/   *She's still very young and not quite ready to settle down yet.*

stand out (phr v) /stænd aʊt/   *We all agreed that he stood out from all the other candidates.*

stay put (phr) /steɪ pʊt/   *Let's stay put for a while.*

stumble into (phr) /ˈstʌmbl ˈɪntuː/   *Jewellery making is just something he stumbled into.*

uphill struggle (phr) /ˌʌpˈhɪl ˈstrʌgl/   *It's been an uphill struggle to make a profit in the current climate.*

1 Match the beginnings of the sentences 1–8 with the endings a–h.
  1 He had a bright future with that company,
  2 She has embarked on a new stage in her life,
  3 If you feel that you're at a crossroads in your life,
  4 The job has very strict entry requirements;
  5 After feeling stuck for a few years,
  6 She knows that it's a backward step,
  7 I think it's time you settled down;
  8 It was an uphill struggle to get our business started,

  a but she's keen to have less responsibility.
  b it's not something you can just stumble into.
  c you never stay put anywhere for more than a year!
  d and no longer wants to just follow the crowd.
  e he decided to do his own thing and go travelling.
  f but our marketing plan really helped us stand out from the crowd.
  g but decided to move on, to further his career.
  h why don't you get away from it all for a bit?

Vocabulary reference

UNIT 4B

catchy tune (phr) /ə ˈkætʃi tjuːn/ catchy chorus (phr) /ˈkætʃi ˈkɔːrəs/ *That song's got such a catchy chorus, I can't stop singing it!*

go to a gig / a live performance (phr) /gəʊ tuː ə gɪg / ə laɪv pəˈfɔːməns/ *We went to a fantastic gig last night by a band I'd never heard of.*

an instant hit (phr) /ən ˈɪnstənt hɪt/ *It's a great song – I'm sure it'll be an instant hit.*

lyrics (n) /ˈlɪrɪks/ *The song lyrics are beautiful.*

(my) music tastes have evolved (phr) /maɪ ˈmjuːzɪk teɪsts həv ɪˈvɒlvd/ *I used to love whatever was in the charts, but my music tastes have evolved since then.*

(the song is) on everywhere (phr) /ɒn ˈevriweə/ *Not that song again! It's on everywhere!*

stream music (phr) /striːm ˈmjuːzɪk/ *I stream music to my phone when I'm on a run.*

top the charts (phr) /tɒp ðə tʃɑːts/ *Their latest song topped the charts for six weeks.*

track (n) /træk/ *This is the third track on the album.*

(be) trending (phr) /(biː) ˈtrendɪŋ/ *His podcast is trending in India.*

1 Complete the conversation with the correct form of the words and phrases from the word list.
A: When was the last time you ¹_____?
B: Actually, I saw my favourite band just last night. And it was amazing. Did you know that their latest song is ²_____ at the moment?
A: Of course I did! It's been number 1 for three weeks. That ³_____ – you can't escape from it!
B: I know. I think it was ⁴_____ on social media on the day that it was released. It was an ⁵_____.
A: It's weird, though. I mean, it's quite a good song, but it's not the best ⁶_____ on the album.
B: Seriously? It's such a ⁷_____ tune, though.
A: Yeah, I know, but the ⁸_____ are a bit boring, aren't they? Maybe it's just that my ⁹_____ … I don't love the band as much as I used to.

2 Work in pairs. Say if you agree or disagree with these statements and explain why.
1 The lyrics are as important as the tune in a song.
2 You can't fully appreciate a band or a singer until you hear them give a live performance.
3 Streaming music is killing the music industry.

UNIT 4C

(our) ancestors (n) /ˈænsestəz/ *My ancestors came from a remote island off the coast of Ireland.*

based on (facts) (phr) /beɪst ɒn/ *The book is based on true events from the Second World War.*

historically accurate (phr) /hɪsˈtɒrɪkli ˈækjʊrət/ *Although the film may not be entirely historically accurate, it's certainly entertaining.*

indigenous peoples (phr) /ɪnˈdɪdʒɪnəs ˈpiːpəlz/ *The indigenous peoples of Canada have created their own map to show the different nations.*

pass down/on (traditions) (phr) /pɑːs daʊn/ɒn (trəˈdɪʃənz)/ *These stories have been passed down from generation to generation.*

preserve for future generations (phr) /prɪˈzɜːv fə ˈfjuːtʃə ˌdʒenəˈreɪʃənz/ *We want to preserve our stories for future generations to hear.*

records of a distant past (phr) /ˈrekɔːdz əv ə ˈdɪstənt pɑːst/ *The tales serve as records of a distant past.*

share stories/legends (phr) /ʃeə ˈstɔːriz/ˈledʒəndz/ *They would sit around the fire and share ancient legends.*

storytelling traditions (phr) /ˈstɔːrɪˌtelɪŋ trəˈdɪʃənz/ *Many cultures have their own storytelling traditions.*

transcend time (phr) /trænˈsend taɪm/ *Many of the messages from these folk tales transcend time.*

1 Complete the text with the correct form of some of the words from the word list.
Many societies and ¹_____ around the world have their own ²_____. These stories are often ³_____ orally – through voice, gestures or song – and they have been a way for different cultures to keep ⁴_____ of the past and honour their ⁵_____ – all the generations that have come before them. Although these stories are often ⁶_____ real events, they are not always ⁷_____, and you are unlikely to find the experiences they describe in history books. Often they include morals, advice, or values that ⁸_____ and still have meaning to people today. When we share ⁹_____ like these, we can help ¹⁰_____ our culture for future generations.

2 Complete these sentences with your own ideas. Then compare with a partner.
1 Some traditions that have been passed down in my family include …
2 One of the great things about oral storytelling is …
3 An example of a story that transcends time is …

UNIT 5B

calories (n) /ˈkæləriz/   *If you eat more calories than you use up, your body stores the surplus as body fat.*

immune system (n) /ɪˈmjuːn ˈsɪstəm/   *Our immune system helps protect our bodies from disease.*

insomnia (n) /ɪnˈsɒmnɪə/   *I've got terrible insomnia at the moment – I don't sleep more than three or four hours a night.*

inappropriate (adj) /ˌɪnəˈprəʊprɪət/   *Please don't use inappropriate language in front of the children.*

infectious (adj) /ɪnˈfekʃəs/   *This illness is highly infectious, so you must avoid contact with other people.*

open-minded (adj) /ˈəʊpən ˈmaɪndɪd/   *I wish you could be a bit more open-minded about other people's life choices.*

social interaction (phr) /ˈsəʊʃəl ˌɪntərˈækʃən/   *Social interaction can help young children develop their language skills.*

tolerance (n) /ˈtɒlərəns/   *She has a very low tolerance to pain.*

1 Complete the sentences with the correct word or phrase from the word list.
   1 After living on his own for so long, he sometimes found _____ difficult.
   2 It was _____ to tell that joke to my grandparents.
   3 This cake is absolutely delicious. I don't care how many _____ there are in it!
   4 People who drink a lot of coffee develop a high _____ to its effects.
   5 He's never suffered from _____ – in fact he could sleep through anything.
   6 She thinks she's very _____, but actually she can be pretty judgemental.
   7 Eating fresh, healthy food and drinking plenty of water can be good for your _____.
   8 Although this disease isn't _____, it would probably be best for you to stay at home for the next few days.

2 Read the message. Write a reply using at least four words and expressions from the word list.

> I've been feeling a bit down and tired recently. I haven't been sleeping well and I keep getting colds. I think it's probably time to change my lifestyle. Have you got any suggestions?

UNIT 5C

analytical (adj) /ˌænəˈlɪtɪkəl/   *She has a very analytical mind, but she isn't very creative.*

availability (n) /əˌveɪləˈbɪlɪti/   *All our prices depend on the seasonal availability of materials.*

humanity (n) /hjuˈmænɪti/   *Humanity has survived many great challenges in the past.*

individuality (n) /ˌɪndɪˌvɪdjʊˈælɪti/   *Everyone should have the right to express their individuality.*

informative (adj) /ɪnˈfɔːmətɪv/   *It was an informative film – I now understand the issues better.*

manipulative (adj) /məˈnɪpjʊlətɪv/   *That 'caring' gesture was just a manipulative attempt by the company to increase sales.*

personal (adj) /ˈpɜːsənl/   *I don't represent the school – this is just my personal opinion.*

persuasive (adj) /pəˈsweɪsɪv/   *Her argument was very persuasive and most of the audience agreed with her.*

statistical (adj) /stəˈtɪstɪkəl/   *Despite the statistical evidence against it, he bought the product.*

1 Choose the correct option.
   1 The sales assistant was very *persuasive*, / *personal*, but in the end we decided not to buy it.
   2 Could you please let me know about the *humanity* / *availability* of this product?
   3 His *informative* / *analytical* approach helped him spot several errors in their financial forecasts.
   4 The *persuasive* / *statistical* data proves that this new medication is 20% more effective.
   5 At this school we support *individuality* / *availability* by understanding each child's needs and strengths.
   6 *Manipulative* / *Statistical* advertising often uses our desire to do better than our peers to sell products.
   7 Many people believe that global heating is a threat to the future of *individuality* / *humanity*.
   8 Thank you for your very *manipulative* / *informative* lecture about the history of mediaeval medicine.
   9 From a(n) *analytical* / *personal* point of view, I will be very sad when this company relocates.

2 Work in pairs. Discuss the questions.
   1 Think of three ways that someone might use manipulative behaviour to get you to do something.
   2 What do you think is humanity's greatest achievement and why?
   3 Are there any disadvantages to always relying on statistical evidence?
   4 Give an example of a persuasive advertisement you have seen recently.

Vocabulary reference

UNIT 6B

change people's perceptions (phr) /tʃeɪndʒ 'piːpəlz pə'sepʃənz/ *We need to change people's perceptions of disability.*

diversity (n) /daɪ'vɜːsɪti/ *Our company is committed to improving diversity in the workplace.*

emphasize (v) /'emfəsaɪz/ *She emphasized the fact that she had plenty of previous experience.*

highlight (v) /'haɪˌlaɪt/ *The report highlights the lack of facilities in the area.*

inclusivity (n) /ˌɪnkluː'sɪvəti/ *This college promotes the values of tolerance and inclusivity.*

negative stereotypes (phr) /'neɡətɪv 'sterɪətaɪps/ *We should try to avoid using negative stereotypes when we talk about teenagers.*

prominent (adj) /'prɒmɪnənt/ *They put up posters in prominent places all around the city.*

represent (v) /ˌreprɪ'zent/ *This image represents nature and the environment.*

resemble (v) /rɪ'zembl/ *People say that I really resemble my grandmother both in looks and personality.*

unrepresentative (adj) /ˌʌnˌreprɪ'zentətɪv/ *His comments were unrepresentative of our beliefs and principles.*

1 **Choose the correct options to complete the text.**
In today's workshop we shall be talking about ¹*inclusivity / perceptions* and how we can provide equal access to all. A(n) ²*unrepresentative / prominent* part of the discussion will be focused on how to ³*change / emphasize* people's perceptions around the topic of disability. It will also examine why the portrayal of people with disabilities in the media is still often ⁴*negative / unrepresentative* of the community. We hope to ⁵*highlight / resemble* the different ways that we can ⁶*represent / emphasize* people with disabilities to avoid ⁷*prominent / negative* stereotypes and ⁸*change / emphasize* the positive experiences and achievements of the disability community. We will also look at how organizations can benefit from ⁹*stereotypes / diversity* by gaining a variety of different perspectives and how, when people see others who ¹⁰*resemble / emphasize* them in the workplace, they feel less invisible and more included in society.

2 **Work in pairs. Discuss the questions.**
1 How can organizations support inclusivity and diversity when they recruit new staff?
2 Think of three different ways that you could change people's perceptions of you.

UNIT 6C

artificial (adj) /ˌɑːtɪ'fɪʃ(ə)l/ *Those flowers are artificial.*

compatible (adj) /kəm'pætəbl/ *Is this printer compatible with my old laptop?*

everyday (adj) /'evrɪˌdeɪ/ *Making the bed is an everyday task which even young children can do.*

fragile (adj) /'frædʒaɪl/ *This fabric is very old and fragile.*

functional (adj) /'fʌŋkʃənəl/ *It's a simple, functional design that is both practical and attractive.*

illogical (adj) /ɪ'lɒdʒɪkəl/ *They all agreed that his decision was illogical and didn't make any sense.*

impractical (adj) /ɪm'præktɪkəl/ *It's a beautiful coat, but completely impractical for a day's hiking.*

in the way (phr) /ɪn ðə weɪ/ *My dog follows me around everywhere and always gets in the way.*

looks (n) /lʊks/ *Personality is more important than looks.*

pointless (adj) /'pɔɪntləs/ *It's pointless doing lots of research then just buying the cheapest model.*

striking (adj) /'straɪkɪŋ/ *The design of the house is very striking and modern, but not everyone would love it.*

unreliable (adj) /ˌʌnrɪ'laɪəbl/ *My laptop has crashed again! It's so unreliable.*

user-friendly (adj) /'juːzə 'frendli/ *It's a very user-friendly app, so anyone can understand how it works.*

1 **Complete the sentences with the correct word from the word list.**
1 There are no _____ flavours in the dish.
2 Pack the bowl carefully as it is _____.
3 She has dark hair and _____ blue eyes.
4 The device was popular because it was stylish but also _____ and easy to operate.
5 Don't believe everything he says – his stories can be very _____.
6 I'm looking for a smartwatch that is _____ with my phone.
7 It's not particularly elegant, but it's fine for _____ use.
8 Having pockets you can't use is _____.
9 The rules seem to be completely _____ and no one really understands them.
10 Don't buy it because of its _____ – make sure it's also _____.
11 That's a great idea in theory, but it seems quite _____.
12 Can we move the printer? It gets _____ where it is.

2 **Write a description of an app you use regularly.**

UNIT 7B

approximate (adj) /əˈprɒksɪmət/ *I'm afraid we can only give an approximate date for completion of the work.*

broadly (adv) /ˈbrɔːdli/ *Salaries are still broadly the same as they were five years ago.*

dramatic (adj) /drəˈmætɪk/ *There has been a dramatic improvement in your son's behaviour.*

marginally (adv) /ˈmɑːdʒɪnəli/ *This year's results are marginally better than last year's.*

notable (adj) /ˈnəʊtəbl/ *Giving employees a longer lunchbreak has made a notable difference to their productivity.*

radically (adv) /ˈrædɪkli/ *Teaching has changed radically since I was at school.*

roughly (adv) /ˈrʌfli/ *There are roughly 100 billion neurons in the human brain.*

slightly (adv) /ˈslaɪtli/ *Tania is slightly taller than me.*

strikingly (adv) /ˈstraɪkɪŋli/ *Your answers in the test are strikingly similar to Gregor's.*

subtle (adj) /ˈsʌtl/ *A professional food taster can perceive even the most subtle differences in flavours.*

1 Read sentence a, then choose the correct option for sentence b so that the meaning is the same.
 1 a She has changed radically since she gave up her old job.
  b There has been a *dramatic / subtle* difference in her since she gave up her old job.
 2 a We now have an approximate figure for the numbers of people attending.
  b We know *roughly / marginally* how many people will be attending.
 3 a The results are broadly what we had expected.
  b The results *are / aren't* strikingly different from what we had expected.
 4 a The situation has improved slightly since we last spoke.
  b There has been a *subtle / notable* improvement since we last spoke.

2 Write sentences with your own ideas. Then compare your answers in pairs.
 1 Name two towns/cities you know that are radically different from each other. Explain how they differ.
 2 Describe a subtle change that has happened to someone you know.
 3 Think of one improvement that you would like to make to your life. Is it dramatic or subtle? Why do you want to make it?

UNIT 7C

give someone a voice (phr) /ɡɪv ˈsʌmwʌn ə vɔɪs/ *It's important to give minorities a voice in the decision-making process.*

lower your voice (phr) /ˈləʊə jɔː vɔɪs / *Could you please lower your voice – I'm trying to work.*

moan about (v) /məʊn əˈbaʊt/ *She's always moaning about her neighbours.*

mumble (v) /ˈmʌmbl/ *I can't understand what you're saying when you mumble.*

raise your voice /reɪz jɔː vɔɪs/ *There's no need to raise your voice – please try to stay calm.*

speak at the top of your voice (phr) /spiːk ət ðə tɒp əv jɔː vɔɪs/ *The music was so loud we had to speak at the top of our voices.*

speak out (phr v) /spiːk aʊt/ *It's important to speak out about these issues.*

speak up (v) /spiːk ʌp/ *Could you speak up, please? I'm a little deaf.*

voice recognition (phr) /vɔɪs ˌrekəɡˈnɪʃən/ *I've installed some new voice recognition software.*

you're breaking up (phr) /jʊə ˈbreɪkɪŋ ʌp/ *I'm sorry, I can't hear you – you're breaking up.*

1 Complete the conversation with the correct form of a word or phrase from the word list.
 A: Hi Tomoko, I just wanted to chat to you about the meeting. I was glad we ¹_____ about the problem at last.
 B: Yes, absolutely. I know some people think we just ²_____ about the same old issues, but this is important. The good thing is that nobody got angry or ³_____.
 A: Yes, I really hope we see some changes this time. The new ⁴_____ app should make the group more accessible.
 B: You're right. And it's so important to ⁵_____ to all those people who usually get ignored.
 A: Sorry, what was that? Can you ⁶_____ a bit?
 B: I'm probably ⁷_____ as usual! I'll try to speak more clearly. ... Any better?
 A: Sorry, I still can't hear you. Can you speak any louder at all?
 B: Not really. I'm speaking ⁸_____! I think it's a bad line.
 A: Hello? Hello? You're ⁹_____.
 B: OK, I'll ring you back.

Vocabulary reference

UNIT 8B

be a born (leader) (phr) /biː ə bɔːn 'liːdə /   *He's a born leader and tends to take charge of a situation.*

be a first-rate (musician) (phr) /biː ə fɜːst reɪt mjuˈzɪʃn/   *He's a first-rate nurse and very caring.*

be an accomplished (athlete) (phr) /biː ən əˈkʌmplɪʃt ˈæθliːt/   *The twins are both accomplished artists.*

be a natural (phr) /biː ə 'nætʃrəl/   *She's never played football before, but you can tell she's a natural.*

(not) be cut out for (phr) /(nɒt) biː kʌt aʊt fɔː/   *I don't think you're cut out for a job in banking.*

be deeply committed (to) (phr) /biː 'diːpli kəˈmɪtɪd (tuː)/   *We are deeply committed to fairness.*

be driven (phr) /biː 'drɪvn/   *She's very driven and rarely takes a break during her working day.*

be in the genes (phr) /biː ɪn ðə dʒiːnz/   *Both of my parents were musicians, so music is in my genes.*

be persistent (phr) /biː pəˈsɪstənt/   *If you want to do well in this industry, you have to be persistent.*

have drive (phr) /hæv draɪv/   *I have drive and energy and am determined to be a success.*

have (an) innate / (a) natural talent (for) (phr) /hæv (ən) ɪˈneɪt / (ə) 'nætʃrəl 'tælənt (fɔː)/   *They have an innate talent for ballet.*

have (a) flair (for) (phr) /hæv ə fleə fɔː/   *He has a flair for music and can play four different instruments.*

1 Choose the correct option to complete the sentences.
1 He's scared of dogs, so he's *a born / not really cut out to be a* vet.
2 She was very *accomplished / persistent* and kept emailing them until they offered her an interview.
3 The child showed *an innate / a driven* talent for chess from a very early age.
4 He's a *born / persistent* entertainer and has always enjoyed making people laugh.
5 You have to be a(n) *innate / very accomplished* chef with several years of experience to work here.
6 All four brothers have become doctors, so medicine must be *driven / in their genes*.
7 He's very *driven / innate* and will stop at nothing to get to the top.
8 She was a *first-rate / natural* lawyer thanks to studying hard for many years and being *persistent / deeply committed* to her work.
9 I'm obviously *a born / a natural* at driving: I passed my test after only five lessons.
10 She is a really hard worker, but she needs more *flair / drive* to be good designer.

UNIT 8C

crash (v) /kræʃ/   *I could hear the waves crashing.*

crystal clear (phr) /'krɪstl klɪə/   *We couldn't wait to swim in the crystal clear water.*

immersed (adj) /ɪˈmɜːst/   *They were immersed in conversation and didn't hear us come in.*

impressive landmark (phr) /ɪmˈpresɪv 'lændmɑːk/   *The tall tower on the horizon was an impressive landmark.*

lush green vegetation (phr) /lʌʃ griːn ˌvedʒɪˈteɪʃən/   *Months of heavy rainfall has led to the area being covered in lush green vegetation.*

memorable moment (phr) /'memərəbl 'məʊmənt/   *Taking a hot air balloon ride was the most memorable moment of the holiday.*

picturesque (adj) /ˌpɪktʃəˈresk /   *Between the two mountains, there was a picturesque valley.*

rocky cliffs (phr) /'rɒki klɪfs/   *We stood at the top of the rocky cliffs and looked down to the sea.*

scenic route (phr) /'siːnɪk ruːt/   *Let's take the scenic route to the campsite.*

summit (n) /'sʌmɪt/   *We won't reach the summit today.*

tranquil (adj) /'træŋkwɪl/   *They stopped for a picnic lunch in the tranquil woods.*

unspoiled (adj) /ʌnˈspɔɪlt/   *Fortunately very few people know about the unspoiled countryside around here.*

untouched (adj) /ʌnˈtʌtʃt/   *The island was untouched and no one had lived there for centuries.*

vastness (n) /'vɑːstnəs/   *We were amazed by the vastness of the ocean.*

witness (v) /'wɪtnɪs/   *Did he witness the accident?*

1 Complete the texts with these words and phrases.

---
impressive landmark   memorable moment   picturesque valley   scenic route   unspoilt   vastness   witnessed

---

Avoiding the motorway, we decided to take the [1] _____ to our hotel, through the [2] _____ and then on to a lovely little [3] _____ village with some beautiful old buildings. We stopped to take some photographs of the castle – a(n) [4] _____ which could be seen from miles away. By the time we arrived at our destination, it was already dark, and as we stared up at the [5] _____ of space, we [6] _____ a shooting star moving through the night sky. It was a truly [7] _____ and a wonderful beginning to our holiday.

UNIT 9B

be back in fashion (phr) /biː bæk ɪn ˈfæʃən/   *Don't throw the dress out – that style is back in fashion.*

dress code (n phr) /dres kəʊd/   *Do you know what the dress code is for the dinner party tonight?*

flattering (adj) /ˈflætərɪŋ/   *It's a lovely colour, but it isn't very flattering on you.*

formal (adj) /ˈfɔːməl/   *I think the event will be quite formal, so don't wear jeans.*

glamorous (adj) /ˈɡlæmərəs/   *She always looks very glamorous, even to go to the supermarket.*

outfit (n) /ˈaʊtfɪt/   *I love your outfit – very smart!*

practical (adj) /ˈpræktɪkəl/   *Please wear practical clothes for the hike.*

scruffy (adj) /ˈskrʌfi/   *I need a new pair of shoes – these ones are beginning to look very scruffy.*

see better days (phr) /siː ˈbetə deɪz/   *This bag has seen better days – it's quite worn and the zip is broken.*

smart casual (adj) /smɑːt ˈkæʒʊəl/   *You don't need to wear a suit – smart casual is fine.*

trendy (adj) /ˈtrendi/   *I know this style is very trendy at the moment, but I really don't like it.*

unconventional (adj) /ˌʌnkənˈvenʃənəl/   *Her ideas were interesting and very unconventional.*

1 Choose the correct options to complete the email.

Did I tell you about my aunt's birthday party? For some reason, I didn't realize that there was a strict ¹*outfit / dress code*. All the other guests were wearing very ²*formal / scruffy* clothes. My aunt was looking very ³*glamorous / practical* (as usual!) in a beautiful silk dress. Anyway, I turned up in an old leather jacket that was a bit ⁴*flattering / scruffy* and had definitely ⁵*seen better days / been back in fashion* and some rather ⁶*trendy / unconventional* trousers, that are not very fashionable, but I love because they are very ⁷*formal / flattering* and they make my legs look longer. Everyone was staring at me, and I felt very embarrassed, but my aunt thought it was hilarious, because the jacket actually used to be hers! She bought it in the 1970s, when that style was really ⁸*trendy / unconventional* and she was thrilled to see that it ⁹*was back in fashion / had seen better days*.

In other news … I start my new job tomorrow! I need to think of a(n) ¹⁰*outfit / dress code* that will be ¹¹*glamorous / smart casual* for the office, but also ¹²*trendy / practical* because I'll be cycling there and back. Any ideas?

UNIT 9C

biodegradable (adj) /ˌbaɪəʊdɪˈɡreɪdəb(ə)l/   *This bag is made of biodegradable materials.*

carbon emission (phr) /ˈkɑːbən ɪˈmɪʃən/   *We are concerned that carbon emissions have not been reduced sufficiently.*

catch on (phr v) /kætʃ ɒn/   *I like the design, but I'm not convinced that it will catch on.*

competitive (adj) /kəmˈpetɪtɪv/   *The market for eco-friendly products is very competitive.*

consumer demand (phr) /kənˈsjuːmə dɪˈmɑːnd/   *Consumer demand for electric cars has increased.*

energy company (phr) /ˈenədʒi ˈkʌmpəni/   *Most energy companies have increased their prices.*

fossil fuel (phr) /ˈfɒsl fjʊəl/   *We need to reduce our reliance on fossil fuels like coal and oil.*

investor (n) /ɪnˈvestə/   *You need to show investors in your business that there is a market for your products.*

natural resources (phr) /ˈnætʃrəl rɪˈzɔːsɪz/   *We should do more to protect our natural resources.*

refillable bottle (phr) /ˌriːˈfɪləbl ˈbɒtəl/   *I always take a refillable bottle with me when I travel.*

renewable energy (phr) /rɪˈnjuːəbəl ˈenədʒi/   *From next year all our offices are going to use renewable energy.*

switch (v) /swɪtʃ/   *If you aren't happy with your current suppliers, you should switch to a different company.*

upward trend (phr) /ˈʌpwəd trend/   *The figures show an upward trend in sales of organic vegetables.*

1 Match the beginnings of the sentences (1-6) with the endings (a-f)

1 Our app will help you to compare energy companies and
2 There has been a significant increase in carbon emissions from
3 In the last twenty years, there has been an upward trend in the use of
4 The idea has really caught on and there is now considerable
5 Our investors showed a lot of interest in these
6 This biodegradable plastic has been manufactured using only

a fossil fuels in the last one hundred years.
b consumer demand for our product.
c natural resources and is produced using renewable energy.
d refillable bottles and we will be launching our new design in the summer.
e switch to the most competitive supplier in your area.
f renewable energy like solar or wind power.

Vocabulary reference

UNIT 10B

for the time being (phr) /fə ðə taɪm ˈbiːɪŋ/   *I will be teaching you for the time being while Ms Dale is away.*

in no time (phr) /ɪn nəʊ taɪm/   *Fortunately, she was able to fix the problem in no time.*

it's about time (phr) /ɪts əˈbaʊt taɪm/   *It's about time someone told him that his behaviour is unacceptable.*

long-time (adj) /ˈlɒŋ taɪm/   *They are long-time colleagues and have worked together for many years.*

make up for lost time (phr) /meɪk ʌp fə lɒst ˈtaɪm/   *I'm working hard now to make up for lost time.*

only a matter of time (phr) /ˈəʊnli ə ˈmætər əv taɪm/   *It is only a matter of time before she finds out the truth.*

take things one at a time (phr) /teɪk θɪŋz wʌn ət ə taɪm/   *I know you want to start immediately, but let's just take things one at a time.*

time-consuming (adj) /taɪm kənˈsjuːmɪŋ/   *I'm afraid it is too time-consuming to answer every email personally.*

1 Complete the sentences with the correct word or phrase from the word list.
  1 I'm running a bit late, but I'm on the train now, so I'll be there _____.
  2 I've decided to stay in my current job _____ until the economy improves.
  3 We hadn't seen each other for months, but we _____ and chatted for hours.
  4 Rather than trying to do everything straight away, why don't we _____?
  5 _____ you stopped being so selfish and started thinking more about other people.
  6 Preparing this dish is very _____, but it's so delicious that it's worth it!
  7 Mary was a _____ friend of his and he knew he could trust her.
  8 You should really fix that ladder – it's _____ before someone has an accident.

2 Work in pairs. Discuss the questions.
  1 Describe a time-consuming activity that you have to do but don't enjoy.
  2 Tell your partner about a long-time friend or colleague. How did you first meet? How long have you known each other?
  3 Are you the kind of person who prefers to take things one at a time or do you prefer to take on several tasks at the same time? Give examples.
  4 Imagine you were rescued from a desert island where you had been stranded for five years. How would you make up for lost time?

UNIT 10C

ahead of schedule (phr) /əˈhed əv ˈʃedjuːl/   *With a lot of hard work, we managed to finish the project ahead of schedule.*

at the last minute (phr) /æt ðə lɑːst ˈmɪnɪt/   *Unfortunately, they cancelled the appointment at the last minute.*

elapse (v) /ɪˈlæps/   *A lot of time has elapsed since we last met.*

perception (n) /pəˈsepʃən/   *Our perception of taste is affected by what we see and smell.*

tedious (adj) /ˈtiːdiəs/   *The play was very tedious and I nearly fell asleep.*

the passage of time (phr) /ðə ˈpæsɪdʒ əv taɪm/   *I know that you feel unhappy now, but with the passage of time, things will start to get better.*

slow motion (phr) /sləʊ ˈməʊʃən/   *If you watch that again in slow motion, you will see that he touched the ball with his hand.*

swiftly (adv) /ˈswɪftli/   *Time seems to pass much more swiftly when you are enjoying yourself.*

1 Complete the conversation with the correct words and phrases from the word list.
  A: What's your book about?
  B: It's about a family in the mid-west and how, gradually, the ¹_____ changes their ²_____ of each other and alters their relationships.
  A: Are you enjoying it?
  B: The first section was a bit ³_____ and dull. But in this second part, ten years have ⁴_____ and a lot of things have happened, so it's a bit more interesting. The problem is that I have to read it quite ⁵_____ because we're discussing it at book club tomorrow.
  A: Why do you always do everything ⁶_____? You should have started reading it earlier.
  B: Well yes, you're probably right. You're much better than I am at doing things ⁷_____.

2 Complete the sentences with your own ideas. Then compare with a partner.
  1 I often / rarely … ahead of schedule because …
  2 Time passes more swiftly for me when …
  3 I think … can affect people's perception of each other.

Grammar reference

UNIT 1

1B Grammar: Perfect structures

Perfect structures are used to look back at a past event from a later time. There are six perfect tenses:

Present perfect simple

- Use the present perfect simple to describe events or actions in the past that still have a link to the present.
- To form the present perfect simple, use *have* + past participle.

  Miguel doesn't live here any more, he's moved to France.

Present perfect continuous

- Use the present perfect continuous to describe events or actions that started in the past and are still continuing in the present.
- To form the present perfect continuous, use *have been* + verb +-*ing*

  He's been working on that project since January.

Past perfect simple

- Use the past perfect simple to describe events or actions that happened before the main event.
- To form the past perfect simple, use *had* + past participle.

  She had met him once before, but he seemed different this time.

- Sometimes you can use either the past perfect or the past simple to describe two events in the past. Using the past perfect emphasizes the completion of the first event.

  He ate / had eaten lunch before he went out.

Past perfect continuous

- Use the past perfect continuous to describe longer events or actions that were in progress before, continued up to, or were interrupted by the main event in the past.
- To form the past perfect continuous, use *had been* + verb +-*ing*

  We'd been walking for a while when it started to rain.

Future perfect simple

- Use the future perfect simple to describe something that will be completed by a point in the future.
- To form the future perfect simple, use *will have* + past participle

  She'll have read your email by now.

Future perfect continuous

- Use the future perfect continuous to describe something that will be in progress up to a point in the future.
- To form the future perfect continuous, use *will have been* + verb +-*ing*

  I've just realized that next week, we will have been living together for a whole year.

Other perfect structures:

Perfect infinitive

- Use *to have* + past participle after verbs and phrases that take *to* + infinitive, e.g. *expect, hope, prefer, pretend, seem,* etc.

  We hope to have finished the work on the house before winter.

  He seemed to have got his foot stuck, so I offered to help him.

- Use the infinitive without *to* after modal verbs, *had better* and *would rather*.

  I would rather have seen her, but it was still lovely to speak over the phone.

  You can't have expected them to be happy with that result.

Perfect with *-ing* forms

- Use *having* + past participle after verbs and phrases that take *-ing*, e.g. *deny, have difficulty, miss,* etc. and after certain prepositions, e.g. *after, before, without.*

  He denied having broken her phone.

- You can often use an *-ing* form or a perfect *-ing* form with no change in meaning.

  After having speaking / having spoken to him, she decided to change her plans.

- You can also use *having* + past participle to describe two actions in the past, when one action happens before, or is the cause of another action that follows it.

  Having read the reviews, we agreed to buy tickets to the show.

  I didn't want to go to the cinema, having seen the film twice already.

- If the subject of the main clause and the subordinate clause are different, use *it* or the subject of the subordinate clause before the present participle.

  All the trains were delayed, it having rained heavily the day before.

  We had to buy a new cover for our sofa, the dog having destroyed the old one.

1 Complete the sentences with the correct perfect form of the verbs in brackets.

1 We must _____ (take) a wrong turning.

2 _____ (watch) the film, I'd now really like to read the book.

3 By next year, I _____ (learn) English for ten years.

4 She thanked them for _____ (give) her so much support after the accident.

5 I pretended to _____ (lose) my phone and said that I _____ (look) for it for days.

6 By the time she gets your letter, she _____ (forget) all about the argument.

Grammar reference

2 Choose the correct options to complete the conversation.

A: What happened to you? I [1]*'ve been / 'd been* waiting for you for forty minutes.

B: I'm really sorry. I [2]*haven't / hadn't* realized that there is only one bus on Sunday mornings. I know I should [3]*have checked / have been checking* the timetable.

A: Oh well, never mind. But I think the film will [4]*have started / have been starting* by now. Maybe we could just go for a coffee instead.

B: Yes, that's a good idea. I could do with something to drink, after [5]*have / having* run all the way here from the bus stop! Where do you want to go?

A: I [6]*'d been / will have been* hoping to check out that coffee shop near the library, but it appears [7]*to have / having* closed.

B: Oh, that's a pity. I [8]*'d heard / 'd been hearing* that it was really good. Well, let's just walk in that direction anyway and see what we can find.

1C Focus on: Distinguishing between words with similar meanings

There are a number of words in English which have a similar, but not exactly the same, meaning. Some examples include:

awake / evoke

- If something *awakes* feelings or memories, it suggests that the feelings and memories were always there but perhaps you were trying to forget them.

- If something *evokes* feelings or memories, there is no suggestion that you were trying to forget them. The feelings it evokes could be new ones.

  *The smell of roses in the garden **evoked** a feeling of calm, but seeing the house again **awoke** less happy memories.*

vivid / vibrant

- *Vivid* means particularly bright and alive. You can talk about *vivid images, dreams* or *a vivid imagination*. *Vibrant* means lively and exciting.

- You can talk about *a vibrant atmosphere, economy* or *town*. Colours can be *vivid* or *vibrant*.

  *Your son has a very **vivid** imagination and would thrive in the **vibrant**, caring atmosphere of our school.*

emotional / sentimental

- *Emotional* means experiencing a strong emotion. If you feel emotional about something, your emotion might be anger, sadness, happiness, pride, etc. *Sentimental* means feeling too much emotion, in a way that is not quite appropriate, or goes against reason or logic.

- *Sentimental* is often (but not always) related to romantic love and usually refers to feelings of happiness, sadness or nostalgia.

  *I still feel quite **emotional** today when I think about all those silly **sentimental** messages I sent him.*

vague / ambiguous

- If something is *vague*, it is not clear or not quite defined, with not enough details. If something is *ambiguous*, it can be interpreted in a number of different ways.

- If you *feel ambiguous* about something, it means you haven't made up your mind yet. If you *feel vague* about something, you don't quite remember it or understand the details.

  *She felt **ambiguous** about the job offer – it sounded interesting, but it was also rather **vague** and she needed to find out more details.*

broad / wide

- Both *broad* and *wide* can be used in measurements and to describe streets, roads and rivers. *Broad* can also be used to describe a person's build and implies strength.

- You also use *wide* and *broad* to talk about a big range, but *wide* refers more specifically to quantity, while *broad* is used to suggest quality as well.

  *The man with the **broad** shoulders walked slowly over the bridge that crossed the **wide** river.*

rare / scarce

- *Rare* can refer to things that don't happen very often – *a rare occurrence*, or to things which are difficult to find or exist only in small quantities – *a rare mineral*.

- *Scarce* means not enough, while *rare* means very few or very infrequent. You can talk about *rare animals*, but not ~~scarce animals~~.

- *Scarce* is also usually only used at the end of a sentence, rather than before the noun it describes, while *rare* can be in both positions.

  *Money was **scarce** and on the **rare** occasion that we went out, we were careful not to spend too much.*

1 Choose the correct option to complete the sentences.

1 At the moment, more information about the new policy is *scarce / rare*.

2 His poems were popular at the time, but are now seen as dated and *emotional / sentimental*.

3 The details of the holiday are all a bit *ambiguous / vague* right now.

4 I have a fairly *wide / broad* taste in books and enjoy many different genres and authors.

5 Seeing the painting for the first time *evoked / awoke* long-forgotten memories.

6 The centre of town is an exciting, *vivid / vibrant* area, with lots of cafés, and independent shops.

2 Read the sentences and decide if the underlined word is used correctly (✓) or incorrectly (✗). Where necessary, replace with the more appropriate word.

1 I have a <u>vague</u> memory of having met him before.
2 We didn't have much money and holidays were very <u>scarce</u> when I was growing up.
3 You wrote such a <u>vibrant</u> description of the wedding in your email that I almost felt I was there!
4 They offer a <u>wide</u> range of food and drinks.
5 Scientists have shown that music can <u>awake</u> at least thirteen distinct emotions.
6 I feel quite <u>emotional</u> when I think about leaving college in July.

UNIT 2

2B Grammar: Multi-word verbs

Multi-word verbs are verbs which are followed by one or two particles or prepositions.

Phrasal verbs

- Phrasal verbs are followed by one or two adverb particles. The adverb particles change the meaning of the verb.
  *I think you need to **clear up** this misunderstanding.*
- Phrasal verbs are usually used in colloquial, informal and spoken English.

Transitive phrasal verbs

- Transitive phrasal verbs must be followed by a direct object. Most transitive phrasal verbs are **separable**. This means that the particle can either come after the verb or the object.
  *I **looked up** the word in the dictionary.*
  *I **looked** the word **up** in the dictionary.*
- When the object of a separable phrasal verb is a pronoun, the particle <u>must</u> come after the object.
  *I **looked** it **up** in the dictionary.* NOT ~~I looked up it in the dictionary.~~
- When the object of a verb is a long noun phrase, the particle usually comes before the object.
  *We need to **pick up** my dad's heavy tent before we leave.*
- When the phrasal verb is part of a relative clause, the particle comes after the verb.
  *The drawing that he **threw away** was a birthday present from his little brother.*
- When the verb is modified by an adverb, the adverb comes either at the end of the clause ...
  *She **paid back** the loan **immediately**.*
  or before the verb.
  *She **immediately paid back** the loan.*

Intransitive phrasal verbs

- Intransitive phrasal verbs do not take a direct object. Intransitive phrasal verbs are always **inseparable**.
  *We didn't think the idea would **catch on**, but sales are really **taking off!***

Transitive phrasal verbs	Intransitive phrasal verbs
bring up	break down
check out	catch on
clear up	eat out
look up	get by
pay back	keep away
pick up	pass out
put off	sell out
throw away	show off

Remember!
Some verbs have more than one meaning and some can have both a transitive and an intransitive meaning:
*I hope the plane **takes off** on time.*
*Please **take** your coat **off**.*

Prepositional verbs

- Prepositional verbs are followed by a preposition, e.g. *after, for, round*. They are always transitive and must be followed by a direct object. Prepositional verbs are **inseparable**. The direct object always comes after the preposition, even when it is a pronoun.
  *Both Sergei and Viktor **take after** their father. They **take after** him.*
- When a prepositional verb is modified by an adverb, the adverb cannot come after the preposition:
  *She **coped with** the crisis **magnificently**.*
  *She **coped magnificently with** the crisis.*
  ~~She coped with magnificently the crisis.~~

Phrasal-prepositional verbs

- Phrasal-prepositional verbs are followed by a particle and then a preposition. The particle and the preposition must always stay together.
  *He's **come up with** an incredible invention. He **came up with** it last month.*

Prepositional verbs	Prepositional-phrasal verbs
break into	catch up with
cope with	come up with
count on	do away with
deal with	face up to
get over	get away with
get rid of	look down on
go over	look forward to
take after	put up with

Grammar reference

1 Put the words in order to make sentences. Sometimes more than one answer is possible.

1 this / forward / I've / looking / months / to / party / for / been

2 put / let's / it / tomorrow / off / until.

3 car / has / that's / the / down / third time / week / my / broken / this

4 break / into / they / how / did / garage / manage / your / to / father's?

5 problem / the / he / brilliantly / dealt / with

6 check / home / I'll / out / I / it / get / when

2 Find and correct the mistakes in the sentences.

1 He went over patiently the explanation one more time.

2 She needs to face up what she has done to.

3 He brought up them on his own after his wife died.

4 I don't know why he looks down her on so much.

5 I don't feel like cooking – let's eat it out.

6 You need to get rid this rubbish of.

2C Focus on: Irreversible word pairs

An irreversible word pair (also known as a binomial word pair) is an expression that is made from a pair of words of the same type, e.g. two nouns, two adjectives or two verbs. These two words are usually joined by *and* or *or*.

The word order is fixed. The pairs of words are often words with a similar or related meaning, e.g. *clean and tidy* or words with an opposite meaning, e.g. *on and off*. Some of them are alliterative (the first letter of each word is the same), e.g. *safe and sound* and some rhyme, e.g. *meet and greet*.

Word pairs with *and*	Word pairs with *or*	Other types of word pairs
back and forth	give or take	all in all
clean and tidy	life or death	back to front
first and foremost	more or less	bit by bit
in and out	rain or shine	day in, day out
on and off	sooner or later	little by little
peace and quiet	win or lose	heart to heart
pick and choose		
plain and simple		
pros and cons		
safe and sound		
tried and tested		

1 Complete the email with these expressions.

back and forth	clean and tidy	little by little
out and about	peace and quiet	rain or shine
safe and sound		

Hi Marlee

Thanks for your email. I've settled in my new home really well, thank you, and am loving the ¹_____ of the countryside, far away from the chaos of urban life! I haven't had much time yet to get ²_____ and check out the area, but I know there are some beautiful villages around here.

I feel as if I'm surrounded by boxes, but, ³_____, I'm managing to get things unpacked – a few every day. I can't wait until everything is ⁴_____ – you know how much I hate mess! Anyway, come ⁵_____, I am determined to have all my friends round for a moving-in party on Saturday. I really hope you can come.

How is life with you? I was relieved to hear that you are back ⁶_____ from your holiday. That journey home sounded really scary! Are you still going ⁷_____ to London every day? I really hope you get some news about that transfer soon.

Hope to see you on Saturday night.

Kaye

2 Match the beginnings of the word pairs (1–6) with the endings (a–f). Then check your answers in a dictionary.

1 ups and   a wide
2 short and   b learn
3 far and   c ends
4 live and   d downs
5 odds and   e match
6 mix and   f sweet

UNIT 3

3B Grammar: Modals and related verbs

Modal verbs

- Modal verbs are used to express modalities like obligation, permission, necessity, ability, advice and speculation.
- Modal verbs do not change their form and are always followed by the infinitive.

Remember!
You do not use *do/does/did* with modal verbs.
*She knew they **must have left** because she **couldn't hear** them.*

can and could

- *Can and could* are used to express ability and permission. *Could* is the past tense of *can*.
- You can only use *could* to describe general ability, not ability on specific occasions.
  *I **could swim** before I could walk, but I still **can't dive**.*
  *The theatre was fully booked so we **couldn't** go, but luckily we ~~could~~ were able to get into the cinema.*
- *Could* and *can't* (but not *can*) are also used to express speculation.
  *That jacket **can't be** Marta's – it's too small – but it ~~can~~ **could be** Sairah's.*

may and might

- *May* and *might* are used to express speculation.
  *She **may be** at work or she **might have gone** to the gym.*
- *May* is also used to request or give permission.
  ***May** I **open** a window please – it's very hot in here.*

will and shall

- *Will* and *shall* are used to express the future, express willingness, announce decisions and make offers and promises.
  *They**'ll call** you back after lunch.*
- *Shall* is only used with *I* and *we*, and is more formal than *will*. It is usually used in the question form to make offers or suggestions.
  ***Shall** I **send** this parcel to the main office?*

must

- *Must* is used to express obligation (in the present) or certainty (in the present or perfect forms).
  *You **must tell** the office if you're going to be late.*
  *They **must have taken** the bus because their car's still here.*

should

- *Should* is used to express advice (in the present) or regret (in the perfect form).
  *It's going to rain later, so you **should take** an umbrella.*
  *I **shouldn't have forgotten** my grandmother's birthday.*
- You can also use *should* to express expectations.
  *I think the parcel **should arrive** tomorrow.*

would

- *Would* is the past tense of *will*.
  *She **wouldn't** even **read** his email.*
- *Would* is also used to make polite requests and offers and to express speculation.
  *I wish I had seen that show – I **would have loved** it.*

You can also use **semi-modal verbs** and other phrases to express some of the same modalities. These semi-modal verbs do not change their form, but otherwise they behave more like main verbs.

ought to and had better

- Use *ought to* and *had better* + infinitive to express advice.
  *You**'d better** / You **ought to** apologize to him now.*

- You can also use *ought to have* + past participle to express regret.
  *I **ought to have** apologized before he went out.*

be able to

- Use *be able to* to express ability, particularly on a specific occasion. It is used instead of *can* after other modals or after verbs that take the infinitive or the *-ing* form.
  *They **were able to break** the window and save the child.*
  *I remember **being able to understand** a film in German for the first time – it was amazing!*
  *You **will be able to** contact them after the 15th of August.*

be allowed to, be permitted to

- Use *be allowed to* and *be permitted to* to express permission. *Be permitted to* is more formal than *be allowed to*.
  *The children **aren't allowed to run** in the corridors.*
  *Members **are permitted to borrow** a maximum of five books at one time.*

be supposed to

- Use *be supposed to* to express obligations and arrangements.
  *You**'re supposed to buy** your ticket before you get on the bus.*
- You can also use it to express expectations.
  *It's **supposed to be** a beautiful day tomorrow.*
- When used in the negative form, it is weaker than *be allowed to*.
  *The children **aren't supposed to watch** TV before breakfast, but they often do at the weekend.*

have to

- Use *have to* to express obligation. While *must* suggests a self-imposed obligation, *have to* implies that there is an external obligation. You can use it to express the past or future, and after verbs that take the infinitive or *-ing* form.
  *You **have to complete** all the work before you can send your invoice.*
  *He**'ll have to talk** to his manager if he wants the day off.*
  *She **had to study** very hard during the holidays.*

don't have to, don't need to, needn't

- Use *don't have to* or *needn't* to express a lack of obligation. There is a slight difference in meaning between the two. *Don't have to* suggests that the activity is optional. *Needn't* suggests that it is not necessary.
  *Students **don't have to wear** a uniform at this school.*
  *You **needn't bring** a packed lunch – food is provided.*
- Use *needn't have* + past participle to say that something wasn't necessary but still happened. Use *didn't need to* + infinitive to say that something wasn't necessary but it might or might not have happened.
  *Jun **needn't have gone** to the supermarket; we had already been.* (Jun went to the supermarket)
  *I **didn't need to go** to the supermarket, so I stayed at home.* (I didn't go to the supermarket)

Grammar reference

Remember!
Your choice of modal can affect how formal a phrase sounds or the strength of its meaning.
*We **are supposed to** be there at five* is more informal and less strong than *We **have** to be there at five.*

1 Rewrite the sentences using these words.

| better | can't | might | needn't | ought | permitted |

1 It won't be necessary for us to bring our laptops to class.
   _____.

2 I would strongly advise you to wear smart clothes.
   _____.

3 Maybe they forgot about our meeting.
   _____.

4 It's not possible that he missed the train.
   _____.

5 You should hurry up if you don't want to be late.
   _____.

6 It is illegal to ride a motorbike without wearing a helmet.
   _____.

2 Decide whether the sentences have the same (S) or a different (D) meaning.

1 a She should have left earlier. _____
   b She ought to have left earlier. _____
2 a We didn't have to pay to get in. _____
   b We needn't have paid to get in. _____
3 a Could I look at your notes? _____
   b May I look at your notes? _____
4 a They might not have heard him. _____
   b They can't have heard him. _____

3C Focus on: Hedging in spoken English

Hedging – using cautious language – is used when you want to soften or reduce the effect of what you are saying. There are different ways to hedge.

Verbs

- You can use verbs like *seem to, appear to, tend to* to make what you say sound less certain or direct.
- *You can also begin statements with I think, I would suggest that, It appears to me, I feel* or *I suppose* to make opinions less direct.

Hedging	Direct
This product **seems to** be extremely popular.	This product is extremely popular.
Users **tend to** prefer the old software.	Users prefer the old software.
It appears to me to be a waste of money.	It's a waste of money.
I feel you're always late.	You're always late.

Adverbs

- Use modifying adverbs and expressions like *a bit, a little, almost, (not) really, rather, slightly, somewhat* to reduce the strength of a verb or an adjective. You can also use *not/never + very* and *(not) particularly/amazingly/super. Amazingly* and *super* are more colloquial.
- Use adverbs like *arguably, perhaps, probably,* or *maybe* to seem less certain about your statement.
- Use adverbs like *seemingly, apparently, allegedly,* to make statements less definite or direct.
- Use adverbs and adverb phrases like *sort of, kind of,* and (more formally) *somewhat* to make your statements more vague.

Hedging	Direct
The décor is **a little** old-fashioned	The décor is old-fashioned.
It isn't **really** very effective.	It isn't very effective.
We're **not particularly** impressed.	We're unimpressed.
Perhaps he's not happy here.	He's not happy here.
Apparently, it doesn't work.	It doesn't work.
She's **sort of** strange.	She's strange.
The room is **somewhat** small.	The room is small.

Expressions

Use the following expressions to limit the information or reduce the strength of what you are saying:

Hedging	Direct
I wouldn't really say that it's successful.	It isn't successful.
I don't know if I can say (that) I agree.	I disagree.
In all likelihood, it's broken.	It's broken.
To my knowledge, it hasn't been popular.	It hasn't been popular.
It isn't useful, **at least, not to me**.	It isn't useful.

1 Rewrite the statements to make them softer or less certain. Use the words in brackets.

1 She doesn't like the idea. (I wouldn't really say)

_____.

2 It's difficult to understand. (rather)

_____.

3 You need to check your information. (suggest)

_____.

4 The sofa is uncomfortable. (not amazingly)

_____.

5 They've never won a competition. (knowledge)

_____.

6 The garden is a mess. (appear)

_____.

2 Complete the short conversations with these expressions.

a little	It appears that
It wasn't particularly	I wouldn't really say
to my knowledge	

1 A: I hear that Lukas has been promoted.
  B: _____ it's a promotion. More of a change of role.

2 A: _____ you've annoyed quite a few people with your recent post.
  B: Well, I didn't mean to. But it's important to speak your mind.

3 A: What do your colleagues think about the new computer system?
  B: There haven't been any complaints, _____.

4 A: What do you think of this jacket?
  B: It's very unusual, but it's _____ too bright for me.

5 A: Did you learn a lot at the conference last weekend?
  B: _____ informative, but I met some very interesting people there.

UNIT 4

4B Grammar: Discourse markers

Discourse markers are words and expressions that organize or connect ideas, or express opinions when you speak. They can make you seem more fluent. You can also use discourse markers in writing, but these tend to be more formal.

Organizing ideas

Use these expressions to organize an argument or to begin, add to or end a list of ideas or suggestions: *for starters, to begin with, for one thing, secondly, on top of that, what's more.*

To begin with, I'm sure that he didn't mean to upset you. Ice skates would be a great gift, and, what's more, nobody else will have had the same idea.

Showing attitude or opinion

Use these expressions to show how you feel or to indicate the strength of your opinion: *to be perfectly honest, to say the least, literally, you name it, to tell (you) the truth, I must admit, if you ask me.*

I was literally crying with laughter. (to add emphasis)
Whatever you want to eat – you name it, he can make it for you. (used after an example or a list, to show it's one of many)

Clarifying

Use these expressions to make what you are saying clearer or to summarize your thoughts: *come to think of it, basically, so to speak, you know, I mean, as such, in fact, in other words, actually.*

She's not unfriendly, as such, it's just that she comes across as a bit distant.
They were walking along that street, you know, the street with all the cafes.

Introducing a different idea

Use these expressions to introduce a new or a different idea about the same topic into the conversation: *as a matter of fact, come to think of it, mind you, well, now you come to mention it, actually.*

Come to think of it, I was watching a documentary about that just the other day. (to show that one thing has reminded you of another)
He says he's finished it all. Mind you, there wasn't that much to do, was there?. (to make less of the thing you just mentioned)

Changing the direction of a conversation

Use these expressions to signal that you are moving from one topic to another: *anyway, at any rate.*

At any rate, we're not going to agree, so let's leave the decision to Freda.

Showing that you are listening/agreeing

Use these expressions to show that you are listening and that you agree with the speaker: *right, OK, fine, great, absolutely, definitely*

A: So, I think we're ready to go ahead with the project.
B: Right, well, let's get started.

1 Choose the correct option to complete the conversation. (The conversation continues on page 152).

A: Why are you so annoyed with Hisato?
B: Well, ¹*for starters, / mind you,* he forgot my birthday. And ²*so to speak / I must admit,* I was pretty upset about that – I know you reminded him a week ago.

Grammar reference

A: Oh dear. Yes, I did. ³*At any rate, / As a matter of fact,* I even sent him a text because I know he never listens to his voice messages.

B: ⁴*Absolutely / Basically.* There's no point in leaving him voice messages. And then, ⁵*to tell you the truth, / on top of that,* I saw on social media that he'd invited loads of our friends round to his place last night, but not us.

A: Really? Maybe he's just being a bit thoughtless. ⁶*I mean, / For one thing,* he's not trying to be unkind, is he?

A: Perhaps you're right. ⁷*Anyway, / Literally,* let's talk about what we're going to do this weekend.

2 Complete the exchanges with the most appropriate expression. Sometimes more than one answer is possible.

as a matter of fact	definitely	you know
to be perfectly honest	what's more	

1 A: How do you think Jon is coping with the new job?
  B: _____, I don't think he's coping at all well.

2 A: I love the new office design, don't you?
  B: _____. I think it's a huge improvement.

3 A: We need to spend more time listening to our customers.
  B: Yes, and, _____, we also need to give our staff more training.

4 A: It's the building on the corner, _____, the one with the red door.
  B: Oh yes – I've been there before. _____, I think my cousin works there.

4C   Focus on: Using the present tense to tell stories

You can use the present simple and the present continuous to tell stories in an informal or conversational context.

The use of the present tense can make a story seem more immediate to the reader or listener and can bring it to life. A story written in the present tense can convey the sense that the writer is actually speaking to us.

I'm walking along the street and suddenly I hear a loud noise. But where's it coming from? I look behind me, in front of me, to the left and to the right. Nothing. Then I hear the noise again. It's coming from above me.

You can also use the present tenses in the following ways:

To tell a joke
A man walks into a library and orders a cup of coffee. The librarian replies, 'This is a library.' The man apologizes and then whispers, 'Can I have a cup of coffee, please?'

To summarize the plot of a film or book
I've just read this book about a woman who moves to Australia and then tries to set up a surfing school.

To relate a fable
A hare and a tortoise are arguing about which of them is the fastest. Finally, they decide to have a race …

To describe events on a timeline
The first wind turbines are built in around 600 CE. Just one hundred years later, the Chinese invent gunpowder and fireworks.

1 Write a short story from the prompts, using present tenses.

One day / hungry fox / in a garden / see / delicious grapes / try to jump up / can't reach / finally / give up / say / grapes / very sour

_____

_____

UNIT 5

5B   Grammar: Adding emphasis with cleft sentences

Cleft sentences can be used to add emphasis to certain words or ideas. Made up of two clauses, there are three main types:

It + be + emphasized word or phrase + relative pronoun + relative clause

• With this structure, the word or phrase you want to emphasize comes after *It + be* and before the relative pronoun.
  *It was **Kyoto** where I first fell in love.*
  *It was **Yukio** whom I fell in love with.*
  *It was **his sense of humour** that I liked about him.*

• Even if the word you want to emphasize is plural, you still use the singular form of the verb *be*.
  *It was **his bright purple shoes** that I first noticed.*

The + category word + relative pronoun, relative clause + be + emphasized word or phrase

• With this structure, mention the category of thing in the first clause with the correct relative pronoun, then the thing you want to emphasize at the end of the second clause.
  *The place where I first fell in love was **Kyoto**.*
  *The person who I fell in love with was **Yukio**.*
  *The thing that I liked about him was **his sense of humour**.*
  *The reason why we split up was that **I had to return to Australia**.*
  *The time when we were together was **the best time in my life**.*

Wh- clause + *be* + emphasized word or phrase.

- With this structure, the thing you want to emphasize goes at the end of the sentence. The most common *wh* word used here is *What.*

  What I liked about him was **his amazing sense of humour.**

  Why we split up was because **I had to return to Australia.**

- You can also use *All / Something / One thing / The thing* in place of *What.*

  One thing (that) I regret was that I didn't keep in touch with him.

- If you want to emphasize an action, use the structure *What + subject + do + be (to) + infinitive… or What + happened + be (that) + clause.*

  What he did was (to) send me flowers every week.

  What happened was (that) he sent me flowers every week.

1 Find and correct the mistakes in the sentences.

1 The day when she passed her driving test it was the proudest day of her life.

2 All I want to say that I completely disagree with you.

3 It were the photographs that they first noticed.

4 What I couldn't understand that why he was so angry.

5 What she does is posting every detail of her life on social media.

6 The person what impressed them the most was a young architecture student.

2 Rewrite the sentences using cleft structures.

1 They enjoyed the beautiful music.
  What _____.

2 The expression on his face scared her.
  It was _____.

3 They forgot to switch it on.
  What happened
  _____.

4 I used to work in a tiny office in the city centre.
  The place _____.

5 She could only wait for their reply.
  All she _____.

5C Focus on: Negative and limiting adverbials

- You can use inversion with negative and limiting adverbials to add emphasis to the verb. Examples of adverbials include: *hardly /scarcely … before/when, in no way, little, never, never before, no sooner … than, not only … but also, nowhere, seldom.*

- The word order of the inverted sentence is: adverbial + auxiliary verb + subject.

  She had hardly left the room before they started laughing.

  → *Hardly had she left* the room before they started laughing.

  He borrowed my laptop without asking me and then broke it!

  → *Not only did he borrow* my laptop without asking me, but he also broke it.

- If the auxiliary verb is negative in the original sentence, it becomes positive in the inverted sentence.

  I don't agree with you.

  → *In no way do I agree* with you.

  They didn't know that the document had already been copied.

  → *Little did they know* that the document had already been copied.

- In sentences with two clauses, the negative adverbial is placed before the subordinate clause and the inversion happens in the main clause.

main clause		subordinate clause

  I only realized I had been burgled when I saw the window.

  → *Not until* I saw the window *did I realize* that I had been burgled.

  → *Only when* I saw the window, *did I realize* that I had been burgled.

1 Rewrite the sentences to make them more emphatic.

1 She had never been so scared before.
  Never before _____.

2 The phone rang as soon as I had started to eat.
  No sooner _____.

3 They had never been anywhere that was so cold.
  Never _____.

4 We didn't know that we were being watched.
  Little _____.

5 I didn't mean to upset you.
  In no way _____.

6 They only stopped for lunch after they had been travelling for four hours.
  Only after _____.

2 Match the beginnings of the sentences (1-6) with the endings (a-f)

1 Never before have I

2 Scarcely had she

3 In no way do I

4 No sooner had he come on stage

5 Not only did they apologize,

6 Little did they

a left the house when the storm began.

b they also bought him a gift.

c felt so angry.

d than all the lights went out.

e realize that all the money had been spent.

f want to suggest she was to blame.

Grammar reference

UNIT 6

6B Grammar: Alternative conditionals

Conditional structures are used to speculate about what could happen or might have happened.

- The conditional clause usually begins with *if* and describes the condition. The other clause describes the result.
- The sentence can start with the conditional clause or the result clause. If it starts with the result clause clause, you don't put a comma between the clauses.

There are four main types of conditional sentences.

Zero conditional

- The zero (or real) conditional describes a real condition that leads to an inevitable result. It is usually used for general truths.
- To form the zero conditional, you usually use *If/When* + present simple, … present simple.

  If I **stay** *up too late, I* **feel** *terrible the next day.*

- You can also use other tenses in zero conditional sentences such as:

If/When + present continuous, … present continuous

  If he **'s checking** *his social media all the time, he* **'s not** *really* **focusing** *on his work.*

If/When + past simple, past simple

  When they worked on Sundays, they **were** *paid more.*

If/When + past continuous, … past simple

  If it **was raining**, *she always* **took** *the bus to school.*

First conditional

- The first conditional describes the likely result of an imagined situation in the future.
- To form the first conditional, you usually use *If/When* + present simple/present continuous/present perfect, … *will/going to* + infinitive.

  If he **gets** *the promotion, he* **'s going to move** *closer to the office.*
  I'll call you when I get the news.

- You can also use other modal verbs, such as *shall/could/should/would/can/may/might* in the result clause or an imperative form.

  If he **isn't replying** *to your emails, (you* **should***) call him.*
  If you **haven't finished** *the work yet,* **don't expect** *payment.*

Second conditional

- The second conditional describes a possible but less likely result of an imagined situation in the present or future.
- To form the second conditional, you usually use *If* + past simple/past continuous, … *would* + infinitive.

  If you **were working** *for a bigger company, you* **'d have** *far less independence.*
  I'd buy a new car if I had more money.

- You can use *were to* + infinitive as an alternative to the past simple in the condition clause. The use of *were to* often emphasizes the improbability of the condition.

  If you **were to lose** *this money, it* **would be** *a disaster.*

- You can also use other modal verbs such as *should/could/might* in the result clause.

  If you were listening, you **might understand** *the lesson.*

Third conditional

- The third conditional describes the imagined results of past events or situations that didn't actually happen.
- To form the third conditional, you usually use *If* + past perfect/past perfect continuous, … *would have* + past participle.

  If I'd seen you, I **would have said** *hello.*

- You can also use other modal verbs such as *should have/could have/might have* in the result clause.

  If we **'d been living** *in that house at the time, we* **might have met** *him.*

- You can also start a sentence in the third conditional and end it using the second conditional. See 'Mixed conditionals'.

Mixed conditionals

Mixed conditionals are used to refer to different times in the condition clause and the result clause.

Past	Present
If you had paid more attention in class,	*you wouldn't be panicking about your exams now.*

Future	Past
If you're going to leave the country,	*you should have sorted out your visa.*

Present	Past
If you were taller,	*you could have played for the school basketball team.*

Alternatives to *if*

You can use other words and phrases to introduce the conditional clauses:

- *Unless* means 'if not'.
  I won't open the window **unless** *you turn down the music.*
- *As long as* or *provided (that)* are used to describe a specific condition needed for a result to take place.
  You can borrow my laptop **as long as** *you give it back by tomorrow lunchtime.*
- *Supposing* or *assuming* mean 'imagine if'.
  Supposing *they didn't return your call – what would you do then?*

1 Rewrite the sentences using a conditional structure and the word in brackets.

1 If you can't afford to buy it, what will you do? (supposing)

_____

2 She didn't answer the teacher's question and now she is in trouble. (if)

_____.

3 I'd be surprised if I won that competition. (were to)

_____.

4 You can go to your friend's house, but you have to call me when you get there. (as long as)

_____.

5 If you don't think it's important, you shouldn't waste time on it. (unless)

_____.

6 They didn't read the instructions and now the machine isn't working. (if)

_____.

2 Complete the sentences with *unless*, *supposing* or *provided that*.

1 I wouldn't have called you _____ it was urgent.

2 _____ you win the prize, what will you do?

3 _____ you can give us more information, we really can't help you.

4 She'll accept the position _____ they offer her a bonus.

5 _____ you get the work done in time, you can start whenever you want to.

6 _____ the bus doesn't come soon - should we call a taxi?

6C Focus on: Compound adjectives

Compound adjectives are made up of two or more words.

- When the adjective comes before the noun, use hyphens between the adjectives to make it clear that they are all modifying the same noun.

  *I've read the **twenty-five-page** document.* (I've read one document with twenty-five pages.)

  *I've read the twenty **five-page** documents.* (I've read twenty documents, each with five pages.)

  Remember!
  With compound nouns made up of a number + a noun, the noun remains singular. NOT ~~the twenty-five-pages document.~~

- However, if the adjective follows the noun, hyphens are generally not used.

  *He's a **well-known** singer.*

  *That singer is very **well known**.*

- Compound adjectives can be formed by:

noun + noun

*It's a **part-time** job.*

noun + adjective

*Welcome to our **family-friendly** restaurant.*

noun + present participle

*This is a **time-saving** device.*

noun + past participle

*It's got a **solar-powered** battery.*

adjective + noun

*I've booked a **last-minute** holiday.*

adjective + present participle

*There is a lot of **slow-moving** traffic tonight.*

adjective + past participle

*My grandmother was a very **kind-hearted** woman.*

adverb + present participle

*This is beginning to feel like a **never-ending** nightmare.*

adverb + past participle

*You have a very **well-equipped** kitchen.*

However, you don't need a hyphen with an -ly adverb.

*We live in a **densely populated** part of the city.*

1 Complete the sentences with these words.

behaved	famous	fashioned
minded	catching	to-date

1 You need to make sure that you're using the most up-_____ information.

2 She's not a very well-_____ child, and often gets into trouble at school.

3 My aunt was a very open-_____ woman and always listened to other people's opinions.

4 No-one could miss the bright, eye-_____ poster that was on the classroom door.

5 It's quite an old-_____ restaurant – in fact, I don't think the menu has changed for years!

6 She's a world-_____ soprano and she will be performing at the City Hall next month.

2 Match the beginnings (1-6) with the endings (a-f).

1 We now have a two-

2 I tried a fat-

3 He's certainly a very good-

4 My sister has got a meat-

5 Congratulations on your record-

6 Snakes, bees, frogs and sharks are all examples of cold-

a looking man, but he's thinks a lot of himself.

b breaking achievement.

c week wait until we find out the results of the election.

d blooded animals.

e eating plant in her bedroom.

f free frozen yoghurt yesterday and it was a bit tasteless.

Grammar reference

UNIT 7

7B Grammar: Continuous aspect

Form the continuous aspect with *be + -ing*. Use the continuous aspect in past, present or future tenses to describe:

Actions that continue for some time

They've been working on that project for months.
He's joined an expedition to Norway and will be sailing around the Oslo Fjord for the next month.

Actions that are in progress at a specific time or during another, sometimes shorter, action

We'll definitely be in tomorrow evening as we'll be watching the football match on TV.
I dropped my phone while I was looking out of the window.

Actions that are repeated

The use of the continuous aspect often implies irritation from the speaker.

I've been trying to call you since eight o'clock this morning.
He's always losing his glasses.

Temporary situations

We're staying in a hotel until we can find longer-term accommodation.
He'll be working in the Frankfurt office for the next couple of months.

Changing situations

Your work has been improving recently.
That crack on the wall is getting bigger.

Future arrangements

We're meeting at the cinema tomorrow afternoon.
Will you be joining us for supper?

State verbs

Some verbs are not usually used in the continuous aspect when they describe a state:

- Verbs of perception, e.g. *hear, recognize, notice, see, smell, taste, feel,* etc.
- Verbs of thinking, e.g. *agree, believe, expect, forget, know, mind, realize, remember, suppose, think, understand,* etc.
- Verbs of possession, e.g. *belong to, contain, have, own, owe, possess,* etc.
- Verbs of emotion, e.g. *dislike, forgive, hate, like, love, prefer, refuse, want, wish,* etc.
  I want to get a new phone.

However, they are sometimes used in the continuous form if the speaker wants to emphasize the temporary nature of the action or in more colloquial speech.

He's been having a difficult time recently.
I've been wanting to get a new phone for months.
I'm liking the hair cut!

- Some verbs e.g. *think, hear, taste* can also be used in the continuous with a slightly different meaning.

What do you think of my jacket?
  She's thinking of changing her university course.
We heard them return.
  We've been hearing a lot about this latest trend.
It tastes really sweet.
  She's tasting the soup, to make sure that it's got enough salt in it.

1 Choose the correct option to complete the sentences.

1 *Do you remember / Are you remembering* your first day at school?
2 I *think / 'm thinking* of moving to Ecuador.
3 This pudding *tastes / is tasting* delicious.
4 I think you *are / are being* a bit selfish about this.
5 *Do they see / Are they seeing* their grandmother tomorrow?
6 We *hadn't realized / hadn't been realizing* that the laptop was so expensive.

2 Complete the sentences with the correct continuous form of the verbs in brackets.

1 He cut himself while he _____ (prepare) supper.
2 Why are you so late? I _____ (wait) for you for twenty minutes!
3 She _____ (try) to call them for hours when she realized that she had the wrong number.
4 I _____ (work) on my project all morning tomorrow, so I can't see you until the afternoon.
5 They _____ (always / complain) about the weather.
6 He _____ (teach) our class this term while our usual teacher is on maternity leave.

7C Focus on: Homophones and homographs

Homophones

Homophones are words that are spelled differently and have a different meaning, but have the same pronunciation.

/naɪt/	knight, night
/ˈflaʊə/	flour, flower
/həʊl/	hole, whole
/ˈaʊə/	hour, our
/dɪə/	dear, deer
/hɪə/	hear, here
/piːs/	peace, piece
/pɔː/	poor, pour

Homographs

Homographs are words that are spelled the same, but have a different meaning.

- Some homographs have a different pronunciation, e.g. *row* /rəʊ/ and *row* /raʊ/

  *All the chairs were arranged in a **row** /rəʊ/.*
  *We had a huge **row** /raʊ/ with our neighbours about their noisy dog.*

- Some homographs have the same pronunciation, e.g. *bat* /bæt/.

  I saw a bat /bæt/ fly out of the old shed.
  I hit the ball with my bat /bæt/.

1 Read the pairs of sentences. Decide if the underlined homographs have the same (S) or a different (D) pronunciation.

1 a I could see a <u>tear</u> on her cheek.
  b Be careful! You're going to <u>tear</u> your jacket.

2 a We <u>live</u> in a small apartment by the river.
  b I saw this band perform <u>live</u> at the Nippon Budokan in Tokyo.

3 a I enjoyed the film, but I really couldn't <u>bear</u> the music.
  b My favourite toy when I was a child was a small brown teddy <u>bear</u>.

4 a Let's light the candle. Have you got a <u>match</u>?
  b Did you watch the football <u>match</u> last night?

5 a It's very stormy tonight. I can hear the <u>wind</u> in the trees.
  b You need to <u>wind</u> the rope around the post several times.

6 a She is tall, with <u>fair</u> hair and blue eyes.
  b Our college is holding a <u>fair</u> at the weekend to raise money for charity.

2 Complete the sentences with the correct word from these pairs of homophones.

---

allowed / aloud   bare / bear   berries / buries
genes / jeans   brake / break   weather / whether

---

1 What's the _____ going to be like tomorrow?
2 I love walking on the grass in my _____ feet.
3 I'm pretty good at music – I guess it must be in my _____.
4 You've been working all morning – I think you should take a _____.
5 Our dog always _____ his toys in the garden.
6 Using mobile phones is not _____ in the library.

UNIT 8

8B Grammar: Dependent prepositions

Some nouns, verbs, and adjectives are always followed by specific prepositions. These prepositions come before the object of the verb. Dependent prepositions are either followed by a noun …

  *She **apologized for** her behaviour.*
  *He's really **terrified of** spiders.*
  *It was the **result of** many years of hard work.*

or a gerund (*-ing* form of a verb).

  *She **apologized for shouting** at them.*
  *He's really **terrified of finding** a spider in his room.*
  *It was the **result of working** hard for many years.*

noun + preposition	verb + preposition	adjective + preposition
attitude towards	believe in	fed up with
commitment to	commit to	good at
demand for	choose between	guilty of
flair for	concentrate on	keen on
impact on	focus on	opposed to
mastery of	insist on	popular with
passion for	laugh at	serious about
reaction to	refer to	skilled in
reduction in	stem from	suspicious of
talent for	succeed at	unaware of

1 Complete the sentences with these prepositions. Then check your answers in a dictionary.

---

about   for   from   in   of   to

---

1 She's simply incapable _____ making any decisions.
2 He suffers _____ very bad migraines.
3 There's been a sharp decrease _____ sales over the last year.
4 Who is responsible _____ health and safety in this office?
5 We've all been feeling very anxious _____ the exams next week.
6 Can anyone suggest a solution _____ this problem?

Grammar reference

2 Complete the text with the correct prepositions.

How to be a Success!

Do you have a passion [1] _____ your job, but at the same time, sometimes find it difficult to concentrate [2] _____ your work? Many people are unaware [3] _____ the simple, but effective strategies that can help them become more successful. In our one-day workshop, we will teach you some techniques to help you focus [4] _____ the important things in life and avoid all the distractions. If you're serious [5] _____ reaching the next level in your career or in your studies, book a place on our workshop now!

'Dan's one-day workshop had an incredible impact [6] _____ my life. I would recommend it to anyone!'

8C Focus on: Using the definite article with natural features

Use the definite article, *the* before:

- plural countries
  *the Netherlands, **the** Philippines*
- groups of islands (but not individual islands, except the Isle of Man/Wight, etc.)
  *the British Isles, **the** Florida Keys*
- countries whose names include *Republic, Kingdom, States*
  *the Czech Republic, **the** Kingdom of Bahrain, **the** United States of America*
- points on the globe or specific geographical areas
  *the South Pole, **the** West Coast of Italy, **the** Highlands of Scotland, **the** North*
- rivers, seas, and oceans
  *the River Danube, **the** Atlantic Ocean, **the** Caspian Sea*
- groups of lakes (but not individual lakes)
  *the Lake District, **the** Italian Lakes*
  ~~the~~ Lake Windemere, ~~the~~ Lake Como
- mountain ranges (but not individual mountains)
  *the Rockies, **the** Pyrenees*
  ~~the~~ Mount Elbert, ~~the~~ Mount Perdido
- deserts, forests, gulfs, and peninsulas
  *the Sahara Desert, **the** Black Forest, **the** Gulf of Mexico, **the** Baja Peninsula*
- names of buildings (but not airports, stations, or most universities)
  *the Colosseum, **the** Pentagon*
  ~~the~~ Paddington Station, ~~the~~ Tokyo Haneda Airport, ~~the~~ Cambridge University

proper nouns that include *of*
  *the Gardens of Babylon, **the** Bay of Biscay*

- You also use the definite article with a singular noun to refer to a whole group of items, for example, names of animals or plants. (If you use a plural noun, don't use *the*.)
  The blue whale is the largest mammal alive today.
  Insects usually have six legs and three body parts. NOT ~~The insects~~ …
  The redwood tree can grow to over 100 metres in height.
- Don't use an article before streets, roads, cities, towns, lakes, continents, most countries, islands or waterfalls.

1 Read the travel blog and add *the* where necessary.

We're really enjoying our tour around [1] _____ west coast of [2] _____ Ireland. Yesterday we went to [3] _____ Galway – it's a beautiful city. We spent the morning checking out all the cool shops on [4] _____ Quay Street, before having lunch at a charming restaurant by [5] _____ River Corrib. Today we've booked a 90-minute boat trip to [6] _____ Inis Mór on [7] _____ Aran Islands. Can't wait! I'm hoping we'll get to [8] _____ Cliffs of Moher tomorrow – they were in *Harry Potter*!

2 Find and correct the mistakes in the sentences.

1 Palace of Versailles, in the Paris, is a place that I've always wanted to visit.
2 Last time I visited United States, I climbed to the top of the Mount Michell in the Appalachian Mountains.
3 Asian elephant lives in India and South East Asia.
4 Equator passes through 13 countries, including the Uganda and Maldives.
5 Have you ever swum in the Lake Bled in Slovenia?
6 Ionian Islands are situated in Ionian Sea, to the west of Greece.

UNIT 9

9B Grammar: Ellipsis and substitution

In English, especially in informal conversation, you can often leave out unnecessary words and expressions or replace them with shorter words. When you leave out parts of the language, this is called *ellipsis*. When you replace words and phrases with other, shorter, words or phrases, this is called *substitution*.

Ellipsis

- After linkers. You can leave out a repeated subject after the linkers *and, but, then* and *or*.
  We went to the beach and (we) swam in the sea.
  He understood what I was saying, but (he) didn't reply.

- After auxiliary verbs. You can leave out a repeated verb or verb phrases after an auxiliary or a modal verb.

  They all thought it was hilarious but I didn't (think it was hilarious).

  You may not want to work tomorrow, but I think you should (work tomorrow).

  A: He can't possibly eat that whole cake.

  B: He just did (eat that whole cake)!

- After verb + *to* infinitive. You can leave out a repeated infinitive after a verb + *to* infinitive.

  I wouldn't talk to him again even if he begged me to (talk to him).

  A: Will you be at the party tomorrow?

  B: Yes, I intend to (be at the party).

- With relative clauses. You can reduce relative clauses in different ways. You can delete the relative pronoun and the verb *be* when:

  the main verb is in the active voice and in a continuous tense

  The man (who was) swimming in the sea looked tired.

  My sister, (who was) not concentrating, missed the turning.

  the main verb is in the passive voice and in a simple or continuous tense.

  I live in a house (that is) covered in ivy.

  I'm enjoying the series (which is) being shown on Netflix at the moment.

  We read a book (that had been) written by our teacher.

- in informal spoken English. In conversation, you often leave out words that are assumed to be obvious from the context. These include …

  pronouns and auxiliary verbs.

  (I'm) Going out for a walk. (Do you) Want to come?

  (Have you) Seen the latest Spielberg film?

  the first word or words in fixed expressions.

  (As a) Matter of fact, I've never really understood why it's so popular.

  definite articles at the beginning of short sentences a.

  (The) Sofa's looking a bit dirty.

  (The) Window cleaner's outside. (He) Says he's got a message for you.

Substitution

- With *so* and *not*. After verbs of thinking, e.g. *imagine*, *suppose*, *think*, *assume*, *believe*, *expect*, *guess*, *hope*, use *so* to substitute positive clauses.

  A: Did she listen to your suggestion?

  *B: I think she listened to it. → 'I think **so**.*

- After the verbs *assume*, *guess*, *hope* and *imagine*, use *not* to substitute negative clauses.

  A: Are you going to be late again?

  *B: I hope I'm not going to be late again. → I hope **not**.*

- After other verbs of thinking, you usually use the negative form of the verb followed by *so* to substitute negative clauses.

  A: Will you be there tomorrow?

  *B: I suppose I won't be there tomorrow. → I **don't** suppose **so**.*

- With *do*. You can substitute a verb and the phrase that follows it with *do, do the same, do so* or *do too*.

  A: They often take the bus to school.

  *B: We often take the bus to school too. → We **do too**. / We **do the same**. / So do we.*

- You can use *either* + the negative form of the verb, or *neither* to make the clause negative.

  A: They never drive to school

  *B: We also never drive to school. → **Neither do** we. / We **don't either**.*

1 Use ellipsis to make the sentences shorter.

1 I can tell that she doesn't understand me, even though she pretends to understand me.

2 The car which is being fixed doesn't belong to me.

3 She's been to Los Angeles three times, but her sister hasn't been to Los Angeles.

4 The taxi's here!

5 I ordered a dress that had been designed by Versace.

6 A: Why don't you ask for a pay rise?

   B: I can't ask for a pay rise. I've only been working here for two months.

2 Complete the conversation with these phrases.

I guess not   Neither do I   I do too
I assume so   You have too

Maja: Do you think Inés is annoyed with us?

Freja: ¹ _____. I don't know why, though.

Maja: ² _____. But she hasn't replied to my last three texts. I hate it when she gets like this.

Freja: ³ _____. It really gets me down. And she probably won't come to the party tomorrow.

Maja: ⁴ _____. Well, it's a real pity, because I think you've tried really hard to include her in things.

Freja: ⁵ _____. We've all made a big effort. Oh well, let's not give up!

9C Focus on: Expressing change and trends

Continuous structures

- You can use continuous structures to focus on the changing nature of an activity (see also the notes for 7B).

  They're building a new development in the city centre. (Buildings are being added).

  He's been spending more time with his sister recently. (He didn't use to spend so much time with her.)

  We were starting to feel unwelcome. (Previously we had felt welcome).

Grammar reference

Verbs to describe general change: *become* and *get*

- The verbs *become* and *get* can both be used to express change. *Get* is used more informally.

  *Towards the end of summer, the days suddenly **got** much warmer.*

  *It **became** impossible to understand what he was doing.*

Verbs to describe changes in appearance or behaviour: *go, turn*

- You can often use the verb *go* to describe changes in appearance or behaviour, or changes to food.

  *She's **going** grey.*

  *These bananas are **going** off.*

- Use the verb *turn* to describe sudden or extreme changes in appearance or behaviour.

  *He **turned** bright red and left the room.*

  *The atmosphere in the room suddenly **turned** hostile.*

Verbs to describe upward and downward changes

Verbs to describe upward trends	Verbs to describe downward trends
increase	decrease
climb	drop
grow	decline
rise	fall
improve	worsen
reach a peak	hit a low

*After **increasing** steadily over several months, sales **reached a peak** in February and then **dropped** suddenly, **falling** to just 20% of their monthly average in April.*

Verbs to describe general changes

- Other verbs to describe change include: *transform, adapt, alter, convert, modify, revise*

  *The house was **transformed** after the garage was **converted** to a fourth bedroom.*

Nouns to describe upward and downward changes

Nouns to describe upward trends	Nouns to describe downward trends
increase	decrease
growth	drop
rise	fall

*The **decrease** in popularity of these toys has been unexpected, but we are optimistic about a possible **growth** in interest following the recent viral video.*

Nouns to describe general changes

- Other nouns to describe change include: *change, adaptation, modification.*

  *They had to make several **adaptations** to the product before it was ready for market.*

1 Complete the description of this graph with these words.

---

drop   growth   low   peak   falling   rose

Annual Sales

Monthly sales in January were at $10000. They
1 _____ to $15,000 in February but then there
was a steady 2 _____ until May, where they hit
a 3 _____ of $8000. From May to July, there
was another 4 _____ in sales, and after suddenly
5 _____ sharply to $10,000 in August, they
reached a 6 _____ of $18,000 in September.

2 Choose the correct option to complete the sentences.

1 Don't eat that bread! It's *going / becoming* mouldy.

2 Things have *gone / got* rather difficult since I lost my job.

3 I hardly recognized the area. It's been *transformed / adapted* in the last couple of years!

4 Electric cars are *becoming / declining* increasingly popular.

5 She suddenly *turned / went* nasty when she saw the evidence.

6 Although the figures are low now, we're optimistic that they will *improve / worsen* soon.

UNIT 10

10B Grammar: The future in the past

To describe predictions or plans for the future which were made in the past, use the past continuous, the past tense of *will* or *going to*; or the past tense of future time expressions.

Plans or arrangements made in the past

- To describe set arrangements made in the past, use the past continuous.

  *You knew what the plans were – you **were meeting** us in the café after the film.*

  *I had an early night as the following day I **was catching** a six a.m. train to Italy.*

- To describe plans made in the past, use *was/were going to* + infinitive.

  *She **was going to call** them as soon as she got to her hotel.*

  *What **were** you **going to do** if we hadn't been there?*

Predictions made in the past

- To describe predictions, offers or promises made in the past, use *would/wouldn't*.

  *We thought he **would be** famous by the time he was thirty.*

  *They promised they **would return** home before dark.*

  *She said she **would help** me look for my bag.*

Past tense of future time expressions

- You can also use the past tense of certain time expressions to express the future in the past.

- To describe something that was going to happen very soon in the past, use *was/were about to* + infinitive; *was/were on the point of* + -ing or *was/were on the verge of* + -ing.

  *We **were about to leave** when we realized that we hadn't closed the window.*

  *He **was on the point of giving up** when he saw her in the distance.*

  *I was **on the verge of leaving** when they finally turned up.*

- To describe something that was probably going to happen in the past, use *was/were likely* or *unlikely to* + infinitive.

  *With its limited budget, the school **was unlikely to invest** in new computers.*

  *As **it was likely to rain** in the afternoon, we decided to stay at home.*

- To describe something that was extremely likely to happen in the past, use *was/were bound to* + infinitive.

  *They **were bound to find out** that she had been lying.*

  *We all knew he was **bound to be** furious.*

- To describe an obligation or an arrangement in the past, particularly in a formal context, use *was/were to* + infinitive.

  *We **were to collect** the documents from the embassy before six o'clock that evening.*

  *He **was to begin** his new job that September.*

1 Rewrite the sentences using the words in brackets.

1 She planned to travel by bus across India. (going to)
   She _____.

2 He made a promise to send a postcard to his grandmother. (would)
   He promised _____.

3 It was extremely likely that we were going to get into trouble (bound)
   We _____.

4 They probably weren't going to pass the exam. (unlikely)
   They _____.

5 We had to send our financial report to them by the end of the week. (were to)
   We _____.

6 The flight was timetabled to depart at 14.00 the next day. (departing)
   The flight _____.

2 Choose the correct options to complete the story.

We had made all our plans. We ¹*were going to take / were on the point of taking* the Trans-Siberian Express from Moscow to Vladivostok. The train ²*was leaving / was likely to leave* Moscow Station at eight in the morning and we couldn't wait. We knew we ³*were to / were bound to* meet new people, see amazing sights and have exciting new experiences. My uncle and aunt had promised they ⁴*were meeting / would meet* us at Vladivostok and take us on a tour of the city. We got up very early that morning and were ⁵*on the verge of leaving / bound to leave* our hostel room when I suddenly realized that my purse, with our tickets in, was missing. I ⁶*would start / was about to start* panicking when my phone rang. It was the manager of the hostel. 'You left your purse at the reception desk last night,' he said.

Grammar reference

10C Focus on: Expressions with *take*

There are many different expressions that include the verb *take*.

take up

- You can use *take up* to mean 'start' a hobby or a sport.
  *I've recently **taken up** skateboarding.*
- You can also use *take up* to mean 'fill an amount of' space, time or attention.
  *The wardrobe **takes up** too much space in this room.*
  *Our whole afternoon was completely **taken up with** boring meetings.*

take over

- If something *takes over (something)*, it becomes bigger or more important than something else.
  *We've allowed this issue to **take over** our lives.*

Take over also means 'assume control of' a business, a country or a group.

  *He has **taken over** as manager of the company.*

take into account

- When you *take something into account*, you consider or include it when you're judging or deciding about something else.
  *It's important to **take into account** all the money we've spent on advertising.*
  *You should **take** her personal situation **into account** before you criticize her.*

take someone's word for it

- Use this fixed expression to mean 'believe what someone says'.
  *You don't have **to take my word for it** – just look at the results.*
  *He promised that he wasn't involved and I'm prepared to **take his word for it**.*

take one's time

- When you tell someone to *take their time*, you are saying that they don't need to hurry.
  ***Take your time** – we're not expecting a reply before next week.*
- You can also say that someone *took their time* to imply that they didn't make an effort to hurry.
  *I'm glad that you're here now, but you certainly **took your time**!*

1 Complete the sentences with the correct form of one of the expressions with *take* from the examples above.

1 You should always _____ the weather _____ when you are planning a hike.
2 You can _____, this is going to be a very popular event.
3 Our organization _____ by a large corporation last year.
4 I'm afraid my time is completely _____ with work at the moment.
5 If you relax and _____, you should be able to work out the answer.

2 Match the beginnings of the sentences (1-6) with the endings (a-f)

1 Please don't take
2 You should take
3 You didn't take
4 Don't let your feelings take
5 I know that a lot of your time is taken

a his feelings into account when you wrote that email.
b up with your studies, but don't forget to see your friends.
c my word for it – try it out for yourself.
d your time before you make a decision like this.
e over – just try to stay calm.

Irregular verbs

INFINITIVE	PAST SIMPLE	PAST PARTICIPLE
be	was / were	been
beat	beat	beaten
become	became	become
begin	began	begun
bite	bit	bitten
blow	blew	blown
break	broke	broken
bring	brought	brought
build	built	built
burn	burned / burnt	burned / burnt
buy	bought	bought
catch	caught	caught
choose	chose	chosen
come	came	come
cost	cost	cost
cut	cut	cut
deal	dealt	dealt
dig	dug	dug
do	did	done
dream	dreamed / dreamt	dreamed / dreamt
drink	drank	drunk
drive	drove	driven
eat	ate	eaten
fall	fell	fallen
feel	felt	felt
fight	fought	fought

INFINITIVE	PAST SIMPLE	PAST PARTICIPLE
find	found	found
fly	flew	flown
forget	forgot	forgotten
forgive	forgave	forgiven
freeze	froze	frozen
get	got	got
give	gave	given
go	went	gone
grow	grew	grown
have	had	had
hear	heard	heard
hide	hid	hidden
hit	hit	hit
hold	held	held
hurt	hurt	hurt
keep	kept	kept
know	knew	known
lay	laid	laid
lead	led	led
leave	left	left
learn	learned / learnt	learned / learnt
lend	lent	lent
let	let	let
lie	lay	lain
lose	lost	lost
make	made	made

Irregular verbs

INFINITIVE	PAST SIMPLE	PAST PARTICIPLE
mean	meant	meant
meet	met	met
pay	paid	paid
put	put	put
read	read	read
ride	rode	ridden
ring	rang	rung
rise	rose	risen
run	ran	run
say	said	said
see	saw	seen
sell	sold	sold
send	sent	sent
set	set	set
shake	shook	shaken
shine	shone	shone
shoot	shot	shot
show	showed	shown
shut	shut	shut
sing	sang	sung
sit	sat	sat
sleep	slept	slept
smell	smelled / smelt	smelled / smelt
speak	spoke	spoken
spell	spelled / spelt	spelled / spelt

INFINITIVE	PAST SIMPLE	PAST PARTICIPLE
spend	spent	spent
spoil	spoiled / spoilt	spoiled / spoilt
spread	spread	spread
stand	stood	stood
steal	stole	stolen
stick	stuck	stuck
swear	swore	sworn
swim	swam	swum
take	took	taken
teach	taught	taught
tell	told	told
think	thought	thought
throw	threw	thrown
understand	understood	understood
wake	woke	woken
wear	wore	worn
win	won	won
write	wrote	written

Extra speaking tasks

PAGE 18, 1D, EXERCISE 3

QUIZ ANSWERS

Mostly As and Ds: Dominance

You have a strong personality and winning and achieving is important to you. You're honest and direct and you speak up when you see a problem. You're determined and confident and you have high expectations of the people around you. You're also not afraid to take risks in order to get to where you need to be. You don't like being weak and losing control, but ultimately it is the end goal that drives you.

Mostly As and Cs: influence

You are a very charming and sociable person who probably has many friends. Your warmth and enthusiasm motivates the people around you and you always try to see the best in a bad situation. You express yourself well and you can be very convincing when you want to be. You care a lot about what people think of you and sometimes struggle to stay focused on one thing for a long period of time.

Mostly Bs and Cs: Steadiness

You are a patient and loyal friend and a great listener. Your friends know that they can always rely on you to be there for them. You're modest and easy-going, and people don't feel intimidated by you. You always put the needs of others before your own and you don't often talk about your own needs and feelings. Your accommodating nature can be taken advantage of at times. You're not keen on changes and you prioritize harmony and stability.

Mostly Bs and Ds: Conscientiousness

You are organized and you're good at understanding the rules and following them. Accuracy is very important to you and so you're meticulous and cautious. People around you can depend on the fact that the things you say are usually based on research and facts, and that the work you produce is usually of high quality. You also expect the same high standards of the people around you, although you might not always voice those thoughts and feelings.

PAGE 74, 6B EXERCISE 1

So easy to open, even a man can do it!

PAGE 30, 2D, EXERCISE 3

One possible solution to the matchstick puzzle:

We could move the top and bottom matchsticks from the zero to make a one to the left of the five ...

And then when we turn the page upside down, we'll get ...

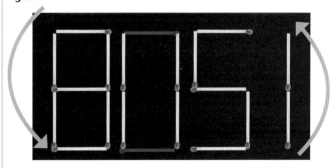

PAGE 127, 10D EXERCISE 9

Student A

Scenario 1: You are Zeki and you want to discuss your proposal with your friends.

Scenario 2: You are Karin. You work for a clothing company. Your colleagues are talking about the best ways for your company to save money and you have some really good ideas that you'd like to contribute.

Scenario 3: You are Huifang. You've been looking forward to this meetup with your English club friends and you really want to practise speaking English. You're determined to find ways to join in the conversation this time.

Extra speaking tasks

PAGE 53, 4C, EXERCISE 8

The Rainbow Serpent: Aboriginal Story from Australia

One day, it started to rain. And it rained like it had never rained before. Rain fell for days and days and the world was becoming flooded with water.

Two young men, Bil-bil, or the Rainbow Lorikeet brothers, <u>had</u> no shelter so they <u>came</u> to Goorialla, the Rainbow Serpent. They <u>asked</u> for help sheltering from the rain. The rainbow serpent <u>was</u> hungry and <u>tricked</u> the young men "I have no shelter, but you can hide in my mouth. You'll be safe from the rain in there." The young men <u>climbed</u> into Goorialla's mouth and he <u>closed</u> it shut, swallowing both men.

He soon <u>realized</u> that people <u>would</u> notice the young men missing and come looking for them. He <u>knew</u> they <u>would</u> find their tracks leading right into his mouth. He <u>didn't</u> want to be caught and so <u>decided</u> to hide in the only place he <u>knew</u> he <u>would</u> be safe: the sky. He <u>saw</u> people's sadness at losing these two young men, so he <u>decided</u> to try and make them happy again by turning his body into a big arc of beautiful colours.

Now, just after it rains, you can see the Rainbow Serpent sharing his beautiful colours with the people on the ground as his way of saying sorry for taking those Rainbow Lorikeet brothers.

PAGE 72, 6A, EXERCISE 3

Example concept map

PAGE 89, 7C, EXERCISE 10

Student A

1 There are a few **minute** details that we need to discuss.
2 My mother would make me wear a **bow** in my hair.
3 I honestly have no idea how we **wound** up here.
4 Our dog will start biting his **tail** and then turning around in circles.

PAGE 99, 8B, EXERCISE 10

Student A

1 You've got to <u>choose</u>.
2 It's in your <u>g</u>enes.
3 The defender hit him right on the <u>ch</u>in.
4 Apparently, these <u>sh</u>oes will help you train harder.
5 You need to ca<u>sh</u> it quickly.

PAGE 115, 9D, EXERCISE 8

Student A

Scenario 2

You are Özlem. You're meeting Gabriel for coffee and you're feeling really upset because your manager told you off this morning for something you didn't do. You feel you're being treated unfairly because he doesn't like you. You want to confide in Gabriel, but you also want to show that you're not self-absorbed and that you're a good listener. Find a way to balance talking about your problem with focusing on Gabriel and showing that you care about him too.

Scenario 3

You are Saif. You're in a one-to-one meeting with Drina talking about a work project. You want to build your relationship with her. You know that she admires you and thinks you never get stressed with any problems and you want to show her your vulnerability. You also want to ask her about inviting you to the dinners she organizes.

PAGE 127, 10D EXERCISE 9

Student B

Scenario 1: You are Nik. You want to tell your friends stories about you and your experiences.

Scenario 2: You are Karin's colleague. You work for a clothing company. Your colleagues are discussing the best ways for your company to save money. You think this is totally unnecessary and you try to interrupt to focus the conversation on how you should make money instead.

Scenario 3: You are a member of Huifang's English club. You get bored easily and so you are constantly interrupting to change the topic of conversation to something that you think is more interesting.

PAGE 89, 7C, EXERCISE 10

Student B

1 When I was a child, my dad would tell us amazing **tales** about our family's past.
2 If you just give me a **minute**, I'll be right with you.
3 All the actors **bowed** to loud applause from the audience.
4 My little sister fell off her bike and now has this horrible **wound** on her right leg.

PAGE 99, 8B, EXERCISE 10

Student B

1 Apparently, this juice will help you train harder.
2 The defender hit him right on the <u>sh</u>in.
3 It's on your <u>ch</u>in.
4 You've got the <u>sh</u>oes.
5 You need to cat<u>ch</u> it quickly.

PAGE 115, 9D, EXERCISE 8

Student B

Scenario 2

You are Gabriel. You're meeting Özlem for coffee and you can see that she seems upset about something. You want to show her that you care, but you're also tired of conversations that focus on her negative emotions. You've been doing a lot of overtime this week trying to meet deadlines and you're tired of the mountain of work you have. You want to talk to Özlem about this, but you're not sure if she's able to listen.

Scenario 3

You are Drina. You're in a one-to-one meeting with Saif, talking about a work project. You just came back from an awful meeting with a client and you're in a really bad mood. Find an opportunity to share this with Saif and ask for his thoughts on this.

PAGE 127, 10D EXERCISE 9

Student C

Scenario 1: You are Zeki and Nik's friend. You really enjoy Nik's stories and you keep trying to bring the conversation back to Nik's stories.

Scenario 2: You are Karin's colleague. You work for a clothing company. You and your colleagues are discussing the best ways for your company to save money. You have some really good ideas and you keep interrupting to try and get them to listen to your ideas.

Scenario 3: You are a member of Huifang's English club. You are confident about your English ability and you have an opinion about any topic that comes up in conversation. You try to take over the conversation with a good story every time there's a change of topic.

PAGE 123, 10B, EXERCISE 6

However, …

changing this one thing in the past was [6]*bound to / wasn't to* alter the future in more than one way, and sure enough, when he returned to 2011, he was no longer in a relationship with Helena as he [7]*had hoped / would hope* he would be and he had fallen out with his long-time friend and business partner Otávio.

Things [8]*were / were to be* a mess. Wishing to try again to change the past events that he thought [9]*had ruined / will ruin* his life, he made another trip back in time. Things [10]*get / were to get* worse – and more confusing – before they got better, but in the end, João and Helena made up for lost time and [11]*found / were going to find* happiness in the past, present and future.

If you're wondering where this story [12]*was to come / comes* from, it's the plot of a Brazilian film called *O Homem do Futuro* – or, In English, *The Man from the Future.*

PAGE 30, 2D, EXERCISE 2

Clue: You can make a five-digit number and then turn the page upside down.

PAGE 36, 3A, EXERCISE 8

<u>**Proposals under discussion regarding the need for change in Prior Park**</u>

This municipal park in the city centre is popular with walkers, athletes, families and local residents as a place to enjoy the outdoors and to do exercise. However, Prior Park Users' Association recently concluded that the park no longer adequately meets the needs of some of the local residents. Consequently, three proposals have been put forward for improving the park's facilities:

a Build a large adventure playground to make the park more attractive to older children and teenagers.

b Add a running track around the edge of the park, which will also leave the middle of the park freer for other people to enjoy.

c Create an indoor space in the park to serve as a meeting place for different groups, e.g. older people and parents with pre-school children. This would be especially useful in winter.

Audioscripts

UNIT 1

🎧 1.1

1
A: We used to see each other all the time … In the cafeteria, in the car park, everywhere.
B: That's right, but you only introduced yourself at that HR meeting.
A: Oh yeah.
B: I still don't understand why we'd never said hello until that day.
A: I was a bit scared of you, I think.
B: Scared of me?!
A: Ha ha, I know.

2
C: I'm really pleased to have met you …
D: Me too.
C: … but this is my stop.
D: Oh right, yeah. I'll say goodbye, and, er …
C: Hey, why don't I give you my number?
D: Good idea. What is it? I'll type it in …

3
E: You know Evgeny and Lily are getting married?
F: Really? After having insisted they would wait at least five years?
E: I know! And they've only been together a year.
F: I wonder why?
E: Who knows?

4
G: I hear you've got a new job. Congratulations!
H: Thanks, but how do you know about that? Who have you been talking to?
G: Leila told me just now.
H: OK, but how did she know?!

5
I: Are you going to speak to João today?
J: Actually, I've already seen him.
I: But it's only nine a.m!
J: I know! I bumped into him at the supermarket at six o'clock.
I: You were at the supermarket at six?
J: Yeah, I couldn't sleep. I decided I might as well go to the supermarket, having woken up at four. Anyway, I think it's more surprising that João was there at that time, don't you?

6
K: I really want to know if Pepe and Carmen can come.
L: To the wedding?
K: Yes, maybe I'll call them tomorrow.
L: Tomorrow's too soon. The invitation won't have arrived by then. Call them next week to be sure.
K: I can't wait that long.
L: You'll have to!

🎧 1.3

Mike: In general, I do not collect a lot of possessions, but, instead, I try to collect and retain memories of experiences. I've been very fortunate to build a career out of unique experiences and adventures that span the globe — including distant, wild places that few humans get to experience.

I think one reason I have not taken to collecting material objects from my work and travels is that I found, early on, that the importance of such objects fades for me and pales in comparison to the memory that can be evoked from, say, a photograph or a story shared with loved ones.

Having said that, I think objects can serve as powerful symbols that evoke strong emotions in people. There's one object in particular, a truly remarkable seashell, which my wife and I came across just a few months before we got married, that fills me with a deep feeling of gratitude.

This particular shell belonged to an abalone, a large marine invertebrate that people love to eat. But because this species is so sought after, it is strictly protected in certain areas and during certain times of the year.

In this case, we found the shell alone, among the intertidal rocks, meaning its owner had died of natural causes sometime before we had arrived. But what it left for us to discover was one of nature's masterpieces: the shell shape is unique and has a line of distinct holes in it, through which its animal host could breathe and move its tentacles. On the underside of the shell, where the animal body would reside is a mix of iridescent emerald and silver that glimmers in the sun. It's truly beautiful, which is why we decided to keep it.

However, its meaning has now expanded beyond its aesthetics. Years have now passed, and we have since moved far from the awe-inspiring California coastline. Along with that move, we have left behind a great deal of beloved people and places, now immortalized in our memories. This abalone shell, perhaps more vividly than any other precious object we've found, evokes these memories, and through this combination of positive thoughts, it gives me a feeling of tranquility and gratitude.

I'd also say that the objects, or lack of objects, that surround an individual can serve as a manifestation of what that individual holds dear. For example, speaking personally, I think I'm happiest when I'm surrounded by objects that either remind me of the people, places and experiences that have shaped who I am, or that inspire me to think big about the future and the ways I can help the world, moving forward.

1 I have a vivid recollection of the day I found this seashell.
2 This old photo has great sentimental value for me.
3 My house is really crammed with furniture of all shapes and sizes.
4 I only need to touch this ticket to evoke memories of that trip.
5 I feel deeply attached to this old toy.

🔊 1.5

1

Min-woo's manager Cara often seems impatient and abrupt. This morning, when she told Min-woo not to be late for meetings again, Min-woo started explaining his reasons for being late and Cara cut him off and started talking to someone else.

2

Min-woo finds his colleague Soha very loud and egocentric. When working on a project together, Soha keeps telling funny stories and distracting him from the statistics he's trying to present to her. Min-woo finds it hard to get any work done with Soha and starts to lose interest in the project.

3

Lev is Soha's brother's best friend but Soha often finds conversations with Lev exhausting. She feels like she's being interrogated every time she tries to give an opinion about a topic. Last weekend, when Soha mentioned that she preferred pasta to rice, Lev started asking her why and insisted on listing all the benefits of eating rice.

🔊 1.6

I know you weren't happy with me earlier and I hope you don't mind me being direct but I would have liked the chance to explain myself. The thing is, I'd found out just before the meeting that the meeting room had been double booked by the HR department. So I went over to get them to book a different room. I didn't think you'd have liked our meeting to be disrupted. I know you were probably waiting for me to start the meeting, so in the future, if something like that happens again, I can leave a message to say I'm on my way.

UNIT 2

🔊 2.1

I'd like to tell you a bit about the Freedom Chair. The engineers who came up with the Freedom Chair set out to provide affordable personal transport for people with a disability living in rural Tanzania. Wheelchair users come up against serious practical challenges every day. Getting around in the countryside involves coping with rough roads and doing without luxuries such as lifts or other special arrangements for wheelchair users that we see in the cities. This means they can have real problems reaching any kind of work or educational opportunities, getting food and other necessities, and sometimes just getting out and being active in the community. I'll go over the main features and benefits of the chair.

Let's look at the most significant innovation of this chair. Its main feature is that the user powers it by pushing two long handles forwards and backwards. So, as you can see, they no longer have to move the wheels directly, by hand. This has at least three benefits. Firstly, the main benefit is that it makes the chair much more efficient and easier to move than models where you turn the wheels directly. Users can rely on the chair to get them across rough roads and muddy paths that a traditional wheelchair couldn't handle. Secondly, the motion of the arms is more natural, so it cuts down on injuries and it's a lot less tiring for the user. Thirdly, the users' hands are far away from the wheels, so they're protected from the dirt and mud that sometimes builds up on the wheels.

In terms of the design of the Freedom Chair, I'd like to point out a second feature, which is that it's made of bicycle parts, available at low cost almost everywhere in the world. The main benefit of this is that if the chair breaks down or heavy use wears out some of the parts, replacement parts will be available locally. So in this way they've done away with many of the drawbacks of older, more traditional models, which made them impractical, uncomfortable and expensive to maintain.

🔊 2.3

Francisco: I began looking at meditation when I had a hard time focusing or organizing my thoughts because I had a lot on my plate. It really helps me clear my mind and focus my thoughts on what's most important and what I need to take care of first. I do this come rain or shine, in the morning and evening to start and close my day. Another tried and tested activity that helps me think is driving. It is most useful when I am with someone with whom I can talk things over. I don't know why, but it works for me to be driving when I try to solve problems or develop complex ideas. Ideas come at various times, day or night. I go through phases. When I am in a writing phase, I tend to take a long time to get in the swing of things and, as a result, I get my best ideas late in the day or night. Other times, I have to solve some type of work or life challenge; I have some ideas when I'm up early in the morning, sometimes after a long sleepless night. Occasionally, I get a good idea in the shower too. I typically have a lot of things to do or take care of, which leaves no time for boredom. However, when I am unable to do things because, either I am waiting on something or someone to arrive or do their part, I do get bored, or rather frustrated. When

Audioscripts

that happens, I try to think about other projects or activities that might need my help or contribution as a way of not letting the time go to waste. This has worked quite well for me, many times, as I have been able to dedicate myself to ideas or goals that otherwise would have been put off and that instead turn out to be successful. When that happens, I feel good.

Andrej: Most of my ideas come up late at night, when I'm not actively thinking. Over time, I've learned not to force myself but instead to stay calm and wait for the idea to come – and it always does! Ideas often come to me while I'm solving completely different issues.

During my ordinary working days I often need to clear my head. A lot of stress and uncertainty causes me to feel stuck and then I need a bit of peace and quiet – a walk by the beach or in the forest or some time playing my guitar. Most of my ideas are based on new knowledge or skills I've learned. Reading new papers and discussing them with my colleagues often helps me to get completely unique ideas of how to develop new plans and make them work. In my case, for creative ideas and thinking I need to read a lot and spend a lot of time in good back and forth discussions. I frequently partner with many different institutions and professionals across the globe. Although I consider myself first and foremost an independent researcher with original and unique ideas, collaborations always broaden my horizons and empower me to see problems in a completely different way. So I often come up with new ideas that wouldn't have been possible without collaboration and team work.

2.4

Francisco:
1 another tried and tested activity
2 it works for me to be driving
3 when I try to solve problems or develop complex ideas

Andrej:
4 when I'm not actively thinking
5 Over time, I've learned
6 while I'm solving completely different issues

UNIT 3

3.1

P = Presenter, A = Ana

P: Paul Salopek's 21,000-mile odyssey is a decade-long experiment in slow journalism. Walking at an unhurried pace, Paul is trekking the pathways the first humans who migrated out of Africa in the Stone Age would have taken when they explored the Earth, all the way to Tierra del Fuego in South America.

Along the way he is able to cover the major stories of our time — from climate change to technological innovation, from mass migration to cultural survival — by giving voice to the people who inhabit them every day.

P: This sounds like an incredible project. Ana, you've been following Paul Salopek on his blog since he started. The journey is due to end in South America. Why there?

A: That's the furthest humans made it from Africa on foot in their exploration of the planet. They went in different directions, of course, but in terms of distance, Tierra del Fuego is the furthest.

P: But they couldn't have made a journey right across the world like this, could they?

A: Oh no. This is a journey that took thousands of years and hundreds of generations.

P: I'm fascinated by Paul's reasons for doing it. I guess I'm asking what 'slow journalism' means. What do you understand by that term, Ana?

A: It's like walking has allowed him to take his time and get to know places and people in a more … intimate way than any other form of transport would have.

P: Right.

A: And he's been able to listen carefully to all these stories of human life, you know, as told by villagers, travellers, traders, farmers, even soldiers, people who rarely make the news.

P: One thing I worry about is his safety. He's passing through some potentially dangerous regions, isn't he?

A: Well, of course there could be dangers, but it's interesting how often he is amazed by the goodness in people. How complete strangers, who might have had nothing in common with him, economically, racially, politically, etc. have been prepared to help over and over again.

P: That's wonderful, isn't it? And a valuable lesson in a world where it can seem like there's always fighting.

A: I should say of course he has had encounters that aren't so positive, and times when he hasn't been permitted through certain regions, you know, but the overwhelming majority of his experiences have been positive.

P: That's fantastic. And last question from me, Ana. The journey was scheduled to take 7 years, which means he would have finished by now. But he's not there yet, is he?

A: That's right. He's had a few setbacks, so right now, he's making his way through East Asia, still a long way from Tierra del Fuego. As you're listening to this, who knows where he might be? He ought to arrive at his finishing point sometime in the next two years.

P: The very best of luck to you Paul, wherever you are!

🎧 3.2

1 Paul is trekking the pathways the first humans who migrated out of Africa would have taken when they explored the Earth.

2 They couldn't have made a journey right across the world like this, could they?

3 He has been able to listen carefully to all these stories of human life as told by people who rarely make the news.

4 ... how complete strangers, who might have had nothing in common with him, have been prepared to help ...

5 As you are listening to this, who knows where he might be.

6 He ought to arrive at his finishing point sometime in the next two years.

🎧 3.4

Anusha: I moved a lot as a child, because my dad had a job that involved moving a lot. Maybe because of that, I had to make friends and adapt to new places quickly. I think my adaptability is a handy skill – it doesn't take me long to settle, at least socially, into new jobs. I keep moving around and living in new places every few years. On the other hand, I struggle to feel attached to a place and I don't have a strong emotional attachment to many of the cities where I grew up as a child. What has always been interesting to me is that many of my friends feel strong emotional attachments to their childhood homes (the physical building). I lived in so many apartments and houses growing up that, although I have some emotional and sentimental feelings about leaving a place, I move on quickly. I realize that moving is often scary because we're going into the unknown – but this is also what makes it so exciting! Learning about new cultures, learning new languages, a new place's history and wildlife – these are all things I love about moving around. But I don't know if I can say I'm more of a traveller or a settler. I can see the appeal of both and I've seen my preference change with time. I love travelling, but sometimes it is strange to feel rootless. I'd love to have one rooted home in the long term, and still travel for work and pleasure (as sustainably as possible).

Many people in my family have never left India, but among my cousins, we've almost all travelled abroad. My American friends seem to travel for fun or for temporary work, but rarely live for more than a few months in a new place, except maybe for a study abroad programme during college. My Ecuadorian friends really hesitate to go abroad, and often want to go back home. Though I've lived outside India for nine years, I feel the pull to return there, to root myself there, and study Indian wildlife – because that's really where I feel most comfortable. My family and past and future are in India!

Rebecca: I was born in the United States, but when I was five, my father got a job in England and my family moved overseas. I lived in England for six years and, to be honest it's the only part of my childhood I remember. When I was twelve, my parents decided it was time to move back home. I assumed we would move back to the United States, but my mom is Canadian, and she wanted to be closer to her family. As a result, we ended up moving to a place I had never even heard of: Halifax, Nova Scotia. Nova Scotia is a small province on the Atlantic Ocean and East Coast of Canada. There is a strong Gaelic and Celtic culture in Nova Scotia, which shouldn't be a surprise as Nova Scotia means 'New Scotland'.

Because I moved so much as a child I've never felt super attached to any particular place. After I graduated high school I started moving around a lot. I went to university in a different province and started getting jobs internationally. I struggled to stay in one place for more than a few years. When I meet people, they often ask me 'Where is home?' and I never know what to say. Is home Canada, England or America? It took me time to realize, but for me, home is where my family is. Right now, home is where my partner and parents are. Not associating the idea of home with a place, but rather with people is beautiful to me. There is a saying 'home is where the heart is' and I fully agree. For me, as someone who is constantly moving and doesn't have roots in any specific place, my home is where I am surrounded by the people I love and care about.

🎧 3.5

Two mice, Sniff and Scurry, and two Little people, Hem and Haw, lived in a maze and made a routine out of going to Station C for their supply of cheese. The mice knew that this supply wouldn't last forever, so when they arrived one day to find no cheese at Station C, they immediately set off looking for cheese elsewhere. Hem and Haw however reacted with disbelief and shock. They didn't believe this was happening to them and Hem exclaimed, 'Who moved my cheese?' They came back to Station C the next day hoping that the cheese would

Audioscripts

reappear and when that didn't happen, they stood around shouting and looking for someone to blame. After several days, Haw started imagining himself finding and enjoying new cheese. He decided to leave, realizing that 'movement in a new direction helps you find new cheese'. Meanwhile, Hem stayed in Station C, angry and insistent that whoever moved their cheese would one day have to put it back.

UNIT 4

🎧 4.1

Imogen: Music plays a huge role in my life. My parents growing up would often tell me to turn my music down as I would be constantly listening to it. As a matter of fact, I always joke that I was basically born in the wrong music era as I love music from the 60s, 70s and 80s. I've always been obsessed with The Beatles, so much so that I did a Beatles holiday in Liverpool and went to lots of the different locations where their songs were based. Listening to The Beatles reminds me of being on long car journeys with my dad when I was younger.

Come to think of it, it is actually my mood that defines what I want to listen to. I definitely have my go-to favourites, but I have playlists for different moods and occasions: when I'm walking, exercising, working, cooking, you name it.

When I am working, I find it really hard to listen to music with words. Sometimes I'll listen to the orchestral music from movies as a bit of motivation! My house is always filled with upbeat music, which is perfect for kitchen dancing! Music is literally the fuel to my day. I can put on my big headphones and go for a walk and completely be transported to another place. To be honest, there is no better feeling when you hear a new song you absolutely love.

Mind you, when listening to music on my phone, it's easy to just skip songs and that's why I have a vinyl player at home. For one thing, listening to a whole record really gives you a more complete story and makes you appreciate the music in a whole new way.

🎧 4.4

Alyea: Within the diversity that exists in the Caribbean (Jamaica and Trinidad and Tobago), oral traditions are a common element in cultures throughout the region. They have survived for hundreds of years, changing, adapting and evolving. Oral traditions persist because of their sensitivity to social change and their ability to express some of the most pressing concerns of each era. They are also examples of the survival techniques that developed under colonial rule and slavery to ensure the preservation of those cultures and their future existence. There are many and varied oral storytelling traditions in the Caribbean. One of the most obvious, without doubt, is music. The stories told with the drums (from the bata drums to the steel drums) and the lyrics of the songs, are narrations of the past. This can be seen in calypso, reggae and kaiso) These stories passed down orally serve as important records of a distant past. They hold important lessons, artifacts, and details of our ancestor's experiences. Coming from a people who do not know every ounce of their history due to a painful, problematic history, it is important to help future generations understand where they come from and who they are.

Storytelling traditions in the Caribbean are daily events within local communities. Built into the language is a constant reflection of the past as words and music are a part of the local interaction. Stories are told on beaches, in kitchens, at family events, and in the galleries of homes. Most importantly, these stories are told during Carnival and Mas when history comes to life in the streets. When people share these stories, it is a reminder of the connection to indigenous and native ancestors, how language has transformed due to a melting pot of people on one island, and how stories and legends can transcend time.

Oral storytelling is universal and is as ancient as humankind. Before there was writing, there was storytelling. It occurs in every culture and from every age. Traditional oral stories are different from the written ones because they depend on the speaker. The speaker is crucial. It does not require the speaker or the listener to be 'literate', as local language can be used in oral storytelling to further connect with the audience. It requires the speaker and audience to be in the same place at the same time to fully connect. Traditional oral storytelling is not in set form. The storyteller may change or improvise the story depending on the audience, circumstances, time allotted, mood of the audience, venue, etc. Similar to gospel church music, the use of repetition allows audience members to remember people, places, and actions, while figurative language, vocal dynamics, body movements, clothing, language, and pacing help with captivation.

Not all of these stories are historically accurate or even based on facts or true events. Truth is less important than providing cultural cohesion. It can encompass myths, legends, fables, religion, prayers, proverbs, and instructions, but the primary focus is the passing down of traditions, beliefs and cultural customs.

Oral storytelling traditions are preserved for the next generation because it educates the young of the community. The next generation can understand the history of the tribe, community or group and carry on to teach behaviour, values, and traditions. Without that history, no one knows 'who' they are, 'why' what they do is significant, and 'where' they came from.

4.5

A long time ago there lived a Coyote. One day, he's strolling around. The sun's shining brightly, and Coyote is very hot. 'I would like a cloud', Coyote says. So a cloud comes and makes some shade for Coyote.

But Coyote is not satisfied. 'I would like more clouds', he asks. More clouds come along, and the sky begins to look very stormy. But Coyote is still hot. 'How about some rain?' says Coyote. The clouds begin to sprinkle rain on Coyote. 'More rain', Coyote demands loudly. The rain becomes a downpour.

'I would like a creek to put my feet in', says Coyote. So a creek springs up beside him, and Coyote walks in it to cool off his feet. 'It should be deeper', demands Coyote. The creek becomes a huge, swirling river.

Coyote is swept over and over by the water. Finally, nearly drowned, Coyote is thrown up on the bank far away. And that is how *Nch'i-Wana*, the 'Great River' began.

5.1

1 /ɪ/ immune, system
2 /e/ depression, infectious
3 /ɒ/ tolerance, insomnia
4 /æ/ calories, happy
5 /u:/ improve, mood
6 /i:/ detail, feelings
7 /aɪ/ fight, open-minded
8 /əʊ/ social, inappropriate

5.2

1
I laugh a lot when I'm with my young cousins. What I love is that they have such a fresh view of the world. And they say such unexpected things. I asked my cousin to say his three favourite foods and he said 'Ice cream and two chocolate bars!'

2
The thing that makes me laugh is my grandfather telling a story from his childhood. He always laughs when he tells the story, even if it isn't really a funny story. It's his enjoyment that gets everyone else laughing.

3
I laugh a lot when I'm with my friends, but if I think about it, the reason we laugh is not usually because someone's made a joke – it's just something that happens when we're messing about together. It's like the glue of our friendship!

4
What starts me laughing is knowing I'm not supposed to! Sometimes in a meeting I just get a powerful desire to laugh. I don't really know why that happens!

5
It's when I'm a bit nervous that I tend to laugh – even when something is fairly serious, like when I was giving a presentation last week. In social interactions, when I'm feeling a bit shy, I often laugh, too. It relaxes everyone – especially me!

5.3

Teresa: Open any textbook and you can read about science in the traditional analytical way. When you introduce characters who have relatable goals and the potential to fail, only then do you have a story. Stories are everywhere. Stories are life. So of course there are stories in science. In all the main articles I write, I try to find the narrative. Stories are important because they help people relate and connect. They make information personal. It's a lot easier to connect with a person or family who love each other, with someone trying to reach a goal, with someone trying to survive, etc. because these are fundamental human ambitions that we've all experienced.

I wrote an article about a gene-therapy treatment for a child who had a rare disease. There were many points of connection there — the doctor who did the drug discovery called the day 'better than her wedding day', and the child said the day represented 'hope'. And their ritual of drinking tea in fancy cups before medical appointments, or naming her doctors, like 'Dr. Big Shoes',— are all very human, very relatable things. The characters (her parents, her doctor) were all so touching. Their ritual was also lovely. Everyone can relate to the drive to survive and protect the people you love. But embedded in that narrative was a few informative paragraphs about how gene therapy works. If the reader doesn't remember the technical details, they will definitely remember what it means for the people and for the world. Stories can bridge that connection.

Audioscripts

Popi: When we think about penguins, the image that sometimes comes to our mind is a colony with lots of penguins together. But we must realize that each penguin is an individual with a life, a unique personality, a family, a story. Twelve years ago, when we found Clarita, she was incubating her eggs with a plastic bottle in the back of the nest. Plastic pollution is a problem because animals can get entangled with it. Sometimes they eat plastic pieces that harm them and can even kill them. Clarita stayed together with her partner, Honorio, for eight years and together they raised seven chicks successfully. But unfortunately, after one winter he never came back. Maybe he was caught in a fishing net.

Another threat that is also affecting penguins like Clarita is climate change. It mainly changes the availability of food in the places and moments when it is most needed. Chicks have to be fed very frequently when they are small. If the food is far away from the colony, the adults take longer to get it and by the time they come back, the chicks are dead.

We could tell the previous story in a more traditional scientific and impersonal way, it could be something like this: the main threats affecting penguins in the ocean are climate change, fisheries and marine pollution. A new colony of Magellanic penguins settled down in a location affected by many threats including many caused by humanity. Our actions protected it and the population showed a statistically significant positive growth trend allowing it to reach 3,200 breeding pairs.

But instead of sharing scientific information about the threats affecting penguins, the breeding and population parameters that reflect the impact of our conservation work, I frame it all into the life story of an individual female penguin. It makes the information more persuasive. Through her, I catch people's interest about the challenges that penguins are facing in the real world, and how we are working to help address those threats.

🎧 5.4

In July 1907 when chemist Leo Baekeland was trying to create a flexible covering for electrical wires, little did he know that he would soon make something that would change the world: plastic. When his mixture of chemicals resulted in a product that was hard rather than flexible, he initially thought he had failed. Only when he saw the potential uses for the new product did he realize it might be important. 'Unless I am very much mistaken,' he wrote in his diary, 'this invention will prove important in the future.' Not only was his invention important, it was also an instant success, soon becoming part of everyday life in products from appliances and airplanes to jewellery and toys. Never before had anyone made a completely new material using only chemicals with no natural ingredients. For better or for worse, Baekeland's discovery changed the world.

UNIT 6

🎧 6.1

P = Presenter, R = Rosie

P: So Rosie, you teach the principles of design. What can you tell us about how design has changed in terms of how we represent people?

R: I think two important principles designers are taking into account more are diversity and inclusivity. Design is good design provided it represents the whole of society ... as well as needing to look good and do its job well, of course.

P: I think it will help the listeners if we're all clear on the basic terms. You mentioned inclusivity. Can you explain the difference between that and representation?

R: Yes. So supposing there were no disabled facilities in a school, like toilets or lifts, could a disabled person get the same educational opportunities as an non-disabled person? They are not included. But even if it was physically accessible, they might still feel unrepresented if all the books and the posters on the wall only showed non-disabled children.

P: In other words, you're going to feel represented as long as you recognize people like you in the world around you.

R: Exactly. Design must show the diversity of the people around us. It's about not feeling invisible. So fair representation is what a lot of design is about these days. Supposing you animate an advert for a job, is the character doing the job going to be a man or a woman? Black or white? These are important decisions to be made.

P: OK, so what about this road sign? It's a warning to drivers that older people may want to cross. Both men and women are represented, and the message is very clear, isn't it?

R: True. But how would you feel if you were an older person looking at that?

P: Haha. I've never thought about it before, but the figures in this image do kind of resemble tortoises ...

R: Ha! They do! So the problem with this is it highlights certain negative stereotypes by showing people with curved backs, having difficulty walking and so on.

P: I can see that. If I was an active person in my seventies or eighties, I might feel it didn't represent me.

R: Yeah, it's the same with the disabled access symbol. The most prominent feature is the wheelchair, and the person seems to be unable to move at all, which is totally unrepresentative of most disabled people.

P: Now, symbols like these are getting a makeover, isn't that right, Rosie? Designers are trying to change people's perceptions about these issues.

R: Yes. So, for example, here's a more dynamic image that emphasizes the idea that older people can still be active. But it's not the designers who are leading the way. I don't think design would have started to progress, unless rights groups had campaigned for better representation.

P: That's great. I love the humour in the image, as well – the fact that the woman is leading the man across the road. They look old-fashioned, though. I don't know many older people who wear hats any more.

R: True. The hat is symbolic, another kind of stereotype of older people, if you like. It's not a literal representation. But the key is that this one isn't a negative stereotype.

P: Right. But I wonder how familiar that image of older people is to people in other countries, where fashions might be very different. If you're going to be representative, surely you need to represent all people?

R: Yes, you're right. Sometimes it's really hard to find a symbol that pleases everyone. The solution the tech companies have found for emojis is to provide choice – you know, the emojis are yellow, then you choose the skin tone to suit you. But of course that's not usually possible, when there is just one design.

P: So you can't please everyone! But it's good to see you're doing what you can. Rosie, thanks very much.

🎧 **6.2**

stress on the third syllable from the end
complexity, disparity, diversity, grammatical, impossible, inclusivity, invisible, professional, simplicity, technological, uncomfortable

stress on the second syllable from the end
independence, performance, population, representation

🎧 **6.3**

R: OK, so let's talk about pants. My pants are very different from your pants. Wouldn't you say? … my pockets are smaller. Think about it – when we are walking down Main Street. I have to bring a purse for my wallet and my phone because they don't fit in my pocket.

A: Right.

R: But everything fits in your pocket.

A: I know it's great …

R: But it's not really fair, and it's a terrible design flaw.

A: It seems terrible. Why? Why do they do that?

R: Well, I guess women historically weren't able to carry wallets. So there is a bit of history … but that being said, it is the 21st century.

A: Seems like it's time for somebody to design women's pants with proper pockets.

R: Yeah, we make a new pants style. Women's wallets are generally so much bigger than men's wallets, which makes no sense, given that my pant pockets are smaller.

A: You know what I really hate: products that are just designed, you know, poorly. They don't last. You know what I'm talking about?

R: But, like, can you give me an example?

A: Yeah, I mean, like recently, like, I had this bike bag and, you know, I mean, it's small. It's just meant to hold a few things so I can repair my bike on rides if I need to. And I got it at the beginning of the summer, and it only lasted a couple of months before the zipper exploded.

R: Where on your bike did this bike bag go?

A: You'd hang it off the back under the seat, but you know, the hanging mechanism was fine but the zipper was terrible. And it was like they expect you to buy a new bike bag every couple of months or something, which I mean, it's not sustainable, but it's also bad design. You know, for me, that's, if I'm going to buy something, I want to buy something that that will last forever. Like, I mean, my camera lasts for years and years and years and does everything I need it to do every single time I turn it on. It just, it just works in any condition. Like that for me is good design.

R: OK, so what you're saying is the camera is a very practical design. The bike bag is impractical and doesn't work and is very flawed.

A: Yeah, for me, at least, the bike bag is illogical.

R: Yeah, that's fair. I'll tell you something else that's illogical.

A: Yeah. What's that?

R: OK? You know, when we're on a road trip and I'm hungry, so we buy chips? Yeah. then you get the bag of chips and it's mostly air. It's the most frustrating thing because you spent three or four dollars on this bag of chips, but it's deceptive, it's made to trick you. They filled the bag up mostly with air and not with chips.

A: That's like totally pointless. Where are my chips?

R: And it just makes me sad because I finished the bag and I'm expecting more.

A: Yeah, it's not particularly user friendly. So, yeah, insufficient pockets. Insufficient chips. Yeah, I can, I can see why those things are frustrating.

R: What do we like? The thing that we like the most is our espresso machine. It's stylish, it's practical and we use it every single day. It basically never breaks, except for that one time you put water in the wrong place.

Audioscripts

A: That was, that was a bad move on my part. And like having a really good coffee rather than kind of a mediocre coffee just makes the day better. Starts it off on the right foot.

R: Yeah. Plus, it grinds the coffee beans. It foams the milk. It does three things in one. It's a very efficient, compact little machine. And you didn't even want to buy it in the first place. But now we love it.

A: Well, you know, the other thing that I think would brighten every day, something that I am very much in the market for, is really good tableware … you know, like plates and forks and knives. I mean, all, you know, all the things that go on the table like, right now, you know, the rental house that we have has kind of mediocre plates. I would say.

R: I like the plates!

A: You like the plates … I could like them more. And I think if you have like nice plates, whatever you eat, all of a sudden becomes just a little bit more exciting, a little more elegant. And it's like something that, like in your everyday life, you can just have this, you know, this little touch of beauty.

R: My concern is I break things very easily, so …

A: … so they'll have to be durable.

R: Yeah, they basically should be made of rubber. Otherwise, I don't know. Having nice things is wonderful and having stylish and pretty things, but if you drop them, that's it.

A: We have to find the point where form meets function. You know where it's where it's, where it looks nice and you can't break it …

R: It can pass the break test.

A: Yeah. That's important. Well, so it seems like, you know, in broad strokes, the things that we find important are practical. But you know, with a certain degree of style.

R: Yes, but mostly practical or maybe I am more practical as a person, I care more about practicality than style and you like style.

A: I like them both to go together. I'm interested in the style, but you know, I need it to last.

🎧 6.4
R = Rebecca, A = Alec

1

R: It's the most frustrating thing because you spent three or four dollars on this bag of chips, but it's deceptive, it's made to trick you. They filled the bag up mostly with air and not with chips.

A: That's like totally pointless. Where are my chips?

R: And it just makes me sad because I finished the bag and I'm expecting more.

2

A: Well, you know, the other thing that I think would brighten every day, something that I am very much in the market for, is really good tableware … you know, like plates and forks and knives. I mean, you know, all the things that go on the table like right now, you know, the rental house that we have has kind of mediocre plates. I would say.

3

R: My concern is I break things very easily, so …

A: so they'll have to be durable.

R: Yeah, they basically should be made of rubber. Otherwise, I don't know.

🎧 6.5
J = Jameela, S = Stefan, L = Lorenzo

J: Your new house looks gorgeous! Did you design the rooms yourself?

S: I did. When I bought this house, it was a mess. So I decided I'd do it up myself.

L: You did all this up yourself?

S: Yeah. I brainstormed a few concepts, made up a mood board for each room, sketched out what I wanted, got full-colour renderings done and then got to work.

L: Wow. That's … um ... impressive.

J: Yeah! It must have taken you a lot of time!

S: In this living room for example, just prepping the walls took me days.

J: I can imagine! And prepping the walls isn't the most exciting job.

L: Yeah …

S: The old skirting board was all cracked and chipped. My mum wanted me to just hire a chippie but I said I'd take it up myself. So I ended up putting in a new bevelled-edge MDF one.

L: M … D … F?

J: Good idea. MDF is much easier to paint and so much cheaper than solid wood.

L: Oh …

S: Yeah! I also wanted more plug sockets around the room. Nothing more annoying than having to run your electrical cables across the living room floor, right?

J: I have one plug socket in my bedroom and everything runs from it. I have to get so much trunking to hide all the cables.

L: Trunking …

S: I had to crimp the lugs myself and fit them onto the circuit breaker and the new face plate. It was a real learning curve for me.

J: I wouldn't have known where to start if that had been me. You've done a great job! Wouldn't you say, Lorenzo?

L: Er … yeah … gorgeous house.

🎧 6.6

J = Jameela, S = Stefan, L = Lorenzo

J: Your new house looks gorgeous! Did you design the rooms yourself?

S: I did. When I bought this house, it was a mess. So I decided to do it up myself.

L: You did all this up yourself?

S: Yeah. Basically, I did the interior design of each room. And then I worked on making each room look like how I wanted it to.

L: Wow. That's impressive.

J: Yeah. It must have taken you a long time!

S: I don't know how interested you are in home improvement, but in this living room, for example, I wanted to repaint all the walls, but I had to prep the walls first – you know, peel off the old paint, fill in the cracks, that sort of thing. It took me days.

J: I can imagine! Prepping the walls isn't the most exciting job.

L: Gosh! Thankfully, I don't own a house so I don't have to do that sort of thing.

S: There were lots of other tedious jobs like that that I had to do as well. My mum wanted me to just hire a CHIPPIE – My mum's British and that's what they call a carpenter! A chippie!

L: Really? A chippie is a carpenter? So, did you hire a … 'chippie'?

S: No, I liked being able to do it all myself. Would you have hired a carpenter to do it all instead?

J: Oh definitely. I wouldn't have a clue where to start!

L: You really are amazing – taking all this on by yourself!

S: Oh I had a lot of help! Online DIY videos are my best friend!

L: You can learn to do anything online these days, right?

UNIT 7

🎧 7.1

Carolina: This text evokes feelings of longing and anxiety for leaving a dearly familiar place for the unknown. I can relate to these feelings as I have moved often to pursue dreams – like when she talks about loving her home country 'as one loves a person'. To this day, I remember exactly how I felt the day I first left home. I had mixed feelings, from sadness for leaving everything and everyone I know and loved to anxiety and nervousness about the unknown and the adventures that will be coming ahead. Six years have passed since that day, but I will never forget those feelings and emotions. I think the author evokes these feelings well by describing both her own feelings and emotions, such as her 'severe attack of nostalgia' and by using images like a 'camera eye snapped shut' to talk about the future. Also by how she writes about her surroundings at that moment in a very detailed and vivid way – such as the contrasting sounds of the cheerful band with the sad sound of the foghorn.

After being away from my family and friends for long periods, I start feeling nostalgic when I think about home. I miss being able to hug and embrace my family, or surprise them with random afternoon visits and watch their reaction. However, what I miss the most are the family gatherings every Sunday over lunch. The house is full; my aunts and uncles and cousins are all there talking at the same time about football and catching up, while the smell of freshly baked beans slowly overtakes the living room.

🎧 7.3

A: So how long have you been working here?

B: Let me see, I started when I was 23, so it would be just over twenty years now.

A: Wow! I don't know how you do it. I'm constantly changing jobs. I've only been here for a year, but am already thinking I might need a change.

B: You already dislike it so much?

A: Not at all. I'm loving it. I don't know what it is, to be honest. I'm just restless, I'm always looking for new challenges, like you know, new coding language to learn, new websites to build …

B: But I think you can get those even if you stay at the same company. For example, about a year ago, I started to feel like I wasn't progressing at all. I'd been doing this same job for several years, and it was becoming slightly repetitive, selling the same product, doing sales calls with similar clients day in, day out …

A: Sounds repetitive all right!

B: So I spoke to my boss, and in a few weeks she managed to find a new role for me. I'm now working on launching a new product to the market, building a sales team, so it all requires a different skillset too. I also have to manage people now, so I'm constantly learning new things.

A: Maybe I should try that too! So do you think you'll still be working here when you're, let's say, 65?

Audioscripts

B: Why not?! Look, another great thing is that your salary increases every year.

A: True. So there was never a time when you were thinking: I want to try my luck at a different company?

B: Of course. For example, when I started, I was working really long hours, and the commute was terrible. So I decided to move closer to work.

A: I'd have moved jobs instead!

🎧 7.4

Carolina: I think there is a lot of Latin accent when I speak English. Other people can easily tell I am not a native English speaker by the way I pronounce certain words and I am very happy about that. Actually, I prefer to speak with my accent and I never really want to change it, because having an accent encourages new conversations with people who are genuinely interested in your background. I mean, there is always a background story for why we sound the way we do. For example, I have had the opportunity to live and work in Europe, the US and Australia, and now when I speak English, my accent is a mix of Latin American Spanish with hints of American and Australian accents.

And the same is true of Spanish, my first language. Ecuador is a diverse country with a variety of accents. I am from Guayaquil, a coastal city, and our accent there is very different from those of the people of the capital, Quito. We speak slower and we usually shorten words.

Gabby: I grew up in a rural area of the southeastern United States, so I have a bit of a southern accent when I speak in English. But when I was a kid, I had a teacher who told me that my accent might make some people think I was less educated or less intelligent. This made me feel a bit embarrassed by my accent, and I started trying to mimic the way people without a strong accent spoke and I gradually lost my accent. Now, I do not think that everyone should have a standard accent. Our accents say something about where we are from and they can help connect us with other people by sparking conversations.

When it comes to speaking another language, I started studying Spanish when I was in high school and I definitely struggled with my accent at first. I had a difficult time with certain sounds in Spanish, such as rolling my *r*s. My accent has improved with practice, but it's probably easy to tell that I am not a native speaker. I'm OK with that. I think native speakers appreciate that I'm trying and that I'm interested in their language.

🎧 7.5

VR = Voice recognition software, VC = Voice coach

1

A: Hey Joe!

B: Hey! How are things?

A: Not too bad. Yourself?

B: Pretty good. I'm calling because Klara and I are planning a holiday, and we were wondering …

A: Say that again, Joe. You're breaking up.

B: I said Klara and I are thinking of going away for a week. So wondering if you and Aisha would want to join us?

A: That's awesome. Whereabouts were you thinking?

B: The South coast maybe. Somewhere warm, you know. … Just lie at the beach and get a tan.

A: Listen, the connection is pretty bad. Let me call you back, and we can talk about it a bit more.

2

C: How many Apollo missions were there?

VR: Sorry, I didn't catch that.

C: This is so frustrating, I give up.

D: Hey, what are you doing?

C: So I bought this voice recognition thing yesterday, and I was trying to learn how many Apollo missions there were, but it keeps on saying it can't understand me.

D: Let me try. How many Apollo missions were there?

VR: Sorry, I don't understand your question.

D: Looks like it's not just you this thing can't understand!

3

VC: Our voice is a very powerful tool, but we don't always use it to its full potential. It's surprising how many public speakers think that speaking at the top of their voice will help them get their message across. But there are times when …

E: Can you turn that down?! I'm trying to study here. … Do you mind turning it down a bit? I'm watching a lecture.

F: Oh sorry, didn't realize. I'll put my headphones on.

E: Thanks.

VC: Lowering your voice can be a very powerful technique. Beware not to mumble, though! This will make you more difficult to understand. Some speakers are afraid of it, and they end up rambling on about nothing really just to avoid silence. Don't fall into that trap. So if you want to make your voice heard, practise using its full range and power.

E: This is ridiculous.

UNIT 8

🎧 8.1

So today we're talking about amazingly talented people to see how they became so accomplished. I wanted to start off by talking about the Polgar sisters, female chess superstars from Hungary. One of them, Judit Polgar, was the youngest player to become a grandmaster and the highest ranked female player in history.

So how did they become so good at chess? It seems it wasn't so much about innate talent, as being driven and having long-term commitment to becoming the best. The sisters were home-schooled by their parents, who taught them how to play chess. So from very early on, they were focused on the game and practised every single day.

This is completely in contrast to Stephen Wiltshire, whose amazing talent seems to be in the genes. Stephen is so skilled at drawing and has such an incredible memory that he can draw an entire city landscape after seeing it just once, for example from a plane. In 2005 he famously drew a perfect image of Tokyo after a short flight above it in a helicopter. Where do his amazing abilities stem from? It seems that Stephen is a complete natural. He never went to art school. But already as a child Stephen had a natural talent and a passion for drawing. In fact, it helped him to communicate. Since he was not able to speak, he depended on his drawings to speak for him.

Yet another case is …

🎧 8.3

1

A: It's really crazy how vast it is. You don't realize that when looking at the map.

B: What do you mean bats? I didn't realize there were any bats there.

A: No, not bats, I mean vast, vast, like very big.

2

C: The hike was pretty intense, so before going up to the summit the next day, we set up the camp, collected some wood, made a bonfire.

D: Cool. So what kind of food did you collect? Like mushrooms and stuff?

C: No, we brought our own food.

D: Oh, I thought you said you collected food …

C: I meant we collected wood, sorry, wood, like, you know, to make a bonfire.

🎧 8.4

Jeff: The natural world is full of endless awe-inspiring stories. Like how a bird can fly all the way from Africa to the Arctic to reproduce, and then fly all the way back again each and every year. Or how a seal can hold its breath as it swims like a fish through an underwater kelp forest lush with vegetation. The daily lives of numerous species are truly fascinating. The more you learn about their behaviour, the more interesting they become. I'm passionate about the natural world because it inspires endless curiosity. There are many unspoiled and picturesque places in the world, but the most memorable moments for me are rare or special animal behaviour. One time while working as a biologist and photographer, I witnessed a gelada monkey give birth in the wild. I was working in the mountains of Ethiopia to study this species. We spent many hours every day studying the monkeys as they ate grass and played with each other. Once, I saw a monkey walk away from the herd and followed her because this was strange behaviour. I soon saw that she was very pregnant, and then I quietly watched as she gave birth just a few metres away. It was an awe-inspiring experience to witness something so rare for even biologists to see. It made me reflect about how much we as humans share in common with wildlife, and how precious life is for all creatures.

Maria: The natural world makes me feel alive in my own body. The vastness of the rainforest is especially magnificent, with trees towering over 60 feet in the air and the branches coming together in the sky. On the one hand, it can feel very tranquil, but, on the other, it's buzzing with life – with dazzling plants everywhere, hummingbirds buzzing in the air above the flowers, and maybe a band of white-faced monkeys – capuchins – swinging through the trees or a flash of blue announcing a blue morpho butterfly.
Perhaps, one of my most memorable moments in nature was in the Ecuadorian rainforest. Waterfalls crashing over the rocks into the river, turning the crystal-clear water white, is one of the most impressive natural wonders I have seen. We took our boots off and climbed up the side, gripping rocks as the water splashed on us from the raging torrent. At the top, we balanced on a rock, and then, plucking up courage, we pushed with our legs as hard as we could and jumped into the cool deep pool of water below. We came up for air, and floated in the clear water with green trees circling the pool, enjoying the small freshwater fish flitting by us. Then we pulled ourselves out to climb and jump again.

Audioscripts

It was so impressive because of the power of the water surging over the top of the rocks coupled with the tranquil water below, and then all of this mixed with the lush green of the ferns and the trees. This is getting to be immersed in nature – literally!

8.5

1 we as humans share in common
2 full of endless awe-inspiring stories
3 in the air
4 flash of blue

8.6

Ayana: When I'm alone with Jasmine, she's really sweet and a lot of fun. But when we're in a group, she becomes a different person. She likes to make fun of me in front of the others. She's a nice person by nature and so I'm sure she doesn't mean anything nasty by it … but I don't really like being laughed at. I didn't want to come across as being over-sensitive, so I just didn't say anything about it. Eventually, I started dreading going out in a group with Jasmine and over time, we just stopped being friends. It's a real pity.

Dimitri: László and I were working on a project together, but we just had very different styles of working. He likes to take control of things, he likes to tell us how to do things and he doesn't like to deviate from the plan. And that's hard when we're trying to be creative. The rest of the team found it difficult to work with him, and so I decided to talk to him. I told him that he's not our boss and that he's killing our creativity. He got really defensive and we got into a huge argument. It was even harder to work together after that.

Hardi: Marco and I are housemates, but we have very different tastes in music. We both work from home and he likes working with loud rock music playing in the background whereas I just find that very distracting. It gives me a headache and I can't get any work done. So one day, I told him his music was lovely and that I knew very little about rock music and would love to know more about it, but possibly not when I'm working. He got really angry and said I was being passive aggressive. What does that even mean? I was only trying to ask him nicely! This is not the first time he's reacted this way. There was that time when he got upset because I asked him not to take my food from the fridge. I feel I constantly have to tiptoe around him and I don't feel like I can be honest with him without him getting angry.

8.7

Jeff: Everywhere I have worked – from the US to Ethiopia to Greenland – I've noticed changes. Sometimes new roads bring more people to an area, or forests are cut down to make new buildings. There are now fewer animals at some of the places I work than there were 10 years ago. Some of the most profound environmental changes are the ones I see while studying satellite images. Huge sections of tropical forests are disappearing, sea ice is decreasing in the Arctic Ocean and sea levels are rising, causing coasts to erode. This habitat loss and ecosystem change has a detrimental effect on animals and people all around the world. Even though we can see these changes from space, we also now understand what is causing these changes and what we can do to minimize them. Knowledge and compassion are both important tools for change.

Maria: One potential solution to these environmental issues is sustainable collection. This means that people can still use the forest as they are a part of the ecosystem as well, but they need to do so in a sustainable way. For example, people can collect fruits from palm trees and leave the tree growing. One of the things that I do is make booklets with the people about how they can sustainably use their plants, creating a record with them of their own information.

Also, as we learn to produce sustainably, we also need to empower those with purchasing power to support sustainable collection and production. For those of us who live in cities, we can buy products that are produced sustainably. Those buying often drive the economic incentive, so they can influence the direction of how items are brought, or are banned from coming, to market.

Ultimately, our actions can have a lasting impact on the forests throughout the world.

UNIT 9

9.1

I = interviewer, N = Nora

I: I'm with Nora today. How would you describe your sense of style and attitude to fashion?

N: Hi. I think I'd describe it as laid back and comfortable.

I: And have you always been the same?

N: No, I don't think so. I used to be more focused on what I looked like rather than comfort, but shifted towards more practical clothes, especially when I'm working.

I: So does that mean in terms of what you wear … jeans and that sort of thing?

N: It can do. I love to wear cargo pants. Love the khaki green colour and army-style outfits; the high black boots go well with cargo pants. They're especially useful with all the pockets and versatility.

I: So that's at work? What about at home?

N: When I'm back home, I'm more on the trendy side. But yeah, when I'm digging and out in the desert, there's a touch of scruffy. My colleagues have always commented on how I look trendy. I definitely try to. I roll with the motto of 'look good, feel good'; even when you're in the middle of nowhere!

I: What's one item of clothing you own that you absolutely love?

N: My denim jacket, definitely. I feel like it's so versatile and you can downplay it or dress it up. I like clothes I can wear again and again rather than for one specific occasion or worn in one specific way. And it doesn't go out of fashion.

I: Who out of your friends and family would you describe as particularly stylish?

N: My best friend, Mika, is one of the most glamorous in my circles. Ever since we were kids. We both went through all the trends and fads together. But as we grew older, she definitely cleaned up well and became the stylish one out of the group.

I: There must have been some fads you bought when you were younger and now you look back on with horror, were there?

N: Oh, yes, there were. When I was growing up, neon bright coloured shirts were a thing. I used to wear really bright red or pinks all the time. When I look back now, I can't believe I used to wear all these colours. They made me look like a rainbow.

I: There isn't a photo I can see is there?

N: I hope not! The colours don't suit me with my dark hair, I feel like it looks too harsh. Nowadays, you'll never see me in bright colours, it's almost like a phobia. I prefer monotone shades or nudes. You'll see me in black, whites, greys and if there's any colour it'll be khaki green or beige.

I: You would never wear bright colours?

N: Yes, I would, and I do, but not often. The last occasion I dressed up for was a friend's wedding. I wore a burgundy dress; so as I mentioned, colour is definitely out of my comfort zone. But every now and then, I'll step out of it and wear something different.

9.2

A = Ayla, D = Disha

A: Disha, you study fashion, don't you?

D: Yes I do.

A: Would you say flares are back in fashion again?

D: I think so, yes. I don't have any myself, but I'd like to.

A: Well, I found these gorgeous ones for sale at the second-hand store near me.

D: Get them! Doesn't matter if they're in fashion or not. But will you wear them?

A: I'm sure I will. They're classic seventies fashion.

D: They are, but actually have been around since the 18th century.

A: You joking?

D: Not at all. Sailors in the navy wore wide-legged trousers. The hippies rejected mainstream fashion, so went to the second-hand supply shops …

A: … And found some old sailors' trousers just waiting to be turned into fashion!

D: Bet you don't want to buy them now!

9.4

I = interviewer, R = Rudi Peeters

I: I've been to the supermarket, and in my bag here I have a few eco-design products: This 'Earth shampoo' looks like a bar of soap and it has no plastic packaging. And I was recommended this vegetarian 'Beyond Burger', which is made from pea protein and is supposed to taste even better than meat.
The market for cleaner, greener products and services has been gradually growing for years, but right now we are witnessing a massive acceleration in the area, a trend which many believe could continue for decades.
But what does it mean for a company to become more sustainable? Economist Rudi Peeters …

R: There would seem to be several ways in which companies are going green. First, we have new products. Between 2015 and 2019 eco-design products enjoyed 54% growth in the packaged goods market. Good examples include plant-based meat alternatives and electric vehicles.

I: And is this new green companies taking over old markets?

R: For the most part, it's existing companies moving into green areas. Car companies with their electric versions is a good example. But there have been some exciting green newcomers as well. One example that may be familiar to listeners is TruEarth who make laundry detergent in the form of strips of paper.

I: OK, so that's what the customer sees – the retail experience. But what about behind the scenes?

R: Well, there are promising noises from investors, who are telling their companies loud and clear that they must look beyond short-term profit. Caring for the planet doesn't come easy to some businesses, but it appears that green organizations are offering to help; 'Wrap' is a global charity that helps companies in the food, clothing and packaging businesses use fewer resources and work sustainably. I think we can expect to see more collaboration like this between private businesses and charitable organizations like Wrap in the next few years.

I: So not just a company's product but also the way it works, even its goals? It's not about money anymore?

Audioscripts

R: Er, … well … I wouldn't go that far! I'd say it's easier to act when the environmental goals match your money-making goals. Take renewable energy. Renewable energy has become cheap in the last ten years. Wind power has become 70% cheaper and solar power even more – almost 90% cheaper. So it makes business sense as well as climate-saving sense for a company to switch to renewables.

I: I read that a Danish energy company, 'Ørsted' has been rated the second most sustainable company in the world.

R: Energy companies tend to move very slowly to decarbonize their business model, but yes, Ørsted seems to be really transforming the way it makes electricity. They're switching to renewables like wind and solar power extremely quickly, and they're aiming to become carbon neutral by 2025.

I: That's fantastic. But you don't need to be an energy company to aim for zero carbon emissions. All companies use electricity…

R: Right. Around a fifth of the largest companies now have commitments to reach net zero. Microsoft has pledged to be carbon neutral by 2030 which is probably ambitious enough; but some companies are only aiming to do so by 2050, which will almost certainly be too late.
And then there are a few companies that are showing real leadership.

I: Unilever make a lot of the things we see in the supermarkets, right?

R: Yes, they manufacture thousands of products, especially soap and that kind of thing. They met their 2020 target to reach 100% renewable energy in all their factories. And despite previous criticisms of their environmental record, it's been claimed that their plans to tackle plastic pollution are now very ambitious. They're investing in research and development for things like refillable bottles and biodegradable plastics.

I: So what's in it for companies like Unilever? Presumably replacing plastics can't be a money saver like changing to wind power?

R: Maybe not in the short term. But I think these companies recognize that sustainable business is the future.

I: It seems that the businesses that survive will be those that adapt. What is clear is that the move to more environmentally friendly practices could be THE most exciting trend we are seeing in the business world right now.

🎧 9.5

1 And I was recommended this vegetarian 'Beyond Burger', which is made from pea protein and is supposed to taste even better than meat.

2 The market for cleaner, greener products and services has been gradually growing for years, but right now we are witnessing a massive acceleration in the area, a trend which many believe could continue for decades.

3 I read that a Danish energy company, 'Ørsted' has been rated the second most sustainable company in the world.

4 Microsoft has pledged to be carbon neutral by 2030 which is probably ambitious enough; but some companies are only aiming to do so by 2050, which will almost certainly be too late.

5 Presumably replacing plastics can't be a money saver like changing to wind power?

UNIT 10

🎧 10.2

1
A: What do you feel when you think about time travel?
B: Sorry, but did you say feel or fear?
A: Feel. What do you feel?

2
C: Was he able to hear after the accident?
D: Was he able to … ?
C: Hear. Could he hear after the accident?

3
E: They weren't able to steal the time machine.
F: Pardon? Did you say they couldn't steer it?
E: Sorry, no, I said steal. They couldn't steal it.

4
G: How did the time traveller appear to you?
H: How did he appeal to me?
G: No, sorry, I said appear. How did he appear to you?

🎧 10.3

1
A: I need to stand up and have a little walk around. I'll be quick.
B: Good idea. But take your time, Lea. We're supposed to take regular breaks.
A: Isn't it almost lunchtime?
B: Not even close. It's only ten thirty.
A: Are you serious? It feels like we've been putting paper in envelopes for about three hours!
B: We started forty-five minutes ago.
A: It's just so tedious!
B: You know what they say. Time flies when you're having fun!
A: Haha. And time goes awfully slowly when you're bored!

2
C: Is Simone here yet? We were supposed to meet at four o'clock
D: No, not yet.
C: But it's a quarter past!
D: You know Simone. Always twenty minutes late.
C: Is her perception of time different from everyone else's? She's always twenty minutes late. I mean always. Twenty minutes late for work, twenty minutes late for lunch,

twenty minutes late to the cinema. She's never on time because she's always in the middle of doing two other things and then she leaves getting ready to the last minute. She never takes into account the time it takes to get ready. You know, finding her shoes, choosing the right jacket, locating her keys, the walk to the bus stop.

E: I asked her why she doesn't just get up twenty minutes earlier, or leave twenty minutes earlier than she thinks she needs to, but she doesn't seem to listen. She doesn't even seem to see it as a problem.

3

F: Remember when you were a kid and a year seemed an impossibly long time?

G: Oh, yeah, for sure. Waiting for the holidays. It seemed they'd never come.

F: My sense of time is so different now. A year isn't actually such a long time, you know?

G: Yeah, right. I heard it's because when you're five years old, one year is twenty percent of your life. And when you're ten, a year is ten percent of your life. But at age forty, a year is less than three percent of your life.

F: So a year seems shorter and passes faster because it's a smaller part of your life?

G: That's what I've heard.

4

H: Ella, are you OK? I heard you had a bike accident.

I: I'm fine now – it wasn't that bad.

H: What happened?

I: My wheel went into a hole and I went over the handlebars.

H: Oh, no.

I: It was so strange. It felt like slow motion as I was flying through the air. It seemed to go on forever, but it probably took like a second. I could see every detail of what was going on. And then I landed in a bush, which was super lucky!

H: Wow. I'm really glad it wasn't more serious.

I: Me too!

5

J: Aren't you ready to go?

K: Now? I thought Anna invited us for seven.

J: She did. It's six forty-five now and it will take us ten minutes to walk there. We don't want to be late!

K: Well, no, but … we don't want to be early, either. Isn't it a bit rude to show up early – or even right on time for that matter?

J: You think so? Not for me.

K: I was thinking we should leave a bit after seven and get there for seven fifteen.

J: Are you sure? That seems a bit rude to me.

K: Well, don't take my word for it. We're all from different countries and Anna may see things like you!

🎧 **10.4**

F: My sense of time is so different now. A year isn't actually such a long time, you know?

G: Yeah, right. I heard it's because when you're five years old, one year is twenty percent of your life. And when you're ten, a year is ten percent of your life. But at age forty, a year is less than three percent of your life.

🎧 **10.5**

1 May I have the pill?
2 I need to dry that.
3 He can't find the glue.
4 Was it boring?
5 Look at the train.
6 It was cold.

🎧 **10.6**

1

He walked right up to me, but I didn't know who he was because, you know, I've never met him before, and so, you'll never believe what I did. I just pushed past him and …

2

A: The problem is that it's very expensive. And the training programme takes place over a very long period and …

B: Mikhail, that's definitely one disadvantage to be aware of. But earlier you mentioned some very important benefits and I just wanted to add something else to that list. Maybe we could come back to the disadvantages in a bit? So, basically what I wanted to say was that one key benefit of this programme is …

3

C: I know there are two things I can do about this. I can simply ignore his behaviour and just pretend everything is normal. But that means I'm not dealing with the issue, right? So I'm thinking that …

D: I have a much better idea, why don't you try …

C: Sorry, Eva, could you hold that thought? I just want to say these two things first and then you can tell us your idea?

D: Oh yes, of course!

C: So, as I was saying, there are two things I can do about this, right? One way is to ignore the issue. The second way is …

4

E: So that was what happened. It was absolutely mad. I don't know if I would ever go skydiving again, you know …

F: That sounds like quite the experience, Fabio. You've just reminded me, have you seen this new travel game show on TV? Basically, these guys have to race around the world doing crazy things …

Acknowledgements

The Voices publishing team would like to thank all of the explorers for their time and participation on this course – and for their amazing stories and photos.

The team would also like to thank the following teachers, who provided detailed and invaluable feedback on this course.

Asia

SS. Abdurrosyid, University of Muhammadiyah Tangerang, Banten; Hằng Ánh, Hanoi University of Science Technology, Hanoi; Yoko Atsumi, Seirei Christopher University, Hamamatsu; Dr. Nida Boonma, Assumption University, Bangkok; Portia Chang, SEE Education, New Taipei City; Brian Cullen, Nagoya Institute of Technology, Nagoya; David Daniel, Houhai English, Beijing; Professor Doan, Hanoi University, Hanoi; Kim Huong Duong, HCMC University of Technology, Ho Chi Minh; Natalie Ann Gregory, University of Kota Kinabalu, Sabah; Shawn Greynolds, AUA Language Center, Bangkok; Thi Minh Ly Hoang, University of Economics – Technology for Industries, Hanoi; Mike Honywood, Shinshu University, Nagano; Jessie Huang, National Central University, Taoyuan City; Edward Jones, Nagoya International School, Nagoya; Ajarn Kiangkai, Sirnakarintrawirote University, Bangkok; Zhou Lei, New Oriental Education & Technology Group, Beijing; Louis Liu, METEN, Guangzhou; Jeng-Jia (Caroline) Luo Tunghai University, Taichung City; Thi Ly Luong, Huflit University, Ho Chi Minh City; Michael McCollister, Feng Chia University, Taichung; Robert McLaughlin, Tokoha University, Shizuoka; Hal Miller, Houhai English, Beijing; Jason Moser, Kanto Gakuin University, Yokohama; Hudson Murrell, Baiko Gakuin University, Shimonoseki; Takayuki Nagamine, Nagoya University of Foreign Studies, Nagoya; Sanuch Natalang, Thammasart University, Bangkok; Nguyen Bá Học, Hanoi University of Public Health, Hanoi; Nguyen Cong Tri, Ho Chi Minh City University of Technology, Ho Chi Minh; Nguyen Ngoc Vu, Hoa Sen University, Ho Chi Minh City; Professor Nguyen, Hanoi University, Hanoi; Dr Nguyen, Hao Sen University, Ho Chi Minh City; Nguyễn Quang Vịnh, Hanoi University, Hanoi; Wilaichitra Nilsawaddi, Phranakhon Rajabhat University, Bangkok; Suchada Nimmanit, Rangsit University, Bangkok; Ms. Cao Thien Ai Nuong, Hoa Sen University, Ho Chi Minh City; Donald Patterson, Seirei Christopher University, Shizuoka; Douglas Perkins, Musashino University Junior and Senior High School, Tokyo; Phan The Hung, Van Lang University, Ho Chi Minh City; Fathimah Razman, Northern University, Sintok, Kedah; Bruce Riseley, Holmesglen (Language Centre of University Of Muhammadiyah Tangerang for General English), Jakarta; Anthony Robins, Aichi University of Education, Aichi; Greg Rouault, Hiroshima Shudo University, Hiroshima; Dr Sawaluk, Sirnakarintrawirote University, Bangkok; Dr Supattra, Rangsit University, Lak Hok; Dr Thananchai, Dhurakijbundit University, Bangkok; Thao Le Phuong, Open University, Ho Chi Minh; Thap Doanh Thuong, Thu Dau Mot University, Thu Dau Mot; Kinsella Valies, University of Shizuoka, Shizuoka; Gerrit Van der Westhuizen, Houhai English, Beijing; Dr Viraijitta, Rajjabhat Pranakorn University, Bangkok; Dr Viraijittra, Phranakhon Rajabhat University, Bangkok; Vo Dinh Phuoc, University of Economics, Ho Chi Minh City; Dr Nussara Wajsom, Assumption University, Bangkok; Scott A.Walters, Woosong University, Daejon; Yungkai Weng, PingoSpace & Elite Learning, Beijing; Ray Wu, Wall Street English, Hong Kong.

Europe, Middle East and Africa (EMEA)

Saju Abraham, Sohar University, Sohar; Huda Murad Al Balushi, International Maritime College , Sohar; Salah Al Hanshi, Modern College of Business and Science, Muscat; Victor Alarcón, EOI Badalona, Barcelona; Yana Alaveranova, International House, Kiev; Alexandra Alexandrova, Almaty; Blanca Alvarez, EOI San Sebastian de los Reyes, Madrid; Emma Antolin, EOI San Sebastian de los Reyes, Madrid; Manuela Ayna, Liceo Primo Levi, Bollate, Milan; Elizabeth Beck, British Council, Milan; Charlotte Bentham, Adveti, Sharjah; Carol Butters, Edinburgh College, Edinburgh; Patrizia Cassin, International House, Milan; Elisabet Comelles, EIM - Universitat de Barcelona, Barcelona; Sara De Angeles, Istituto Superiore Giorgi, Milan; Carla Dell'Acqua, Liceo Primo Levi, Bollate, Milan; John Dench, BEET Language Centre, Bournemouth; Angela di Staso, Liceo Banfi, Vimercate, Milan; Sarah Donno, Edinburgh College, Edinburgh, UK; Eugenia Dume, EOI San Sebastian de los Reyes, Madrid; Rory Fergus Duncan; BKC-IH Moscow, Moscow; Ms Evelyn Kandalaft El Moualem, AMIDEAST, Beirut; Raul Pope Farguell, BKC-IH Moscow, Moscow; Chris Farrell, CES, Dublin; Dr Aleksandra, Filipowicz, Warsaw University of Technology, Warsaw; Diana Golovan, Linguist LLC, Kiev, Ukraine; Jaap Gouman, Pieter Zandt, Kampen; Maryam Kamal, British Council, Doha; Galina Kaptug, Moonlight, Minsk; Ms Rebecca Nabil Keedi, College des Peres Antonines, Hadath; Dr. Michael King, Community College of Qatar, Doha; Gabriela Kleckova, University of West Bohemia, Pilsen; Mrs Marija Klečkovska, Pope John Paul II gymnasium, Vilnius; Kate Knight, International Language School, Milan; Natalia Kolina, Moscow; David Koster, P.A.R.K., Brno; Suzanne Littlewood, Zayed University, Dubai; Natalia Lopez, EOI Terrassa, Barcelona; Maria Lopez-Abeijon, EOI Las Rozas, Madrid; Pauline Loriggio, International House London, London; Gabriella Luise, International Language School Milan, Milan; Klara Malowiecka, Lang Ltc, Warsaw; Fernando Martin, EOI Valdemoro, Madrid; Robert Martinez, La Cunza, Gipuzkoa; Mario Martinez, EOI Las Rozas, Madrid; Marina Melnichuk, Financial University, Moscow; Martina Menova, PĚVÁČEK vzdělávací centrum, Prague; Marlene Merkt, Kantonsschule Zurich Nord, Zurich; Iva Meštrović, Učilište Jantar, Zagreb; Silvia Milian, EOI El Prat, Barcelona; Jack Montelatici, British School Milan, Milan; Muntsa Moral, Centre de Formació de Persones Adultes Pere Calders, Barcelona; Julian Oakley, Wimbledon School of English, London; Virginia Pardo, EOI Badalona, Barcelona; William Phillips, Aga Khan Educational Service; Joe Planas, Centre de Formació de Persones Adultes Pere Calders, Barcelona; Carmen Prieto, EOI Carabanchel, Madrid; Sonya Punch, International House, Milan; Magdalena Rasmus,

Cavendish School, Bournemouth; Laura Rodríguez, EOI El Prat, Barcelona; Victoria Samaniego, EOI Pozuelo, Madrid; Beatriz Sanchez, EOI San Sebastian de los Reyes, Madrid; Gigi Saurer, Migros-Genossenschafts-Bund, Zurich; Jonathan Smilow, BKC-IH, Moscow; Prem Sourek, Anderson House, Bergamo; Svitlana Surgai, British Council, Kyiv; Peter Szabo, Libra Books, Budapest; Richard Twigg, International House, Milan; Evgeny Usachev, Moscow International Academy, Moscow; Eric van Luijt, Tilburg University Language Centre, Tilburg; Tanya Varchuk, Fluent English School, Ukraine; Yulia Vershinina, YES Center, Moscow; Małgorzata Witczak, Warsaw University of Technology, Warsaw; Susanna Wright, Stafford House London, London; Chin-Yunn Yang, Padagogische Maturitaetsschule Kreuzlingen, Kreuzlingen; Maria Zarudnaya, Plekhanov Russian University of Economics, Moscow; Michelle Zelenay, KV Winterthur, Winterthur.

Latin America

Jorge Aguilar, Universidad Autónoma de Sinaloa, Culiacán; Carlos Bernardo Anaya, UNIVA Zamora, Zamora; Sergio Balam, Academia Municipal de Inglés, Mérida; Josélia Batista, CCL Centro de Línguas, Fortaleza; Aida Borja, ITESM GDL, Guadalajara; Diego Bruekers Deschamp, Ingles Express, Belo Horizonte; Alejandra Cabrera, Universidad Politécnica de Yucatán, Mérida; Luis Cabrera Rocha, ENNAULT – UNAM, Mexico City; Bruna Caltabiano, Caltabiano Idiomas, São Paulo; Hortensia Camacho, FES Iztacala – UNAM, Mexico City; Gustavo Cruz Torres, Instituto Cultural México – Norteamericano, Guadalajara; Maria Jose D'Alessandro Nogueira, FCM Foundation School, Belo Horizonte; Gabriela da Cunha Barbosa Saldanha, FCM Foundation School, Belo Horizonte; Maria Da Graça Gallina Flack, Challenge School, Porto Alegre; Pedro Venicio da Silva Guerra, U-Talk Idiomas, São Bernardo do Campo; Julice Daijo, JD Language Consultant, Rua Oscar Freire; Olívia de Cássia Scorsafava, U-Talk Idiomas, São Bernardo do Campo; Marcia Del Corona, UNISINOS, Porto Alegre; Carlos Alberto Díaz Najera, Colegio Salesiano Anáhuac Revolución, Guadalajara; Antônio César Ferraz Gomes, 4 Flags, São Bernardo do Campo; Brenda Pérez Ferrer, Universidad Politécnica de Querétaro, Querétaro; Sheila Flores, Cetys Universidad, Mexicali; Ángela Gamboa, Universidad Metropolitana, Mérida; Alejandro Garcia, Colegio Ciencias y Letras, Tepic; Carlos Gomora, CILC, Toluca; Kamila Gonçalves, Challenge School, Porto Alegre; Herivelton Gonçalves, Prime English, Vitória; Idalia Gonzales, Británico, Lima; Marisol Gutiérrez Olaiz, LAMAR Universidad, Guadalajara; Arturo Hernandez, ITESM GDL, Guadalajara; Gabriel Cortés Hernandez, BP- Intitute, Morelia; Daniel Vázquez Hernández, Preparatoria 2, Mérida; Erica Jiménez, Centro Escolar, Tepeyac; Leticia Juárez, FES Acatlán – UNAM, Mexico City; Teresa Martínez, Universidad Iberoamericana, Tijuana; Elsa María del Carmen Mejía Franco, CELE Mex, Toluca; José Alejandro Mejía Tello, CELE Mex, Toluca; Óscar León Mendoza Jimenez, Angloamericano Idiomas, Mexico City; Karla Mera Ubando,

Instituto Cultural, Mexico City; Elena Mioto, UNIVA, Guadalajara; Ana Carolina Moreira Paulino, SENAC, Porto Alegre; Paula Mota, 4 Flags, São Bernardo do Campo; Adila Beatriz Naud de Moura, UNISINOS, Porto Alegre; Monica Navarro Morales, Instituto Cultural, Mexico City; Wilma F Neves, Caltabiano Idiomas, São Paulo; Marcelo Noronha, Caltabiano Idiomas, São Paulo; Enrique Ossio, ITESM Morelia, Morelia; Filipe Pereira Bezerra, U-Talk Idiomas, São Bernardo do Campo; Florencia Pesce, Centro Universitario de Idiomas, Buenos Aires, Argentina; Kamila Pimenta, CCBEU, São Bernardo do Campo; Leopoldo Pinzón Escobar, Universidad Santo Tomás, Bogotá; Mary Ruth Popov Hibas, Ingles Express, Belo Horizonte; Alejandra Prado Barrera, UVM, Mexico City; Letícia Puccinelli Redondo, U-Talk Idiomas, São Bernardo do Campo; Leni Puppin, Centro de Línguas de UFES, Vitória; Maria Fernanda Quijano, Universidad Tec Milenio, Culiacan; Jorge Quintal, Colegio Rogers, Mérida; Sabrina Ramos Gomes, FCM Foundation School, Belo Horizonte; Mariana Roberto Billia, 4 Flags, São Bernardo do Campo; Monalisa Sala de Sá 4 Flags, São Bernardo do Campo; Yamel Sánchez Vízcarra, CELE Mex, Toluca; Vagner Serafim, CCBEU, São Bernardo do Campo; Claudia Serna, UNISER, Mexicali; Alejandro Serna, CCL, Morelia; Simone Teruko Nakamura, U-Talk Idiomas, São Bernardo do Campo; Desirée Carla Troyack, FCM Foundation School, Belo Horizonte; Sandra Vargas Boecher Prates, Centro de Línguas da UFES, Vitória; Carlos Villareal, Facultad de Ingenierías Universidad Autónoma de Querétaro, Querétaro; Rosa Zarco Mondragón, Instituto Cultural, Mexico City.

US and Canada

Rachel Bricker, Arizona State University, Tempe; Jonathan Bronson, Approach International Student Center, Boston; Elaine Brookfield, EC Boston, Boston; Linda Hasenfus, Approach International Language Center, Boston; Andrew Haynes, ELS Boston, Boston; Cheryl House, ILSC, Toronto; Rachel Kadish, FLS International, Boston; Mackenzie Kerby, ELS Language Centers, Boston; Rob McCourt FLS Boston; Haviva Parnes, EC English Language Centres, Boston; Shayla Reid, Approach International Student Center, Boston.

Credits

Illustrations: All illustrations are owned by © Cengage.

Cover © Jelena Jankovic; **3** Alexander Hassenstein/Bongarts/ Getty Images; **4** (tl1) © Neely Ker-Fox, (tl2) © Studio Roosegaarde, (cl) Alexander Hassenstein/Bongarts/Getty Images, (bl1) © Brian Doben, (bl2) Markus Scholz/DPA/Getty Images; **6** (tl1) David Doubilet/National Geographic Image Collection, (tl2) Josie Gealer/Getty Images News/Getty Images, (cl) © The Parahawking Project, (bl1) Julien Behal/PA Images/ Getty Images, (bl2) © Stephen Wilkes; **8-9** (Spread) Robert Harding Picture Library/National Geographic Image Collection; **8** (tl1) © Alec Jacobson, (tl2) Courtesy of Alison Wright, (tr1) © Anusha Shankar, (tr2) © Carolina Chong Montenegro, (cl) Courtesy of Alyea Pierce, (cr) Courtesy of Francisco Estrada-Belli, (bl) © Fernando Caamano, (br) Courtesy of Gabby Salazarr; **9** (tl1) © Eleanor Burfitt, (tl2) Courtesy of Jeffrey Kerby, (tr1) Courtesy of Nora Shawki, (tr2) © Global Penguin Society, (cl) Courtesy of Maria Fadiman, (cr) © Alec Jacobson, (bl) © Mike Gil, (br) © Benjamin Carey; **10-11** (spread) © Neely Ker-Fox; **11** © Mike Gil; **13** (tl) PictureLux/Alamy Stock Photo, (c) Lukasz Szwaj/Shutterstock.com, (br) CBW/Alamy Stock Photo; **15** gilaxia/E+/Getty Images; **16** © Mike Gil; **19** (tc1) ERRER/Shutterstock.com, (tc2) Puckung/Shutterstock.com, (tc3) bungacengkeh/Shutterstock.com, (tc4) AVIcon/Shutterstock. com; **20** Morsa Images/DigitalVision/Getty Images; **22-23** (spread) © Studio Roosegaarde; **23** (br1) Courtesy of Francisco Estrada-Belli, (br2) © Fernando Caamano; **25** AFP/Getty Images; **26** Rob Schuster Illustration; **28** Busà Photography/ Moment/Getty Images; **30** Anuwat Susomwong/EyeEm/Getty Images; **31** S1AETQDKNHAA/Reuters; **33** Dinodia Photo/ Corbis Documentary/Getty Images; **34-35** (spread) Alexander Hassenstein/Bongarts/Getty Images; **35** (br1) © Anusha Shankar, (br2) © Alec Jacobson; **37** (tl) CamRosPhotography/ Shutterstock.com, (c) h.yegho/Shutterstock.com, (bc1) Blue Flourishes/Shutterstock.com, (bc2) 4LUCK/Shutterstock.com, (bc3) Panda Vector/Shutterstock.com, (br) Jose Luis Pelaez/ Stone/Getty Images; **38** (t) © Paul Salopek/National Geographic Image Collection, (tl) Courtesy of Jeff Blossom, Center for Geographic Analysis, Harvard University; **40** (t) Kuliperko/ Shutterstock.com, (tc) Pakhnyushchy/Shutterstock.om; **45** alvarez/E+/Getty Images; **46-47** (spread) © Brian Doben; **47** (br1) Courtesy of Alyea Pierce, (br2) © Eleanor Burfitt; **49** (tl1) (tr) © Alida Missari/Advocate Art, (tl2) Morsa Images/ DigitalVision/Getty Images, (cl) Sam Edwards/OJO Images/ Getty Images, (bl1) StephM2506/iStock/Getty Images, (bl2) James Whitaker/DigitalVision/Getty Images; **50** (cl1) Alexander Ryabintsev/Shutterstock.com, (cl2) Lisa Kolbasa/Shutterstock. com; **52** © Alyea Pierce; **54** Westend61/Getty Images; **57** © Netflix; **58-59** (spread) Markus Scholz/DPA/Getty Images; **59** (br1) © Benjamin Carey, (br2) © Global Penguin Society; **61** (tr) © Lisa Sacks, (cr) © WORKING HANDS; **62** © Szilvia Szakall/ Beehive Illustration; **64** © Pablo Borboroglu; **66** SDI Productions/ E+/Getty Images; **68** (br1) (br2) (br3) (br4) stas11/Shutterstock. com; **69** (tl1) Rvector/Shutterstock.com, (tl2) (tc1) cosmaa/ Shutterstock.com, (tc2) stockhype/Shutterstock.com, (tr1) Maria Korikova/Shutterstock.com, (tr2) smashingstocks/Shutterstock.

com, (tr3) Macrovector/Shutterstock.com; **70-71** (spread) David Doubilet/National Geographic Image Collection; **71** (br1) (br2) © Alec Jacobson; **72** Panther Media GmbH/Alamy Stock Photo; **73** Rob Schuster Illustration; **74** (tl1) ngaga/Shutterstock. com, (tl2) Fast_Cyclone/Shutterstock.com, (tl3) Shawshots/ Alamy Stock Photo, (tl4) Valentina Vectors/Shutterstock.com; **77** © The Uncomfortable; **78** Klaus Vedfelt/DigitalVision/ Getty Images; **80** (tl) (tc) (tr) Fourleaflover/Shutterstock.com, (cr) Gallinago_media/Shutterstock.com; **82-83** (spread) Josie Gealer/Getty Images News/Getty Images; **83** (br1) © Carolina Chong Montenegro, (br2) Courtesy of Gabby Salazar; **85** (t) © Alida Missari/Advocate Art, (br) © Better World Books; **86** (tl) Sviatlana_Koro/Shutterstock.com, (cl) Bardocz Peter/ Shutterstock.com, (bl) Sapann Design/Shutterstock.com; **88** Rawpixel/iStock/Getty Images; **90** GaudiLab/Shutterstock.com; **93** Wavebreakmedia Ltd IP-210527/Alamy Stock Photo; **94-95** (spread) © The Parahawking Project; **95** (br1) Courtesy of Maria Fadiman, (br2) Courtesy of Jeffrey Kerby; **97** Clare Jackson/ EyeEm/Getty Images; **98** tracielouise/E+/Getty Images; **101** © Vivek Venkataraman; **103** triloks/E+/Getty Images; **105** somnuk krobkum/Moment/Getty Images; **106-107** (spread) Julien Behal/ PA Images/Getty Images; **107** courtesy of Nora Shawki; **109** (cr1) Tim Gainey/Alamy Stock Photo, (cr2) Design Pics Inc/Alamy Stock Photo, (br) © Rio Rinaldi Rachmatullah; **110** (tl) Stephen Chung/Alamy Stock Photo, (l) brainpencil/Shutterstock.com; **112** Pako Mera/Alamy Stock Photo; **114** (br1) VoodooDot/ Shutterstock.com, (br2) Vadym Nechyporenko/Shutterstock. com, (br3) Leremy/Shutterstock.com, (br4) art-sonik/ Shutterstock.com, (br5) kaisorn/Shutterstock.com, (br6) 13ree. design/Shutterstock.com; **117** (tl) Gordon Scammell/Alamy Stock Photo, (tc) Plan Shooting 2/Imazins/Getty Images, (tc) Vietnam Stock Images/Shutterstock.com, (tr) Image Source/ Getty Images; **118-119** spread © Stephen Wilkes; **119** Courtesy of Alison Wright; **121** (t) travelbild excl/Alamy Stock Photo, (tc) Oksana8838/Shutterstock.com, (br1) gus Studio/ Shutterstock.com, (br2) smallsketch/Shutterstock.com, (br3) Tatiana Stupak/Dreamstime.com, (br4) ArtMaris/Shutterstock. com, (br5) IvanDbajo/Shutterstock.com; **122** Karwai Tang/ Getty Images Entertainment/Getty Images; **124** GibsonPictures/ E+/Getty Images; **126** Monkey Business Images/Shutterstock. com; **129** © Alison Wright; **130** (tl) © Neely Ker-Fox, (tr) © Studio Roosegaarde; **131** (tl) Alexander Hassenstein/Bongarts/ Getty Images, (tr) © Brian Doben; **132** (tl) Markus Scholz/DPA/ Getty Images, (tr) David Doubilet/National Geographic Image Collection; **133** (tl) Josie Gealer/Getty Images News/Getty Images, (tr) © The Parahawking Project; **134** (tl) Julien Behal/ PA Images/Getty Images, (tr) © Stephen Wilkes; **165** (tr) (cr) Anuwat Susomwong/EyeEm/Getty Images, (bl1) Africa Studio/ Shutterstock.com, (bl2) Ivsanmas/Shutterstock.com, (bl3) Leremy/Shutterstock.com, (bl4) Valentina Vectors/Shutterstock. com; **166** © Rob Schuster/Cengage.

Text: Source: Graphicspedia, https://graphicspedia.net/why-laughter-truly-is-the-best-medicine-infographic; **24** http://www. brainyquote.com/authors/tu-youyou-quotes; **25** Source: https:// www.brainyquote.com/quotes/tu_youyou_931621

26 Source:Tobias Waldau, https://medium.com/@waldau.t/the-benefits-of-reverse-innovation-d7d6a197c152; **28** Source: Mark Twain's Own Autobiography: The Chapters from the North American Review, https://www.goodreads.com/quotes/843880-there-is-no-such-thing-as-a-new-idea-it; **37** Source: Extract from the book 'Invisible women: exposing date bias in a world designed for men', by Caroline Criado Perez, Penguin, Random house, London. ISBN: 9781784741723, 2019; **43** https://www.exeter.ac.uk/media/universityofexeter/humanresources/documents/learningdevelopment/the_change_curve.pdf;
49 https://medium.com/@owenbezick/bot-or-not-ai-generated-poetry-6adf3d789c4; **49** https://www.poemhunter.com/poem/the-old-pond/; **49** https://www.mentalfloss.com/article/75507/what-point-does-novel-become-literature; **53** The American Dream: Native American Myth: Coyote and the Columbia (cmclaughamdream.blogspot.com); **54** Source: https://www.azquotes.com/quote/1438706; **61** Source: https://publishing.rcseng.ac.uk/doi/full/10.1308/rcsbull.2017.172?mobileUi=0 and a pdf is at https://publishing.rcseng.ac.uk/doi/pdf/10.1308/rcsbull.2017.172; **73** https://www.theguardian.com/cities/shortcuts/2015/jun/08/what-does-your-city-smell-like-smellscapes-maps;**85** Source: Lost in Translation. Memoir by Eva Hoffman, Random House. Ebub ISBN: 9781446499566;
88 https://www.timetoshinepodcast.com/6-great-quotes-power-voice/; **108** Source: In the Attic by Hiawyn Oram;
121 https://www.eurekalert.org/pub_releases/2015-06/uoe-hat062615.php; **122** https://www.youtube.com/watch?v=elah3i_WiFI See from about 1:00; **124** https://www.frontiersin.org/articles/10.3389/fpsyg.2012.00196/full;
166 https://dreamtime.net.au/rainbow-serpent-story/